Contemporary Metaphysics

Philip Sidney

On Defense of

Poetry

(An Apology for..)

B

Contemporary Philosophy

Each volume in this series provides a clear, comprehensive and up-to-date introduction to the main philosophical topics of contemporary debate. Written by leading philosophers, the volumes provide an ideal basis for university students and others who want an engaging and accessible account of the subject. While acting as an introduction, each volume offers and defends a distinct position in its own right.

Published Works
Contemporary Philosophy of Social Science
Brian Fay
Contemporary Metaphysics
Michael Jubien
Contemporary Philosophy of Mind
Georges Rey

Forthcoming
Contemporary Philosophy of Thought
Michael Luntley
Contemporary Philosophy of Religion
Charles Taliaferro
Contemporary Philosophy of Law
Dennis Patterson
Contemporary Philosophy of Physics
Simon Saunders
Contemporary Philosophy of Language
Kent Bach
Pluralism and Contemporary Political Philosophy
Daniel Weinstock

Contemporary Metaphysics
An Introduction

Michael Jubien

BLACKWELL Publishers

Copyright © Michael Jubien 1997

The right of Michael Jubien to be identified as author of this work has been asserted in accordance with the Copyright, Designs and Patents Act 1988.

First published 1997
Reprinted 1998 (twice)

Blackwell Publishers Inc.
350 Main Street
Malden, Massachusetts 02148, USA

Blackwell Publishers Ltd
108 Cowley Road
Oxford OX4 1JF
UK

Library of Congress Cataloging in Publication Data
Jubien, Michael.
Contemporary metaphysics / Michael Jubien.
p. cm.—(Contemporary philosophy)
Material presented was originally developed for courses taught by the author at the University of Calif., Davis, Philosophy Dept.
Includes index.
ISBN 1-55786-858-1 (alk. paper). —ISBN 1-55786-859-X (pbk. : alk. paper)
1. Metaphysics. I. Title. II. Series: Contemporary philosophy (Cambridge, Mass.)
BD111.J83   1997
110—dc21   96-52895
                                                CIP

British Library Cataloguing-in-Publication Data

A CIP catalogue record for this book is available from the British Library.

Typeset in 11 on 13pt Garamond 3
by Best-set Typesetter Ltd., Hong Kong
Printed in Great Britain by MPG Books Ltd, Bodmin, Cornwall

This book is printed on acid-free paper

For Sidney

Contents

Preface

The material presented in this book was originally developed for use in two courses I teach in the Philosophy Department at the University of California, Davis. The first, "Introduction to Metaphysics," is intended for a broad undergraduate audience. (It satisfies the "general education" requirement at the University, and usually draws over a hundred students.) The second, "Topics in Metaphysics," is a small upper-division course designed primarily for undergraduate majors and graduate students.

Chapters 1–7, which I use in the introductory course, are, in general, not as difficult as chapters 8–11. Nevertheless, I have sometimes used material from chapters 9 and 11 with good success in the introductory course. In the "Topics" course, I typically cover the material in chapters 1–4 rapidly, in order to provide a methodological background. Chapters 8–10 are then the main focus (usually with supplementary material by myself and other authors). My experience suggests that chapter 8 is probably the most challenging.

This book treats several topics that happen to be very prominent in recent metaphysics. I hope the treatments are not only interesting in their own right, but also serve as good preparation for understanding contemporary discussions. I have tried to present a range of positions on issues, often advocating a particular view, but other times simply presenting alternatives and mentioning strengths and weaknesses. (In some cases the positions I advocate are well known and widely accepted, in others they are not.)

There is an underlying ontological and methodological theme that unites the various discussions in the book: Platonism concerning properties, relations, and propositions. I introduce the theme in chapter 1, where philosophy itself is characterized as the study (and especially the analysis) of certain general concepts, and these concepts in turn are seen as objective entities, typically Platonic properties. In chapter 3, Platonism is defended as a theoretical hypothesis that helps explain a variety of related everyday phenomena, including our ability to have beliefs about our surroundings, the capacity of our language to refer to external entities, and our ability to communicate with each other. (The postulation of these Platonic entities is likened to the postulation of quarks in physics.)

The Platonist theme appears in the remaining chapters as a methodological tool, as when we insist on knowing just what proposition is being expressed or asserted, what possessing such and such a property entails, and the like. I hope it emerges from the book that the acceptance of this Platonist ontology promotes a sharpness of focus on philosophical material in general that is not otherwise so easily obtained.

Two pedagogical decisions should be mentioned. First, I have decided not to include lists of related reading on the various topics, because instructors are better placed to make recommendations that are appropriate for their specific courses and students. Second, I have decided to include "exercises" at many points throughout the book. Some of them are intended to heighten the reader's awareness of the depth of a problem, or to draw attention to further ramifications of a problem, argument, etc. Others are semi-technical exercises along the lines of: "Give an appropriate definition for . . . ;" or "Give a convincing example of . . . ;" and so forth. Other exercises challenge the reader to construct arguments for specific conclusions, or to expose flaws in arguments that have been mentioned in the text. Many are suitable as short paper or term paper topics. (In some cases it may be beneficial to announce that some of the exercises will reappear as exam questions.) The exercises are inserted at the appropriate points in the text rather than collected at the ends of chapters. This has the favorable effect of raising the question precisely when the reader is thinking about the motivating material. Since it might also have the unfavorable effect of interrupting the flow of the text, the exercises have been emboldened and enclosed within square brackets. A reader may then respond to this "signal" in whatever way is most appropriate at the time.

This book has been improved by the comments of many people: colleagues and friends in the profession, teaching assistants, and, of course, students. I am very grateful to David Copp, Fred Feldman, Greg Fitch, Joel Friedman, Dennis Holden, Jeff King, Randy Mayes, Paul Teller, Michael Wedin, Melanie Branca, Melinda Campbell, Stuart Campbell,

Judy Cross, Patrick Findler, Dan Gaskill, Russ Payne, Ron Pritchard, Rick Schubert, and Leslie Stapp. This list is so long that I fear it must be incomplete, and I apologize to anyone I've forgotten. I am also very grateful to the Blackwell readers and to Margaret Aherne and Martin Cutlan for extremely helpful comments. Finally, I would like to thank my wife, Sidney Mannheim Jubien, for her encouragement and understanding.

1
Metaphysics

1.1 A Picture of Philosophy

Metaphysics is one of the main branches of philosophy, the branch that is concerned with the concept of being (that is, existence) and with several other closely related concepts. The study of concepts plays a central role in all of philosophy. In fact it is often held that philosophy is nothing more than the study of certain very general, characteristically "philosophical" concepts – for example, existence, truth, knowledge, justification, mind, and goodness (and a multitude of narrower philosophical concepts closely related to the general ones). These sorts of concepts are rarely explicitly treated in the special sciences and, when they are, they are treated in fundamentally different ways. But philosophical concepts underlie all genuine scientific inquiry because science cannot even begin in the absence of philosophical assumptions and presuppositions. These assumptions are generally not stated explicitly and so may not even be noticed by practicing scientists or students of science. But they are there.

As an example, physics presupposes the following three things: (1) that there exists a physical reality independent of our mental states; (2) that the interactions of the stuff constituting this reality conform to certain general laws; and (3) that we are capable of grasping physical laws and obtaining evidence that favors or disfavors specific proposed laws. These are certainly not the only philosophical presuppositions of physics, but they are good examples for our purposes. The first two are metaphysical in nature while the third is espistemological. It is important to notice two things about them. First, they are not at all self-evidently true, even if we do not normally question them. Each of them may be questioned and, in fact, each

1

of them has been questioned by one prominent philosopher or another. Second, they are not themselves part of the subject matter of physics. They cannot be "theorems" (or even "axioms") of physics because they are not propositions of physics in the first place. But physics as we know it is drained of all significance if any of them is false. Perhaps it could be replaced by a theory of certain sorts of "possible mental phenomena" – for example, those we normally take to be actual observations of external physical events (along with "merely possible" such phenomena). And such a theory could conceivably be based in part on a thorough reinterpretation of physics as it now stands. But these possibilities are very much a matter of speculation.

It was claimed above that philosophy, or at least a good part of it, involves the study of the philosophical concepts and some examples of these concepts were given. But how does this "study" proceed? How do we "do" philosophy? There's no philosophy laboratory – philosophy doesn't seem "empirical" at all. So, is it all just a matter of personal belief or opinion (as some view religion) whereas a discipline like physics is "objective?" These are important questions. When they are left unaddressed, newcomers to philosophy often have a hard time seeing what's going on in philosophical discussion and tend to underestimate its significance. So the next few paragraphs will offer a "picture" of philosophy and the practice of philosophy that answers these questions. To begin, let's imagine that someone claims that physics is "objective" but philosophy is not (and that this reflects badly on philosophy). Let's first try to figure out what this means, and then ask whether it might be true. To start, we need to know what is meant by "objective." Unfortunately, the term can be used in several different ways. So we'll have to do a small survey.

(i) Sometimes "objective" is applied to people and their judgments. To be objective in this sense is, roughly, to be free of bias. This sort of objectivity is certainly desirable in both physics and philosophy, but there is nothing about the nature of either discipline that guarantees it will be pursued without bias. Well-known practitioners of each have sometimes had their conclusions influenced, for example, by politics or by the desire for personal advancement. So if the claim means that physicists are always objective (in this sense), but philosophers are not, then it is simply incorrect.

(ii)   Another conception of objectivity is that only what is "real" is objective. So the worry may be that while physics concerns what is real, philosophy does not. Sometimes this conception of objectivity is paired with the idea that what isn't real is "subjective." For example, beginning philosophy students sometimes say that horses are objective since they really exist, but that unicorns are subjective – "they're just ideas." But unicorns are not ideas any more than horses are. Unicorns are animals that happen not to exist. It's just as wrong to confuse an idea of a unicorn with a unicorn as it is to confuse an idea of a horse with a horse. For notice that ideas really do exist, even ideas of things that don't exist (like unicorns). So, if ideas of unicorns were unicorns, then we would be forced to conclude that unicorns really exist after all, and that they are just as objective as horses on the present account.

Conception (ii) of the objective/subjective distinction is too crude to stand up to careful scrutiny even without the confusion just discussed. The fundamental problem is that it is inconsistent with the idea that there really is an actual phenomenon of subjectivity. The account entails that the subjective is whatever is not objective, so subjectivity and objectivity must exclude each other. But then we get a contradiction if we assume there really is such a thing as subjectivity. For it would have to be both subjective and objective, contrary to the supposed exclusiveness of the two. We could only maintain consistency by denying that subjectivity exists, in other words, by holding that everything is objective. But if everything is objective, then the subject matter of philosophy is objective, assuming it has a subject matter. But of course it does, and we have already listed some of its main concerns.

(iii)   What about retaining the idea that the objective is whatever is real, but viewing the subjective as a special subcategory of the objective? One such conception of subjectivity may be described as follows. Some of the events that actually occur in the world involve the perspective of a subject in a special way – they're intrinsically "from" that perspective. A good example is a (felt) pain. There cannot be a pain without its being some specific subject's pain. Now, if you are presently feeling a pain, then that event is an objective part of reality, but it's also subjective because it has you as its subject. It has a specific "experiencer" built right into it. On this view, the realm of the subjective consists of first-person experiences like this.

3

Now, with conception (iii) in mind, what about physics and philosophy? Well, they must both concern objective matters, since everything real is objective. But philosophy conspicuously concerns certain subjective notions in addition to nonsubjective ones. For example, it treats concepts like intentionality and consciousness. It is hard to see this as a defect since there is clearly a genuine reality corresponding to these notions, and that reality must have some basic nature whatever it may be. Here there could be a contrast with physics, because it may seem that physics concerns only nonsubjective notions. But this certainly isn't obvious. For example, if subjective phenomena are just certain physico-chemical events in the brain, then they ought to be governed by the laws of physics. But even if it did turn out that physics concerns only nonsubjective notions, while philosophy concerns notions of both sorts, that would only be a difference in subject matter, not a difference for which either field should be disparaged.

(iv) This is a variation on conception (iii). Subjectivity is understood as in (iii), still fully real, but it is held not to be objective. So "objective" means *real but not subjective*. Usually this variation is favored by those who argue that experiences are not publicly accessible and hold that the term "objective" should be reserved for publicly accessible entities and events. The difference between (iii) and (iv) is strictly terminological – it reflects a decision about how to use a word. So there is no more reason to see a problem for philosophy under (iv) than there is under (iii).

(v) Another conception sees the objective as the realm of fact and the subjective as the realm of mere "opinion." Sometimes people think that a discipline that, like philosophy, features strong disagreements on fundamental matters cannot be objective. But this isn't right. If it were, then physics would also lack objectivity because its history documents a succession of disagreements about fundamental physical concepts and principles. (Notice also that if philosophy were subjective in this sense, then physics would have to be too since, as we have seen, it depends on philosophical claims like (1)–(3). We'll return to this point shortly.)

The main problem with the idea that disagreement is a symptom of subjectivity is that it is hard to see how genuine disagreement is even possible if there isn't some (objective) fact to disagree about. Genuine opinions are simply beliefs concerning the facts, and sometimes such beliefs are correct. So there is no inevitable conflict between fact and opinion, contrary to the present conception of objectivity and subjectivity. In effect, the realm of opinion really is the realm of fact, though of course opinions about the facts are sometimes right and sometimes wrong. So let's stick with the idea that the objective is the realm of fact (or, if you prefer, "the real"). But let's combine this with the notion of the subjective found in conception (iii): it is a subrealm of the objective, the realm of "experience."

The idea that there is an inherent opposition between fact and opinion is probably encouraged by the following familiar type of occurrence. People often engage in seemingly endless and fruitless "arguments" about who was "the greatest" practitioner of this or that expertise. Was Van Gogh greater than Rembrandt? Was Aaron greater than Ruth? Was Aristotle greater than Plato? And so on. But are these really questions about *facts* or do specific answers to them merely convey personal preferences? Of course there are facts about numbers of home runs, batting averages, and so forth. Real disagreements about these are possible (and can often be settled by appeal to the records). But questions like who was "greater" have no such resolutions. (You just can't "look it up.") So they seem more like mere expressions of personal taste. But notice that if "X was greater than Y" just means that the speaker *prefers* X to Y, then it doesn't contradict another speaker's similar claim that Y was greater than X, so there is no factual basis for a real disagreement.

If the history of philosophy (and, for that matter, the history of physics) is filled with genuine disagreement as opposed to mere personal preference, then that is evidence that its subject matter is objective, not evidence for the contrary. Because many of the same philosophical disputes have been going on for centuries, they can easily seem endless and fruitless. But it should not be concluded that they merely reflect personal preferences, as in the case of Aaron and Ruth. There really is no preference-independent fact as to whether Aaron was greater than Ruth. But there really is a fact of the matter as to whether our minds are nonmaterial entities distinct from our brains, or whether there exist nonphysical entities like numbers, or whether free will is an illusion. Philosophical disagreements are genuine disagreements about just such factual questions. That many of the debates have gone on for quite a long time shows only that they are about very deep and difficult questions – like basic questions of physics – not that they are not genuine debates about matters of fact.

So, if physics and philosophy are both objective, why do they seem so different? We will see that according to the present picture, they are really not that different. Physicists and philosophers are engaged in very similar activities. Physicists produce and try to verify physical theories. These theories offer analyses of physical concepts and contain (proposed) laws that link these concepts in systematic ways. Philosophers do pretty much the same sort of thing. Physical theories analyze and connect, for example, the concepts of force, mass, and acceleration. Philosophical theories analyze and connect, for example, the concepts of reference, meaning, and truth. And the concepts of intention, volition, and moral responsibility. And also the concepts of causation, regularity, necessity, and physical law. And more.

We saw above that physics (as we know it) has certain essential philosophical presuppositions, notably (1)–(3). If we think about this a little more carefully, something very important emerges. Physics is supposed to be the leading example of science at its purest, the epitome of an "empirical" science. This means that its claims are, *in principle*, verifiable by anyone (if verifiable at all). So it goes beyond the idea that the subject matter of physics is objective, adding in effect that it is nonsubjective (in the sense we have just adopted). Physics is not about any features of subjective experience that should happen not to be publicly verifiable. To put it another way, no one is, as a matter of principle, better placed to verify a physical proposition than anyone else. It is this that gives physics its special aura of ultimate respectability. So, for example, whether gravitational forces tend to accelerate objects of different masses at the same rate seems to be an obvious case of just such an empirical question.

But why? Because, we are tempted to reply, the bodies that have the masses are "out there" independently of us, exerting gravitational forces on each other independently of us, and either they are doing this in the uniform manner described, or they are not, quite independently of us. Furthermore, the reply continues, we can obtain empirical evidence on the question by doing the sort of thing that Galileo did at the Tower of Pisa. (Just get a marble, a bowling ball, and the use of a tall building . . .)

But notice that this reply is nothing more than a specific application of presuppositions (1)–(3) to the case at hand. In fact it is hard to see how the claim that physics is empirical could be defended at all without invoking some such philosophical positions. After all, it's a philosophical claim – an objective claim that might actually be false. So the lofty status of physics as an empirical science rests on just such philosophical assumptions.

Suppose we now agree that philosophical theories are objective and are analogous to physical theories in seeking to clarify and connect various distinctive concepts. It may still be thought that there is nothing in philosophy quite like physical experiment, in which theory confronts reality and faces its ultimate test of correctness. So, it is often felt – for example by beginning philosophy students – that even if philosophical theories do make objective claims, there is no way to decide which ones are true and which false. The theories seem to float in a kind of vacuum and it doesn't make much sense to get too worried about which are right since we can never really tell. We can have genuine opinions, but they might as well just be personal preferences since we'll never know whether they're really right.

According to the present picture of philosophy, this pessimistic view is incorrect. There is something very much like physical experimentation in philosophy, something that enables us to test and evaluate philosophical theories. But it doesn't involve any physical manipulation, observation, measurement, or the like. Instead it involves "mental manipulation" – we think as carefully and creatively as we can about the philosophical claim or problem and, if we do it well, the effort can produce genuine progress. Sometimes the thinking takes the form of argumentation. Sometimes it takes the form of finding "counterexamples" to specific claims. Sometimes it takes the form of assessing theoretical simplicity or explanatory power. Sometimes it takes the form of what are actually called "thought experiments." Sometimes it takes the purely logical form of deriving a contradiction. Sometimes it takes the form of a more-or-less arbitrary resolution of vagueness in our concepts. And it may take a variety of other forms as well. It is not easy to give a complete inventory or a general characterization of the sorts of mental manipulations that can be used to support or discredit philosophical positions. It is better to get the idea by being exposed to a variety of different sorts of examples, and that kind of exposure can be found throughout this book. But it is a good idea to offer a couple of examples right away, in order to make it seem at least initially credible that philosophy is not only objective but also capable of genuine "experimental" support, as the picture we are offering contends.

Suppose someone claimed that people are morally responsible for causing injuries only if they cause them intentionally. Now, this is certainly a philosophical claim – the concepts of causation, intention, and moral responsibility are indisputably philosophical concepts. It is a claim that might even seem plausible on first hearing. But a little reflection reveals

7

that it isn't really all that plausible. Let's assume for the sake of this reflection that people really are morally responsible for some of the things that they do, as we normally take them to be. (Of course this itself is a philosophical claim that could be considered in its own right on a different occasion. We won't consider it here.) Now, given this assumption, it is certainly true that people are often morally responsible for injuries that they intentionally cause. And it is also true that people are sometimes not morally responsible for injuries that they cause unintentionally. But it is not hard to think of examples where we find moral responsibility without intent to injure. Cases of gross negligence are probably the clearest examples. Say a pharmacist carelessly fills your prescription with the wrong pills and you take them and die as a result. Here there is no intent to injure, but the pharmacist is morally responsible. Examples of this general sort are easy to multiply. (But even if we could only think of one, it would be enough to discredit the original philosophical claim. The claim that all prime numbers are odd is untrue since 2 is both prime and even. The fact that it is the only such number is not relevant.)

Now, what went on here? Well, let's begin answering this by noting something that did not go on. We did not undertake empirical research in order to find a case in which some actual pharmacist made a fatal error of the sort described and was deemed morally responsible. Whether this sort of thing has ever actually happened has no effect on the evidential value of our recent philosophical thinking. That thinking stands on its own. It was an exercise in what we might as well call "conceptual" experimentation. We were able to satisfy ourselves that a certain philosophical claim was incorrect merely by thinking about the concepts involved. More specifically, we dreamed up a possible situation embodying those concepts in a way that evidently refutes the general claim.

Before turning to another example, a couple of comments are in order. First, it may initially seem too much like magic – and perhaps even arrogance – to think that we can make genuine philosophical progress merely by thinking about philosophical concepts. Are we invoking special powers of insight or intuition here? Not at all. In a rough and ready way, here is why. We speak a language, an evolving language that is the product of a long span of everyday human activity. In particular, the meanings of the words and phrases of our language are the result of the linguistic activity of its (past and present) speakers. To understand these words and phrases is to have a grasp – possibly imperfect – of these meanings. In other words, it is to have some idea of the concepts associated with the terms.

Among these terms are "cause," "intention," and "morally responsible." We cannot be said to know what these terms mean, even roughly, without having some idea of the concepts they express, and hence some idea of the ways in which those concepts fit together. So, it should not be at all surprising that we are often able to discover the relations among various concepts merely by thinking about them. This ability is simply part of what is involved in understanding our own language.

Further, it shouldn't be surprising that this kind of conceptual experimentation is not at all limited to philosophy, and this is the second comment. Conceptual experimentation takes place at all levels of thought ranging from simple everyday reasoning to the most abstruse reaches of physics and mathematics. The practice of theoretical physics, in particular, consists mainly in this sort of mental activity. (In fact, the same is true for experimental physics, but that's another story.) Albert Einstein's special theory of relativity was, overwhelmingly, just the product of his thinking hard and creatively about the concepts involved.

Physical theories of course need to be vindicated by empirical data – if they are deemed incompatible with the data they will be rejected no matter how clever and elegant they may be. But here is an interesting question: Could there be two physical theories, inconsistent with each other, but both consistent with all the empirical data that we could – even in principle – obtain? To put it another way, how do we know that physical theory is not to some extent "underdetermined" by all possible empirical data? It is easy to see how it might be. Contemporary physics apparently postulates entities (or phenomena) that are too small to allow even indirect detection. Any evidence for their actual existence is "theoretical" in the sense that the postulated entities are part of a theory that makes *other* claims that are empirically verifiable. But if we had two incompatible such theories, as described, then although either one would be perfectly acceptable for practical application, at most one of them would really be true. It is not clear that we could ever arrive at the one true theory. What is clear is that we could not do it empirically. If we could do it at all it would have to be the result – at least in part – of conceptual experimentation.

Now let's look at another example of philosophy at work. One of the classic problems of metaphysics is the so-called mind/body problem. Some philosophers claim that in addition to their physical bodies, human beings have a nonphysical component, usually called the soul or mind. There are several variations on this "dualistic" position, but we won't consider details

9

now. Other philosophers deny the existence of any such nonmaterial component. (There are also variations on this "materialist" position.) Now, this dispute is certainly about the nature of reality. It is an objective question whether we have any such nonmaterial component (just as it is an objective question whether protons are made of quarks). But it is obviously not a straightforward empirical question. The fact that souls (if they exist) are nonmaterial removes them from the realm of possible empirical detection. And, perhaps, the fact that quarks (if they exist) are so small removes them from the realm of possible empirical detection. This leads to the initially somewhat surprising idea that the existence of quarks, though it is a perfectly objective question of physics, is nevertheless not an empirical question. So it appears that in addition to empirical matters, physics cannot avoid taking stands on some matters that are not at all empirical. It may also be that philosophy, perhaps only to a minor extent, cannot avoid certain empirical questions. So the idea that physics is empirical but philosophy is not is beginning to look like a misleading oversimplification.

Notice that although the mind/body problem cannot be solved in any directly empirical manner, empirical facts do have a real bearing on the problem. We have brains in our heads, and these brains are extraordinarily complex organs. (It has been claimed – plausibly but unverifiably – that nowhere in spacetime is matter so intricately organized as in the regions occupied by human brains.) Furthermore, there is an impressive amount of correlation between events of certain types in the brain and, for example, reported sensations of certain types. Empirical facts like these clearly have some bearing on the philosophical debate. For one thing, they make materialism seem like a position worthy of serious consideration. If our heads were empty, and no such correlations could be found between mental events and any appropriately complex physical events in our bodies, materialism would seem very unlikely. In fact it might never have emerged as a theory of the mind.

Still, although empirical matters may influence our approach to the mind/body problem, it is fundamentally not an empirical matter. It isn't going to be solved in a laboratory. Any solution must largely be the result of conceptual experimentation. But a solution won't be as easy to find as it was in the case of the careless pharmacist. If it were that simple, we would already have had the answer for a long time. Open-minded philosophers of both persuasions admit that they can imagine that the opposing position is actually correct. So merely reflecting on the concepts of being a human and having a nonmaterial soul is not going to do the trick. The experimentation has to be much more elaborate, involving the fitting together of these with a number of other concepts (while paying due attention to any relevant empirical matters).

An important example of such a concept is that of "immediate" sense experience, as exemplified in the event of actually feeling a pain. A typical dualist will claim that these sorts of events cannot be physical events in the brain. The reason is that pains (etc.) are "private" or "subjective" (in our present sense of the term) – a given person's pain cannot be experienced by anyone else, whereas events going on in the brain are (in principle anyway) open to public inspection. So now we have the further concept of privacy thrown into the mix. A dualist will have to provide some theoretical explanation of the apparently close association of public events in the brain and these private sensations – the problem of mind/body "connection." A materialist may respond in several different ways. One is to bite the bullet and claim that the events in the brain really do have the needed subjective character. But, in turn, it would take a substantial theory to make this seem plausible. A start on such a theory is the claim that it isn't just an event in the brain, but also an event that is embedded in a causal history that exemplifies a number of causal patterns, and that the subjective character is really a localized, "relational" feature of this complex whole. But this is only a bare start, really just an idea that might lead to the sort of comprehensive theory that the position needs for its clarification and ultimate believability. (There are several other materialist approaches to the problem.)

So the mind/body problem evidently requires a solution involving a heady combination of theory and argument. It may be that no conclusive solution can ever be found, but so far no one has provided any special reason for thinking this. After all, it's a difficult problem. And real advances have been made on many difficult philosophical problems (including the mind/body problem). The fact that a given physicist – or generation of physicists – is unlikely to produce the ultimate, true physical theory is not a good reason for not trying. After all, physical reality is extremely complex and difficult to understand. Even small advances can be very valuable and exciting. Things are no different with difficult philosophical problems. Pessimism is as unwarranted in philosophy as it is in physics.

In the pages that follow we will look at a multiplicity of philosophical problems, arguments, and theses. Sometimes things will be relatively easy, as in the case of the careless pharmacist. Other times the difficulty of the issue will be forbidding, as in the mind/body problem. So we will not always be able to reach firm conclusions. In the cases where we cannot, it should not be thought that the effort was wasted. In every case, conclusive or not, it will be possible to gain new insights into the ways in which philosophical concepts are related. And each case will present the opportunity to enhance our ability to think about important questions in a cogent and dispassionate way.

1.2   Concepts

This brings us to our first metaphysical topic: What is a *concept* in the first place? We have been proceeding as if there actually exist certain things called "concepts," and the question asks about their nature. In other words, the question asks what is involved in the concept of a concept! This is a question that can only be correctly answered by an analysis or characterization of the concept of *being a concept*. It is a question about the nature of a very general concept that isn't treated in the special sciences. So it's a good example of a philosophical question – a question that happens to belong to the realm of metaphysics. Unfortunately, the word "concept" is used in two significantly different ways. To make matters worse, the two different ways are closely related. As an illustration, consider the following sentences.

(1)   The concept of mass is fundamental in physics.

(2)   I had no concept of mass until I studied physics.

Sentence (1) *apparently* asserts that there is a specific "something" – whatever is referred to by the phrase "the concept of mass" – and that that something is fundamental in physics. That something may for the moment be thought of as the *property* of having mass, a property that is possessed by many (but not all) physical entities. But what is important now is not so much the exact nature of the something as the fact that it is a nonsubjective aspect of physical reality, a part of the subject matter of physical theory. (We will discuss the nature of the something soon.)

Sentence (2) does not directly concern this nonsubjective something. Instead it concerns something subjective or mental, specifically my own personal "concept of mass" (and my earlier lack of such). It is tempting to say that (2) is about an "idea" – my idea of mass. But this doesn't really help, because "idea" is just as ambiguous as "concept," and in essentially the same way. If we replace "concept" by "idea" in (1), the result sounds like it says the same thing as the original – that there is some nonsubjective thing that plays a basic role in physics. And if we make the parallel replacement in (2), the result also sounds like the original – it says something about a subjective or mental entity.

So the word "concept" (and, for that matter, "idea") can have either a nonsubjective meaning or a subjective meaning. When we say that philosophy (or physics, etc.) is the study of certain concepts, we are certainly using the term in its nonsubjective sense. When we study, say, the concept of causation (or the concept of mass), we are not studying our own subjective states, but rather something that is a mind-independent component of reality, capable of being studied by persons other than ourselves.

There are two reasons why this is potentially very confusing. First of all, we cannot engage in any study at all without having various subjective states, including concepts in the sense of (2). For example, in order to think about the sense-(1) concept of mass, a person must have a sense-(2) concept of mass. Each one of our own sense-(2) concepts of mass serves to represent the one-and-only sense-(1) concept of mass, but none of these subjective entities can actually *be* the nonsubjective one, no matter how accurately they may represent it. For present purposes, we may think of our various sense-(2) concepts as analogous to different photographs of some single object. They each represent the object, but none of them actually is the object (even if the object is a photograph).

A second possible source of confusion is that the sense (1) concepts studied in philosophy are often concepts *of* subjective phenomena such as consciousness, intention, and belief. Just as there is a mind-independent concept of mass, so is there a mind-independent, sense-(1) concept of, say, consciousness. The phenomena to which this concept applies are themselves subjective, but the concept *itself* is not. So, a philosopher who is thinking about consciousness is having certain subjective experiences. Some of these experiences serve to represent the nonsubjective concept of consciousness, which in turn applies only to certain subjective phenomena. (Notice that these phenomena include the mental activity that is the philosopher's actual ongoing thinking about consciousness – it is a series of conscious events.)

The chief source of confusion on this matter is our own informal talk about concepts in everyday life. We tend to classify them according to the kinds of things they apply to. So we talk about mathematical concepts, psychological concepts, physical concepts, and so on. Properly understood, none of this sort of talk implies, say, that a mathematical concept is itself a mathematical entity like a number. That the concept of a vector space is "mathematical" merely means that vector spaces are mathematical, not that the concept itself is some kind of mathematical entity. This may be clear enough in the present case, but things get cloudier when, in doing philosophy, we start talking about, say, "mental concepts." This might mean sense-(2) concepts in general, or it might serve to single out the sense-(1) concepts that apply to things that are mental. So it is a good idea to be very clear about what we are trying to say when we talk about concepts: The term itself is ambiguous, its two main meanings are closely related, and the seeds of philosophical confusion are already present in our everyday use of language.

Now let's return to the question of the exact nature of sense-(1) concepts. Our original examples of philosophical concepts included existence, truth, knowledge, justification, mind, and goodness. To these we have since added the narrower concepts of intentionality, moral responsibility, causation, belief, reference, meaning, volition, regularity, necessity, and physical law. We also mentioned the physical concepts of mass, force, and acceleration, and the everyday concepts of horse and unicorn. But just what sort(s) of entities are these various concepts?

Let's try to think about this question with the help of the specific concepts of mass, horse, and unicorn. We have already rejected the idea that such concepts are subjective, mental entities. They are sense-(1) concepts and hence they are – somehow or other – accessible to us all.

So the concept of mass is nonsubjective. But is it *physical*? It is certainly not an ordinary physical object, even though the concept of mass can only "apply" to physical objects. The same is true of the concepts of horse and unicorn. They are not ordinary physical objects, but they can only apply to physical objects. (It is simply an accident of nature that there are no physical objects to which the concept of unicorn applies.) One very natural picture of what is going on here is that the concepts of mass, horse, and unicorn are *properties* that different physical objects may or may not have (or, in philosophical terminology, "instantiate").

There are a number of different philosophical accounts of properties. Two very different kinds of account are of special interest to us here. According to one of these, properties are "abstract" entities – they exist

14

apart from and independently of their instances. Plato is famous for his detailed version of this position, and this and more modern versions are often called *Platonism* in his honor. (Plato's ancient Greek term for properties is usually translated in English by "forms" (or "ideas") and his account is called the theory of forms.)

A Platonist philosopher who holds that the concept of mass is simply the property of *having mass* therefore thinks that this concept is an abstract entity. It exists independently of any physical objects that happen to instantiate it, and also independently of anyone's mind or mental activity. Although the *instances* of the concept of mass are of course physical, the concept *itself* is not. It does not even occupy spacetime.

The abstractness of properties is surely the hardest feature of Platonism to swallow. Some philosophers have tried to avoid it by holding that the property of having mass is *itself* somehow physical, claiming that it is "in" the entities that "have" it and is dependent on them for its existence. So it would be "located" in a disconnected region of spacetime – roughly, the "sum" of the regions where the things that have mass are located. Proponents of this "physicalist" approach may or may not go so far as to hold that the property itself is (literally) a physical *object*. Although physicalism may succeed in avoiding the problem of abstractness, it has serious problems of its own. One crucial problem is that it seems unable to account for the property of being a unicorn. **[It is a good exercise to try to explain clearly why this is so.]** We will compare Platonist and physicalist accounts of properties in more detail in chapter 3.

So far it has seemed very natural to think that there really are non-subjective concepts, that concepts like the three under discussion are in fact properties, and that the significant issue is whether these properties are abstract or somehow physical. But there is a powerful and seductive alternative position: the view that there really are no such entities as nonsubjective concepts in the first place! According to this "nominalist" view, the term "the concept of mass," as it occurs in sentence (1), should not be understood as referring to some specific entity.

Nominalism is often motivated by comparisons with uncontroversial cases. Consider the sentence:

(3)   The illusion of immortality fades with the blush of youth.

There are probably several plausible understandings of this quasi-poetic offering. But none of them makes a claim that there is some *one specific thing*

15

that fades under certain circumstances. Instead, the term "the illusion of immortality" somehow functions in a more general way, so as to permit (3) to mean something more like the more prosaic observation that young people who have a feeling of immortality generally lose it as they get older. On this view sentence (3) concerns indefinitely many feelings of indefinitely many people, not just some single thing.

A nominalist might claim that "the concept of mass" functions in some such more general way in (1). For example, it might be held that (1) means something like: Everyone who learns physics acquires a (sense-(2)) concept of mass. So then it would be about indefinitely many private mental representations, not about some single public entity. Or it might mean: Physical reality includes bodies that have mass, and this phenomenon of bodies' having mass is a fundamental concern of physics. There are various other potentially nominalist interpretations. [**Exercise: Try to think one up and defend it.**] What is central to the nominalist view is that the apparently literal reference to nonsubjective concepts is held to be just a loose and convenient "manner of speaking." The nominalist of course has to settle on a specific plausible (and uniform) way of interpreting sentences that contain such apparent references – an interpretation that makes it clear that no genuine reference is actually being made. A truly plausible nominalist interpretation may not be easy to find. The history of past efforts is far from glorious.

Nominalism about nonsubjective concepts is, of course, logically consistent with either Platonism or physicalism about properties. But in fact most concept nominalists are also property nominalists. If one really did accept the existence of properties, there would be little motivation for thinking (for example) that the concept of mass was anything other than the property of having mass. (Nominalism about properties will be considered in some depth in chapter 3.)

We have now taken a brief look at three different approaches to the question of the nature of nonsubjective concepts. (There may be others.) It's time to take a stand. Our stand will not be very bold because it will defer the heart of the issue to a later time. In chapter 3 we will argue in favor of Platonism concerning properties, relations, and propositions. Part of the argumentation will be a rejection of both nominalism and physicalism concerning properties (etc.). Now, if there really are properties (etc.), and they really are abstract entities as the Platonist claims, then – as just noted – there is no real point in being a nominalist about (nonsubjective) concepts. (And of course it would simply be wrong to be a physicalist about them.) The natural position would be that concepts like those of mass, horse, and unicorn are simply the respective (abstract) properties of having mass, being a horse, and being a unicorn.

It doesn't follow that all (nonsubjective) concepts are properties. Some are relations. For example, looking at the list above, both moral responsibility and causation seem to be relations. We usually think of moral responsibility as a relation between a person and a state of affairs. In our recent example, the (imaginary) *pharmacist* was morally responsible for *your being dead*. The relation of responsibility held between the person and the state of affairs. Similarly, we usually think of causation as a relation between *events*. For example, *your taking the pill* was one of the (imagined) events that occurred at a certain time and *your dying* was another (that occurred at a later time). When we say that taking the pill caused you to die we are saying that a certain relation, the relation of causation, held between the former event and the latter event. So relations are entities like properties, except that they link two or more things together (in a certain order) instead of applying to things singly. According to Platonism, relations are abstract entities.

Most concepts that are of interest to us are either properties or relations. But not all. Consider the sentence:

(4)   Einstein based the special theory of relativity on the concept of the invariance of the speed of light.

But what *is* this concept? It certainly isn't a property or relation. Rather, it is a *proposition*, specifically, the proposition *that the speed of light is constant relative to all reference frames*. To see this, notice that (4) evidently says the same thing as:

(5)   Einstein based the special theory of relativity on the proposition that the speed of light is constant relative to all reference frames.

Platonists hold that propositions, like properties and relations, are abstract entities whose existence is independent of our mental activity. (We will have much more to say about this in chapter 3.)

Now, here is a small puzzle. Suppose it is true that nonsubjective concepts are entities — like properties — that exist independently of us. Then why do we find it natural to choose such a subjective-sounding *term*? I think the answer is that we do not *always* find it natural. We find it natural only when these entities are being considered in part as objects of our own *thought*. Sentences (1) and (4) provide good examples of such contexts because physics and relativity theory are human *studies* of certain aspects of reality. Consider the following sentences.

(6) The concept of unicorn might have had some instances;

(7) The property of being a unicorn might have had some instances;

(8) The medievals were fascinated by the concept of unicorn;

and

(9) The medievals were fascinated by the property of being a unicorn.

Sentences (6) and (7) say exactly the same thing (on the present account). But (6) nevertheless sounds very odd – compared to (7) – simply because it doesn't treat the property specifically as an object of thought. Something like the opposite happens with (8) and (9), which also have the same meaning. Sentence (9) sounds at least a little strange (compared to (8)) because the property *is* being mentioned as an object of thought.

1.3   Analysis

In Section 1.1 we stressed the importance of the "analysis of concepts" in philosophy (as well as in physics or any other theoretical discipline). In Section 1.2 we settled (conditionally) on a specific account of the nature of concepts. Now it is time to say something about the concept of *analysis*. Not surprisingly, there are several different notions of analysis, both everyday and scientific (or otherwise technical). But when philosophers speak of analysis they are generally thinking about an analysis of a concept, usually a property or relation.

Most properties are complexes of other properties. To give an analysis of a property is to break it down into constituent properties. For example, consider the property of *being a bachelor*. It is composed of the following properties: being unmarried, being an adult, being a male, and being a (human) person. A bachelor is an unmarried adult male person. To have the property of being a bachelor is simply to have the complex property that is

18

composed of the four properties just mentioned. This is surely a correct analysis of the property of being a bachelor, but notice that the four analyzing properties are themselves complex properties, properties for which analyses could be given. For example, being unmarried is a property whose analysis would involve properties and relations reflecting certain social institutions, and being a person is a property whose analysis is very controversial (and is in fact a central problem in metaphysics).

Because our analysis of being a bachelor appealed to other complex properties without analyzing them, we may say that it was not "totally refined." A totally refined analysis would break a property down into "simple" properties, ones that were themselves unanalyzable. But notice that the fact that our analysis is not totally refined does not mean it is in any way incorrect. To be incorrect an analysis must either include as constituent parts some properties that really aren't constituent parts, or else it must omit properties that really are. An example of the former would be the claim that being a bachelor was composed of being unmarried, being an adult, being a male, and being a dog. (For an example of the latter, just delete any of the four original properties from the original list.) The important point is that properties that would appear *explicitly* in a more refined analysis have not been *omitted* in the less refined analysis, since it explicitly includes properties that have them as constituent parts. So analyzing a property is like cutting a pie into pieces. There are many ways to cut a pie into separate pieces without losing any of the pie's parts. But no matter how we do it, some of the pie's parts will be present without being individual pieces – they will be parts of pieces.

Here is a slightly different analysis of being a bachelor: it's the complex property composed of the two properties being unmarried and being a man. This analysis is just as correct as the original, but it's less refined. In effect, the original analysis just incorporates an analysis of being a man as an explicit component. Normally in philosophy we aren't interested in giving totally refined analyses. The level of refinement we seek in a particular case depends on our goals in seeking the analysis. For some purposes a given level may be sufficient, for others it may not. Here's an example. Some philosophers (certain materialists) give roughly this analysis of being a person: the property composed of being a human body, being alive, and functioning properly. Other philosophers (certain dualists) think this analysis is incomplete, and therefore incorrect, because it omits the property of having a soul. Now, if our interest in the analysis is to consider the debate between these dualists and materialists, then the competing analyses are probably refined enough. We simply want to know which analysis is right *regardless* of how the explicit constituents might themselves be analyzed. But if our interest in the analysis concerns the fate of a hospital patient on life-support systems, we will certainly need more refinement. We'll need analyses of being alive and functioning properly.

This discussion strongly suggests that an analysis (in the present sense of the word) is a certain sort of *proposition* – a proposition to the effect that a certain property (etc.) is composed of certain other properties. We have already seen that concepts include propositions as well as properties and relations. So analyses are included among concepts. This should not be too surprising if we think about a sentence like:

(10)   Aristotle's concept of happiness is different from Mill's (concept of happiness).

Here the terms "Aristotle's concept of happiness" and "Mill's (. . .)" do not refer to the property of being happy. If they did, then – according to (10) – there would be at least two properties of being happy. But there is only one property of being happy. When people disagree about it, they are disagreeing about some aspect of this one single property, say its proper analysis or maybe the best way to acquire it or promote it. When philosophers like Aristotle and Mill disagree about such a property, it's usually about its analysis. Then sentence (10) would mean the same as:

(11)   Aristotle's analysis of the concept of happiness is different from Mill's.

In (11) it is clear that "the concept of happiness" refers to the single property of being happy and the sentence says that the two philosophers offered different analyses of this single property. These analyses are simply different propositions as to the constituents of happiness, at most one of which could be correct.

1.4   The Scope of Metaphysics

We have already given a characterization of metaphysics and, in fact, we have even done some metaphysics in the previous three sections. The purpose of this section is to give some indication of the different kinds of questions metaphysicians try to answer. Some of the following matters will be dealt with in this book, others will not.

Persons. Almost all of us think that there are entities in the world called persons. Another way of saying this is to say that most of us include persons in our "ontologies." *Ontology* is the theory of what kinds of things exist, but sometimes the word "ontology" is also used to refer to a philosopher's claimed inventory of what kinds of things exist. So, assuming that we include persons in our ontologies, it is natural to ask for an analysis of the concept of being a person. We have already seen that this is a very controversial question in philosophy, and we have hinted at a couple of the different positions.

Abstract Entities. There are many different sorts of supposed "abstract" entities. We have already mentioned properties, relations, and propositions. Mathematical objects, like numbers, sets, functions, points, lines, and so forth, are also commonly thought to be abstract. The fundamental metaphysical question about such supposed entities is whether they really do exist. Of course it could be that some kinds do and some kinds don't. We will look separately at the cases of properties (etc.) and numbers in this book. We will see that in doing so we must also face the question of the nature of the concept of existing.

Truth and Falsity. There are many metaphysical questions regarding the notion of truth (and falsity). Some of them will be considered in this book and others will not. The most general question about truth is: What is it? That is, what is the analysis of the concept of truth? We will not attempt an analysis, but will content ourselves with the following more modest questions (1) What sorts of things are properly said to be true? (Is it sentences, propositions, utterances, or some other category of things?) (2) Is truth "relative?" A satisfactory analysis of the concept of truth would of course provide answers to these questions, but we will see that answers are possible even in the absence of an analysis. (A satisfactory analysis would also provide a solution to the well-known "paradoxes" of truth. An example of such a paradox is provided by the sentence, "What I am now saying is false." It certainly appears that such an assertion must be both true and false. But this is absurd. How can the absurdity be avoided?)

Causation. Most of us believe that events in the world sometimes cause other events to occur. For example, hurricane winds cause ocean waters to flood coastal areas. Or, for a simpler case, the impact of a moving billiard ball on a stationary ball causes the latter to begin moving. But what is the

21

exact nature of the supposed relation of causation? Some philosophers have thought that there really is no such relation in nature, that it is something we imagine is there but really isn't. Others have tried to supply an analysis of the concept of causation that places it squarely in the realm of things independent of us.

Necessity and Possibility. Any ordinary thing, like a table or a tree, might not have existed. For example, the table I am presently working at might never have been built. The steel and fiberboard of which it is made might have been parts of the deck and trim of a boat, or might never have been made themselves. Is this true of everything? Maybe not. According to most theists, God exists necessarily. That is, God must have existed, could not have failed to exist. And according to Platonists, entities like properties and numbers exist necessarily. Perhaps space and time (or spacetime) exist necessarily, even though the distribution of stuff within them might have been different. The notions of necessity and possibility do not pertain only to the question of existence. A given wooden house may happen to be white, but certainly it could have been some other color. In other words, it isn't necessarily white, it's possibly nonwhite. On the other hand, it does seem to have some of its properties necessarily, for example, being made of wood. It is certainly true that a stone house might have been built where the wooden house sits, and in fact it might have the same owner. But such a house would not have been one and the same house as the one that is actually there. That house couldn't have been made of stone. We have now seen several claims involving the notions of necessity and possibility. Apart from the question of whether these claims are true, there remains the question of what they really mean. To say what they mean is, in effect, to give an analysis of the concepts of necessity and possibility. This is one of the central tasks of metaphysics, and it will be treated in this book.

Determinism and Freedom. We find it natural to think that all events in the physical world are caused by previous events in the physical world. But we also find it natural to think that certain of our physical actions are the products of our own "volition" and are not caused by any physical events outside us. Are these views in conflict or not? If they aren't, how is it that they seem to be? And if they are, which one of them is wrong, and why? We will discuss this issue, and also the related issue of fatalism: Is everything that happens "inevitable?"

God. Metaphysicians have argued about the existence and nature of God since ancient times. We will not treat the topic directly in this book, but we will touch upon it in the chapter on cosmology.

The Nature of Physical Things. What is a thing? For example, what is a table? Is it a three-dimensional, merely spatial object that is "entirely present" at different times? Or is it a four-dimensional, spatiotemporal object only part of which is present at any given time? Could a given thing have failed to have some of its parts (and still have been one and the same thing)? Some things, like disassembled bicycles, are grossly "disconnected." That is, some of their parts are spatially separated from all of the parts that don't overlap them. Yet we still consider such "scattered objects" to be individual things. Then why don't we consider every bunch of similarly separated things as constituting a single scattered object? (For example, your watch and your notebook.) Would there be any harm in doing so? All of these questions will be addressed in this book.

Time. What is time? Does it "pass," and if so, how? What, if anything, does consciousness have to do with it? Does it have an intrinsic "direction?" In what way does the temporal dimension differ from the spatial dimensions (if at all)? Is it logically possible to "travel" in time?

Color. Do things have colors when they are in totally dark vaults? When you look at a fresh, ripe tomato, is the redness you perceive located in the tomato or in your mind? We will look at some different views on this topic in a later chapter.

These topics do not exhaust the scope of metaphysics, but they are certainly among the most widely discussed topics in the history of the subject, and they do provide a good idea of its nature.

2

Numbers

As we noted in chapter 1, *ontology* is the branch of metaphysics devoted to the question of what kinds of things there are, or, in other words, what kinds of things *exist*. At first it may seem ridiculous to worry about such a question because the answer is obvious: There are tables and chairs, mountains and rivers, clouds and trees, stars and planets, dogs and cats, and so on. But if we think about it for a moment, a list of *these* sorts of things, even if we extended it indefinitely, would omit lots of other sorts of things whose existence we *apparently* assert and presuppose in ordinary life every day. For example, it would omit *facts, values, ideas, concepts, properties, times, debts, proposals, obligations, likelihoods, relationships, questions, commands, promises, trends, words, rules*, and so on. It would also omit *numbers*. In this chapter the question of the existence of numbers will serve as a case study in ontology, partly for its own intrinsic interest and partly as a warm-up for what will come in chapter 3.

The (supposed) entities of the second list above differ from those of the first because they evidently aren't material things. Despite this, we certainly act (and speak) as if such things really do exist, just as we do regarding the material things on the first list. Now, many people also say that there exist such nonmaterial entities as angels and ghosts. But there is a subtle and important difference between the cases of angels and ghosts, on the one hand, and (for example) those of trends and numbers on the other. We can bring this difference to light by considering the following two sentences:

(1)   Many ghosts have haunted many houses;

and

24

(2)   Many trends have started in California.

The difference is this. A person who happens to believe that (1) is true will nevertheless agree that if there really are no ghosts after all, then (1) would have to be false. To put it a little differently, there is no plausible way to give (1) a literal reading that does not involve a literal assertion of the existence of ghosts. **[Is this really right? It is a good exercise to try to find such a reading and then figure out why it doesn't really capture the meaning of (1).]** On the other hand, a philosopher who thinks there really are no such entities as *trends* will *not* deny the truth of sentence (2). After all, it would border on the absurd to deny (2). Instead, our philosopher will try to provide a literal way of understanding (2) that does not involve a literal assertion of the existence of special entities called trends.

Statements that seemingly assert or presuppose the existence of numbers are more like (2) than (1) in this respect. For example, consider the sentence

(3)   Seven is less than nine.

Everyone who understands (3) will agree it is true, even philosophers who deny that there are special entities called numbers. The superficial grammar of (3) is apparently the same as that of

(4)   Sue is shorter than Kate;

or

(5)   Chicago is west of New York.

But these latter statements presuppose the existence of Sue, Kate, Chicago, and New York. So doesn't (3) presuppose the existence of seven and nine, that is, doesn't it presuppose the existence of certain numbers? If we answer yes, then we have to say something plausible about what these numbers are like and how we come to know about them. On the other hand, if we say no, then we have to explain how it is that (3) can make good sense (and even be true) if there are no numbers. (In other words, we have to give a plausible reading of (3) that doesn't involve entities called numbers.) Following is a sketch of three approaches to the overall "problem of numbers" that have been taken in the past.

(1) *Platonism (or realism) about numbers* is the view that numbers are *abstract* entities that exist independently of any minds. (The term "abstract" is notoriously hard to define, and we won't try to define it here. But one of the key features of abstract entities is that they don't have spatiotemporal locations. Another is that they exist independently of minds and mental activity generally.) According to Platonism, (3) asserts that a certain relation holds between two specific such entities, and (3) is true or false according to whether or not that relation actually does hold between those entities. So Platonists think that the grammatical similarity of (3) to (4) and (5) is no accident — they think each asserts that some relation holds between two actually existing entities.

Some people find the idea of something truly existing, but not existing at any spacetime location, very hard to accept at first. This is often because — whether consciously or not — they have accepted an identification of "reality" or "existence" with *spacetime and its contents*. This identification is sometimes seen as part of what is involved in having a "scientific worldview." The idea that existence might extend beyond the spatiotemporal is wrongly viewed as something that could only be the product of superstition, mysticism, religion or, at any rate, something alien to science. This widespread feeling is extremely ironic because, as was suggested in Section 1.1, the sciences themselves appear to be studies of (nonsubjective) *concepts* — entities that evidently belong on the second list because they are nonmaterial (and hence have no spatiotemporal locations)! In their zeal to defend the scientific worldview against mysticism and superstition, such people may unwittingly be discarding the primary subject matter of science itself. The moral is this: The fact that many supposed nonmaterial entities are the dubious products of mysticism or superstition does not show that there are no scientifically legitimate nonmaterial entities.

People who are prone to making this mistaken inference often say (for example) "But how *could* there be anything that didn't occupy spacetime?" This makes it sound like they think "existing" just *means* occupying spacetime, and hence that Platonists are making a serious "conceptual" error. But this isn't really right. If the concept of *existing* and the concept of *occupying spacetime* were one and the same, then it would be self-contradictory to claim that something exists that doesn't occupy spacetime. Yet many, many people (probably *most* people) believe there exist such things (nonmaterial souls, for example). These people may be wrong, but if they are wrong it isn't because their belief is self-contradictory. If they're wrong it's simply because the things that occupy spacetime are *in fact* the only things that exist. In other words, if they're wrong, they're wrong about a matter of nonlinguistic fact, not about what the word "exist" means. The *normal,* everyday concept of existing really doesn't involve occupying spacetime, even if lots of things that exist do occupy spacetime, in fact even if *everything* that exists occupies spacetime.

Now notice this. Suppose, contrary to what we have claimed, that the word "existing" really did mean occupying spacetime. That still wouldn't be enough to make Platonism go away. It would just mean the Platonist would have to avoid the word "exist." It would still be possible to claim that *some things don't occupy spacetime.* The Platonist would just have to deploy some *other* word to cover both the things that do and the things that don't occupy spacetime. (Of course we would still need to be convinced that some things really don't occupy spacetime. Just as we couldn't refute Platonism by appeal to the meanings of words, we can't prove it that way either.) But rather than introducing a new term, let's just accept what seemed on reflection to be true anyway, namely, that the concept of existing does not involve occupying spacetime. Then one could cheerfully (and consistently) claim that there exist things that don't occupy spacetime, and we can stick with the easier statement of the Platonist's position about numbers.

So it doesn't appear that Platonism is wrong for any simple conceptual reason. But here is an argument that does raise a real difficulty for the theory. (The argument is a *reductio ad absurdum.*)

1   (Suppose:) Platonism is true. **Then:**
2   Numbers aren't located in spacetime. **Hence:**
3   We can't have any causal interactions with numbers. **So:**
4   We can't come to know anything about numbers. **But:**
5   In fact we do know lots of things about numbers (for example, that seven is less than nine). **Therefore:**
6   Platonism cannot be true.

Here the central idea is that one of the consequences of Platonism contradicts the unquestionable fact that we have numerical knowledge. From this it is concluded that Platonism cannot be true (since no true theory can have an absurd consequence). In short, the problem for Platonism is that it leaves no room for us to know anything about numbers. Clearly it is important for any Platonist to come to grips with this sort of criticism.

[Exercise: Analyze the argument. Is it valid? Does it have hidden premises? If so, are they plausible?]

(2) *Conceptualism (about numbers)*, like Platonism, accepts the existence of numbers. But conceptualists do not hold that numbers are independently existing, abstract entities. Instead they say numbers are "concepts," and by this they mean that numbers are ideas in our minds, not that they are properties or propositions (like the "nonsubjective" concepts discussed in chapter 1). Different conceptualists have different views about just what these ideas are like, but we won't go into that. What is important for us is that these ideas, though they might not be located in space, are nevertheless located in time, and they depend on minds for their existence. They're mind-dependent entities.

Conceptualism is very different from Platonism despite their agreement on the existence of numbers. While Platonism seems to isolate us from the numbers in the sharpest of ways, conceptualism puts us into direct contact with them, since we may find them among our own ideas. Though it seemed to be a serious challenge for a Platonist to account for our knowledge of numbers, it seems easy for a conceptualist. We can know about numbers, presumably, just by having certain ideas and paying attention to their features.

On the other hand, the simple version of conceptualism we have so far sketched has a very serious problem of its own – it is apparently in direct conflict with both our common-sense views and our theoretical claims about numbers. For example, we normally think there is only one number seven. And in fact, it is a theorem of arithmetic that there is only one natural number between six and eight, namely seven. To put the matter a little differently, we normally think the term "seven" is the name of a single entity. But if conceptualism is true, then it looks like there has to be an abundance of numbers seven. There's your idea "seven" and my idea "seven." In fact, if ideas are mental *events* (or parts of mental events) then it is clear that no one can have the same, single idea more than once. Of course we can have an idea today that is impossible to distinguish qualitatively from an idea we had yesterday, but it still isn't the same, single idea any more than two consecutive photocopies of the same, single page are the same, single photocopy. One idea happened yesterday, the other did not; one photocopy was made at a certain time, the other somewhat later. Thus not only would different people have different "sevens," but even the same person would have different "sevens" on different occasions. There would be way too many sevens.

A closely related violation of common sense is this. We normally think there are infinitely many numbers. No matter what number we pick, there must always be a larger one. (Of course, this is also a theorem of arithmetic.) For example, we always get a new, larger number when we take a given number and add one to it. So there are infinitely many numbers. But there are apparently only finitely many ideas. Better: Assuming there are only finitely many minds (past, present, and future), and assuming minds are finite, there are only finitely many ideas.

A third problem, also closely related, is that our ordinary conception of numbers construes them as having a kind of constancy that seems impossible if they are anything like "occurrent" ideas. We don't think of numbers as continually popping into and out of existence, according to whether or not someone is thinking about them. Conceptualism thus has problems that are different from but surely as serious as those facing Platonism.

The problems just mentioned, however, are not quite decisive. For one thing, they depend on the assumption that a concept or idea (in the relevant sense) is a temporally circumscribed mental *event* (or else a part of such an event). Now certainly some of our ideas meet this description, but perhaps we also have "ideas" that, while genuinely mental, are nevertheless not of this occurrent sort. Then it might be possible to retain the view that numbers are ideas without giving up the uniqueness of seven or the infinitude of the realm of numbers. Of course, any such defense would depend on a solid account of these supposed nonoccurrent ideas – something that might not be easy to find.

One effort that doesn't depend on the doubtful notion of nonoccurrent ideas but is somewhat similar in approach is this. The conceptualist concedes that numbers are *not* ideas (of any sort) but holds instead that they are certain *properties* – in fact, properties of (occurrent) ideas. So your idea of seven, my idea of seven, and your earlier and later ideas of seven (etc.) all have a certain property in common, and it is this property that is really the number seven. That way we get just one seven, as our normal view of numbers requires. Of course, conceding that numbers aren't ideas would be a major concession for a conceptualist and many would be unwilling to make it, seeing it as a betrayal of the essential spirit of the view. But those willing to make it would hold that the spirit of conceptualism is retained because the properties that are the numbers are properties that can only be instantiated by *ideas*.

A conceptualist who adopts this view will have to say what notion of properties is being invoked. (See Section 1.2.) There are three basic possibilities here, but each of them appears to raise further problems. The possibilities and the problems are as follows.

(i) *Platonism*. If the numbers are Platonic properties of ideas, then they are abstract entities whose existence is independent of any mental activity. They would have existed even if no minds had ever existed and produced ideas to instantiate them. So any claimed conceptualist spirit would be considerably diluted by this choice. After all, it was presumably these very features of abstractness and independence that drove conceptualists away from Platonism about numbers *proper* in the first place.

(ii) *Physicalism*. There are two problems here. First, if the numbers are "physical" properties of ideas, then ideas must be physical entities of some kind. But this evidently commits the conceptualist to a materialist conception of the mind – something that certainly didn't seem to be part of the original bargain. Originally it appeared that conceptualism was quite independent of any particular theory of the mind. Second, although this approach would solve the problem of "too many sevens," it would leave the problems of infinitude and constancy very much intact because the numbers would be dependent on (occurrent) ideas for their existence.

(iii) *Aristotelianism*. This position, inspired by Aristotle, is a generalization of physicalism about properties. It holds that the properties of any entity – *whether physical or not* – are "in" that entity. As with physicalism, one and the same property may be "in" any number of separate entities. Finally, the existence of any property is dependent on its having instances precisely because properties are held to be "in" the things that have them. This is often called the *"in re"* conception of properties. (The Latin phrase means *in the thing*.) General problems of the *in re* conception will be discussed in chapter 3. What is worth noticing here is that a conceptualist could adopt this position without being committed to a materialist view of the mind. Despite this, the problems of infinitude and constancy evidently remain.

(3) *Nominalism (about numbers)* holds that there literally are no numbers at all. Like unicorns and ghosts, they simply don't exist. Hence terms like "seven" and so forth don't refer to any entities, whether abstract or con-

crete, mental or nonmental, or whatever. As noted above, this theory faces the task of saying how it is that sentences like (3) can be true if seven and nine don't even exist. Many different strategies for doing this have been proposed, but none has ever enjoyed wide acceptance. The general nominalist strategy is to have us view ordinary statements that are apparently about numbers as shorthand for more complicated statements that clearly *aren't* about numbers. Thus, for example, if (3) is really shorthand for a statement that plainly doesn't refer to any numbers, then it can be claimed that its truth doesn't depend on the existence of numbers after all.

Here is a sketch of how such a proposal might look in greater detail. Notice first that the word "seven" is used very differently in the sentence

(6)   There were seven elves in the forest,

than it is in sentence (3). In (3) it's a noun that looks like a proper name of some supposed entity. But in (6) it has no such appearance. Instead it's an adjective, apparently modifying the noun "elves." Furthermore, its adjectival function is somewhat unusual. To see this, compare (6) with

(7)   There were happy elves in the forest.

Here the adjective "happy" modifies "elves" with the result that (7) means that (at least) some of the elves in the forest were, as individual elves, happy. But (6) cannot mean that (at least) some of the elves in the forest were, as individual elves, *seven*. It can't mean this because this doesn't even make sense. But (6) makes perfectly good sense. So "seven" (in (6)) doesn't function like "happy" (in (7))

One promising view of what is going on here is that in (6) the adjective "seven" is implicitly describing a *group* of elves − the group consisting of the elves in the forest − rather than describing the individual elves that make up the group. So (6) means that the group consisting of the elves in the forest is a *seven-membered* group. Whereas (7) attributes the property of *being happy* to some individual elves, (6) attributes the property of *being seven-membered* to a group of elves.

The next step in the nominalist strategy is to explain this property without making any reference to supposed entities called "numbers." For example, and to pick a slightly simpler case, we could explain *being three-membered* as follows. A group has the property of being three-membered just in case it has a member, and it also has a member that is different from

31

that member, and it also has a member that is different from either of those members, and it has no other members. (Using variables, we can simplify this to: A group is three-membered just in case it has members x, y, and z, all different, and it has no members other than x, y, and z.) Notice that although this formulation is a little clumsy, it doesn't make any reference to "numbers" at all.

So now let's assume we can make good sense of any statement like "There were seven elves" or "I have three tickets" (etc.) in terms of properties like being three-membered and notably without any assumption that there exist special entities called numbers. (Note that the phrase "being three-membered" does not include an occurrence of the word "three" as a noun. In fact we need not have used "three-membered" at all. Instead we could have used a term like "ternary" or even a totally made-up term. After all, we're simply defining a technical term here, and the point is that it's one that doesn't presuppose the existence of numbers.)

Now back to sentence (3). The nominalist proposal is to treat this as shorthand for a more complicated sentence like:

(8)   If all the members of any seven-membered group are paired off (one-to-one) with members of any nine-membered group, then there will be members of the nine-membered group left over.

(And a sentence like "3 + 2 = 5" will be treated as shorthand for something like: "If A and B are groups with no members in common, and A is three-membered and B is two-membered, then the group consisting of all members of A and B is five-membered.")

Thus it seems that a nominalist may be able to provide a uniform account of the meanings of statements that *apparently* refer to numbers, but without assuming that there really *are* any numbers – an account that has the further virtue of preserving the common-sense truth-values of such statements. But there are problems.

For one thing, it seems to be a serious violation of common sense to believe that, *all along*, statements like "Seven is less than nine" have really been covert statements about groups of things. They don't *appear* to say anything at all about groups, pairing off members of groups, forming aggregate groups, and the like. They just look like statements about relations between numbers. Of course, what we call common sense is often demonstrably incorrect and should be subject to revision in the light of sound science or philosophy. (Still, if sound philosophy on some issue happens to accord with common sense, that is surely a point in its favor.)

A second problem is that the nominalist's account makes heavy apparent use of *properties*. Of course, maybe the nominalist *also* has a nominalistic account of properties. But then the solution to the problem of numbers will depend on this further theory, and we cannot fairly evaluate it until we see that theory. (We will discuss nominalism about properties in chapter 3.)

On the other hand, the appeal to properties may be literal. Then we need to know whether they are Platonic, physicalist, or Aristotelian (just as we did with the variation on conceptualism mentioned above). Of course if they are Platonic, then the nominalist has avoided Platonism about numbers only by embracing Platonism about properties. But most metaphysicians, regardless of ontological persuasion, will agree that the latter theory is much more complicated and poorly understood than the former. So this is a highly unlikely combination of views for a serious nominalist to adopt.

If the properties are Aristotelian (or physicalist), then an ultimate evaluation will depend in part on the question of what kind of thing a *group* is – a question the nominalist must eventually face *anyway*. We will return to this below, but for a moment let's pretend we have a satisfactory answer. Now what if there are only finitely many ordinary things in the universe? Then any group of ordinary things has only finitely many members. But there are supposed to be infinitely many numbers. So there's a number that would be larger than the size of any group of ordinary things. But there is no corresponding *in re* property. This creates a serious difficulty for the nominalist's strategy.

There are three kinds of responses a nominalist might make. One is to allow groups of groups, and groups of groups of groups, etc., in addition to groups of ordinary things. Another is to treat the original claims about groups not as claims about *actual* groups, but as claims about all *possible* groups, so that even if there are no actual n-membered groups (for some large n), there are still (merely) possible n-membered groups. A third approach is to treat the nominalist interpretations of arithmetic statements – such as (8) – *subjunctively* (as described below), in an effort to avoid the issue of actual group existence. Each of these responses has its own difficulties. Very briefly, the difficulties are these.

The groups-of-groups approach comes dangerously close to requiring that the nominalist accept a theory of *sets*, for it is set theory that lays down the principles according to which sets may be gathered into sets. But sets are very commonly viewed Platonistically – as independent abstract entities. So the ontological issue of the status of "numbers" will have been resolved only by raising a parallel – and, incidentally, more difficult – issue about sets.

The possible-groups approach faces a similar problem. For what is a "(merely) possible group" in the first place? Well, evidently it must be a group that includes among its members some "possible things" that aren't actual. But what right do we have to believe in the existence of such merely possible things? Are they abstract entities? They certainly don't occupy actual spatiotemporal regions, so it looks like they're abstract. The possible-groups strategy of defending nominalism may be committed to the existence of abstract entities that are at least as bad as, and probably worse than, numbers. One way in which they are arguably worse is this. We have a mathematical theory that tells us how the numbers interrelate, what numbers (supposedly) exist, and so forth. But, at least so far, there is no parallel theory governing the behavior of merely possible objects. It would be up to the nominalist to provide such a theory before this method of avoiding numbers could be considered a serious alternative to Platonism.

A nominalist might respond by claiming (on one basis or another) that in fact there are infinitely many things in the universe, so that we don't have to worry about groups of groups or about possible groups. Then two comments are appropriate. First, even if there are infinitely many things, it does seem that there *might* have been only finitely many. And it seems that this would not have had any effect on which statements of arithmetic were true. We don't normally think statements of arithmetic are true by accident. We think they're *necessarily* true, and that the same ones would be true no matter how many ordinary things actually existed. Second, the nominalist would still have to tell us something about the nature of groups. Granted, there would be no need for groups of groups (or for merely possible groups), but the notion of a group still sounds very much like a Platonist notion, so that the nominalist would be achieving nominalism about one sort of entity only by embracing Platonism about another.

The idea behind the subjunctive (or "counterfactual") approach is this. Suppose n is, intuitively, some number that is larger than the membership of any actually existing group. Then there is no (*in re*) property of being n-membered. But we all want the sentence "Seven is less than n" to be meaningful (and true). So the strategy is to mimic (8), but put the verbs into the subjunctive mood. This would yield:

(9)   If all the members of any seven-membered group *were* paired off (one-to-one) with members of any n-membered group, then there *would be* members of the n-membered group left over.

(9) can be read so as not to require that any n-membered group (or, for that matter, seven-membered group) actually exist in order for it to be true. In other words, it can be read as synonymous with

(10)   If there were a seven-membered group and an n-membered group, then, if all the members of the former were paired off (one-to-one) with members of the latter, then there would be members of the latter group left over.

The difficulty with this strategy is that it has proved to be a notorious problem in modern philosophy to say exactly what such "counterfactual" suppositions mean. One idea is that (10) means "In any *possible world* where there is a seven-membered group and an n-membered group . . ." But then we are faced with the problem of the nature of "possible worlds." Most accounts of possible worlds are Platonistic. Another approach is to avoid possible worlds, but appeal to Platonic properties. Then *being n-membered* exists even if there are no n-membered groups, and (10) can perhaps be understood as expressing some relation between Platonistic properties. As a general remark, it appears that the counterfactual approach would very likely depend on some other sort of Platonism or else would commit the nominalist to producing a further and more complicated nominalistic theory.

The above discussion of approaches to the problem of numbers is certainly not complete. The goal has been to provide some idea of the depth of the problem and some idea of the nature of ontological issues. It should also give further evidence of the degree to which our everyday lives are permeated by generally unnoticed philosophical problems and presuppositions.

3

Platonism

3.1   Properties, Relations, and Propositions

In chapter 2 we considered the problem of numbers as an example of an issue in ontology. The goal was to provide an understanding of the problem, the main competing proposals, and some of the difficulties they face. But in this chapter we are going to adopt and defend a specific ontological position – one that has a long and honorable history of not appealing to beginning metaphysics students.

It should not be surprising that Platonism, conceptualism, and nominalism may each be adapted for application to ontological issues other than the problem of numbers. (In fact, we got a hint of this in considering *concepts* in Section 1.2.) An especially important and controversial example is provided by the trio of closely related (supposed) entities: *properties*, *relations*, and *propositions*. We will do our best to defend Platonism concerning these entities in this chapter. That means we will argue that these entities really exist, and that their existence is independent of any physical or mental entities or activity. (They are "abstract.")

Let's begin with a few remarks about what these entities are supposed to be like. First, *properties*. The noun "property" has (at least roughly) the same meaning as the nouns "feature," "characteristic," "quality," and "attribute." A property is a way something can be. Here are some randomly selected ways things can be: green, hot, slimy, hungry, four-legged, dead, married, flat, tasty, soluble, valuable, loud, distant, new, boring, two feet wide, difficult, and inspiring. These are all comparatively simple properties. Most Platonists hold that there are innumerably many properties, and some of these are of course much more complicated than the ones just mentioned. An example of a more complicated property is: *being a person who has been thought about on a February 29th by someone who has set foot on all five continents and whose favorite color is orange.* I am sure that, whether they know it or not, a fair number of people have this property. An example of a property that no one has is the property of *having been a female US president before 1997.*

It is very common to say that things "have" certain properties. But what is this "having" all about? For a Platonist, properties are entities that exist apart from and independently of the things that have them. So, if a thing has a property, it must be that the having is a certain relation that holds between the thing and the property. Philosophers usually call this special relation "instantiation." So they say that things *instantiate* properties. Now suppose we have a red rose. Then, according to Platonism, the rose instantiates the property *redness* (i.e., the property of *being red*). Moreover, the fact that the rose instantiates redness is the *very same fact* as the fact that the rose is red. The rose's being red *is* the rose's instantiating redness. There are two important (and related) consequences of this position. One is that it is incorrect to think that instantiating redness *causes* the rose to be red. The other is that it is also wrong to think that instantiating redness *explains why* the rose is red. Because the rose's being red *is* (or, to put it another way, *consists in*) its instantiating redness, it cannot be that the latter causes (or explains) the former – nothing (at least nothing *contingent*) is its own cause. What causes the rose to be red is a chain of biochemical events occurring before and during the development of the rose's petals. *In other words*, what causes the rose to instantiate redness is a chain of biochemical events occurring before and during the development of the rose's petals.

Most Platonists think that *just about* any time we say something about a specific person, place, or thing, we attribute a property to it (whether the thing actually has that property or not). We can put this a little more formally as a principle, which we will call "the predication principle:" (Just about) every declarative sentence that has subject-predicate form attributes a property – the one expressed by the predicate – to an entity – the one denoted by the subject. In this way properties come to serve as the *meanings* of words and phrases of our language. So, if someone says, "The moon is made of green cheese," then the property *being made of green cheese* has been attributed to the moon. If someone says, "Susie has a purple Cadillac," then the property of *having a purple Cadillac* has been attributed to Susie. [A difficult exercise: **Figure out why the qualification "just about" is needed.**]

According to Platonism, properties provide the metaphysical basis for the phenomena of similarity and difference between things in the world. So, if you have a red rose and a red Rolls Royce, then these two objects are similar in both color and ownership. Their similarity in color is accounted for by their both instantiating *redness* and their similarity in ownership by their both instantiating *being owned by you*. On the other hand, there are many differences between these objects. The differences always consist in there being a property that one of them instantiates but the other doesn't. The fundamental *metaphysical* reason for believing in the existence of properties is that they provide this account of similarity and difference.

Relations are like properties, except that instead of applying to single things, they link together pairs or triples (etc.) of things in specific orders. Thus, if Jack loves Jill, then the *love* relation holds between Jack and Jill in that order. (Of course, it doesn't necessarily hold in the reverse order.) And if the rose instantiates redness, then the *instantiation* relation holds between the rose and the property redness. An example of a relation that links triples of things is the *betweenness* relation – "x is between y and z" – in arithmetic. It holds of 5, 3, and 6, in that order. (It also holds in the order 5, 6, and 3, but in no other order.) Of course there is also a *betweenness* relation reflecting the relative physical locations of objects. It's easy to see that if our everyday use of language fits best with a Platonist conception of properties, then it also fits best with a Platonist conception of relations, since they are very much the same sort of thing.

Notice that if we know that Jack loves Jill, then not only can we conclude that the *love* relation holds between them (in a certain order), we can also conclude that Jack and Jill have certain properties: Jack has the property of *loving Jill*, and Jill has the property of *being loved by Jack*. Properties like these are called "relational properties" because anything that has such a property is related to a certain specific thing (or things) by means of a certain specific relation. It is very important to see that relational properties are *not* relations, because they only apply to single things. The distinction between properties and relations concerns only their logical functions – whether they apply to things singly or multiply (in some order).

Also note that some relations, like *loving*, can link a given thing to itself. It may be that Jack not only loves Jill, but also loves himself. On the other hand, some relations never hold between a thing and itself. Examples are the *taller-than* and *parent-of* relations. A certain very special relation always links everything to itself and never links anything to anything other than itself. This is the *identity* relation, which we will discuss in detail in chapter 4.

Propositions are entities that either correctly or incorrectly represent how things are in the world (or in part of the world). Here we are not using the term "proposition" in the sense of a proposal or suggestion for future action. Instead we are using it in the sense in which a proposition is the sort of thing that can be true or false, believed or doubted, affirmed or denied. Just as the predicates of declarative sentences are seen as expressing properties, declarative sentences themselves are seen as expressing (and usually, but not always, asserting) propositions. We may think of this as an extension of the predication principle. We often refer to propositions by using "that-clauses" – the word "that" followed by a declarative sentence. Thus, applying the extended predication principle, the sentence "Snow is white" expresses the proposition *that snow is white*.

The proposition *that snow is white*, as it happens, correctly represents how (some) things are in the world; the proposition *that snow is blue*, though it is a perfectly legitimate proposition, happens not to represent things correctly. When a proposition represents correctly, it's called *true*; otherwise it's called *false*.

It is important to understand very clearly at the outset that the Platonist's properties, relations, and propositions are not *linguistic* entities. So, for example, the proposition *that snow is white* should not be confused with the sentence "Snow is white," even though we *express* it when we utter that sentence and it serves as the *meaning* of the sentence. (We will discuss linguistic entities in more detail in Section 3.3.) Similarly, the property *whiteness* should not be confused with the predicate "is white." According to Platonism, both the proposition and the property would have existed even if no one had ever uttered the sentence or the predicate. In fact, they would have existed even if no one had ever existed and no words had ever been spoken. We will have more to say about this feature of Platonism later.

Platonists see reality (or "the world") as divided into two realms, the spatiotemporal and the nonspatiotemporal or, as we will usually say, the concrete and the abstract. We can represent this division pictorially by depicting things on one side or the other of a horizontal line, which we will call the *Great Line of Being* (GLB). Abstract entities belong above the line, concrete entities below. In figure 3.1, Joe and Flo are depicted below the line and certain properties, relations, and propositions are represented

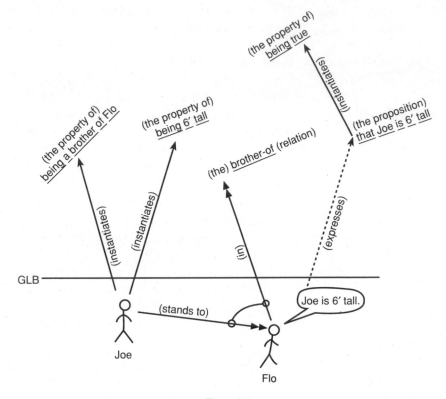

Figure 3.1

above. Also depicted below the line is Flo's utterance of the sentence "Joe is 6' tall." (This utterance is a concrete entity because it consists of vibrations in the air.) Solid, single-headed arrows are used to represent cases in which the instantiation relation holds. Thus we see that Joe instantiates the property of *being 6' tall*. He also instantiates the (relational) property of *being a brother of Flo*. Flo's utterance expresses (and, if she is sincere, asserts) the proposition *that Joe is 6' tall*, and we have used a dotted, single-headed arrow to represent the fact that the *expression* relation holds here between the utterance and the proposition. That proposition also instantiates the property of *being true* (precisely because Joe instantiates *being 6' tall*).

That Joe stands to Flo in the *brother-of* relation (in that order) is represented by a linked pair of solid, double-headed arrows. The one below the GLB connects the two related entities (in the proper order); the one crossing the GLB goes to the relation in which they stand (in that order). [It is tempting to think that it would be better to represent the fact that Joe stands in the *brother-of* relation to Flo by drawing a double-headed arrow first from Joe to the relation and then another from the relation to Flo. It is a challenging but valuable exercise to try to figure out why this method of representation does not generalize smoothly to more complicated cases.] GLB diagrams are often extremely useful in clarifying discussions of Platonism.

There are three major reasons favoring Platonism about these entities. The first is the metaphysical point about similarity and difference just mentioned. The second is that our ordinary use of language appears to be heavily committed to properties and propositions. The third reason is that these entities provide the basis for a very natural and compelling – though presently incomplete – *theory* of how language works. (In particular, a theory about how language connects with the world in such a way as to make fruitful communication possible.) These reasons are closely related, none is conclusive, nor are they conclusive taken together. But many philosophers take them very seriously and think that, ultimately, some elaboration of them might prove to be conclusive. We now turn to a discussion of the latter two.

Every day we say things like, "Shirley and Lee have lots of things in common." This certainly *sounds* like we're asserting that there are many properties that they both have. (Especially since we're prepared to give examples, like *being from New Orleans*, or *being singers*, etc.). We also say things like, "There's at least one thing that Mickey and Sylvia both believe." This certainly *sounds* like we're asserting that there's a proposition that they both accept. (Especially since we will happily give an example, perhaps the proposition *that love is strange*.) Of course there may be other ways of understanding these everyday statements. After all, they don't explicitly use the terms "property" or "proposition" (or any synonyms for these). But notice that we *also* say – outright – things like "Shirley and Lee have several properties in common," or "Mickey and Sylvia both accept that proposition." Here we apparently make an overt commitment to properties and propositions.

So, right off the bat, ordinary things that we do not hesitate to say – and believe – seem committed to the existence of these entities, sometimes only indirectly but other times quite explicitly. Certainly when we utter these sentences we are *sometimes* saying things that are true. It's totally implausible to believe that *every* time we make such an assertion we're

41

simply wrong. So suppose we happen to be right when we utter the sentence

(1)   The candidates disagreed about that proposition.

Now consider the similar sentence

(2)   The neighbors disagreed about that fence,

and also suppose that we're right when we utter it (in a certain situation). Now, it is very clear what is required for our utterance of (2) to be right: First, there must be certain entities – in fact people – whom we refer to with the phrase "the neighbors," and these people must in fact be neighbors. Second, there must be a certain further entity – in fact a fence – which we refer to with the phrase "that fence." Finally, it must be that the former entities really did disagree about the latter entity.

A Platonist believes that what is required for our utterance of (1) to be right is exactly parallel: There must be some entities, in fact people, whom we refer to with the phrase "the candidates," and these people must in fact be candidates. And there must be a further entity – in fact a proposition – which we refer to with the phrase "that proposition." (And of course it must also be true that the former entities disagreed about the latter entity.) Platonists see the indisputable facts about what it takes for the utterance of (2) to be true, together with the fact that the grammatical structure of (1) parallels that of (2), as evidence in favor of their view of what it takes for the utterance of (1) to be true. That is, they take it as evidence for Platonism.

But it is far from conclusive evidence. For one thing, it leaves room for the view that although the truth of (1) may require that there be such things as propositions, it doesn't require that they be *abstract* entities. The possibility that they are (somehow) either *concrete* (or otherwise "*in re*") or *mental* is still wide open. Another wide open possibility is the *nominalist* view that the parallel grammatical structure is misleading, and that the truth of (1) doesn't require the existence of propositions after all. So, although Platonism about properties, relations, and propositions certainly fits very nicely with observed grammatical structure (and with our apparent outright existence assertions), it is far from established. But the case for Platonism becomes much stronger if these alternative possibilities can be eliminated or discredited. Soon we will try to do just that, but we need to say a few more things about Platonism first.

We have already seen the beginnings of a Platonist theory of how language connects with the world: For example, predicates of our sentences express properties, and things in the world either have or don't have these properties. Also, our sentences express propositions that represent the world as being certain ways, and the world either cooperates by being those ways or it doesn't. So our language connects with the world through the medium of Platonic properties, relations, and propositions. Now let's confine our attention to the case of propositions, and think for a moment about the phenomena of belief and communication.

What is going on when you "believe something?" The Platonist picture is that you are standing in a certain relation to a certain abstract entity, a proposition. The proposition is the "object" of your belief. A Platonist would not deny that there may also be something going on in your head (or mind) and that this state or event may be *instrumental* in your having the belief, but would emphatically deny that what is going on in your head *is* the belief. What is going on in your head may be part of your *believing* (or belief activity or belief state), but it isn't part of the thing that you believe, nor is the thing that you believe a part of what's going on in your head.

This position has four (related) major points in its favor. First, it offers a theoretical structure for the connection between what is going on in our heads and what is going on in the world outside our heads: What is going on in our heads enables us to stand in the belief relation to a proposition, and the proposition, in turn, represents what is going on in the world outside our heads. Second, it provides a simple and natural explanation of how you and I can both believe "the same thing" even though the events in our respective heads are entirely distinct, nonoverlapping events – these separate packages of events are instrumental in connecting us both (respectively) to a *single* proposition. Third, it provides an explanation of how sentences in different languages can "mean the same thing." The Spanish sentence "La nieve es blanca," the French sentence "La neige est blanche," and the English sentence "Snow is white," all mean the same thing because they all express the proposition *that snow is white*. Thus propositions provide the basis for interlinguistic translation.

Finally, Platonism also provides a good basis for a theory of communication. Suppose you have offered to pick me up at the airport, but you don't know when my flight arrives. I utter the following sentence to you: "It arrives at 5 p.m. next Friday." Friday rolls around and you head for the airport at 4 p.m. The plane lands and I emerge at a little past 5 o'clock. We meet at the gate.

If you think about it in the abstract, this is really a very striking chain of events. Simply because I created a very brief series of vibrations in the air, in your presence, you were led, several days later, to go to a certain location, where, at a certain time, you found me. How amazing! How could this actually work? The Platonist answer is (very roughly) this: The vibrations in the air express a proposition that I happen to believe but you have no belief about. Your understanding of the language is sufficient for you to know what proposition these vibrations express. And your understanding of the surrounding situation – for example, you know that I'm not acting in a play – results in your believing that I am asserting that proposition, that I believe it (and have good reason to believe it). All of this quickly results in *your* coming to believe *that very proposition*. Several days later that belief (together with lots of other beliefs, for example about cars and the location of the airport) leads you to go and meet me. So, a large part of what is going on in successful communication is that speakers are modifying the beliefs of their hearers by asserting propositions that they believe, in situations that give the hearers reason (or cause) for *also* coming to believe them.

We have now seen a sketch of Platonism (about these entities) and some of the considerations that favor it. It is very useful to think of the case for Platonism as one that is based on "circumstantial" evidence. The prosecution bases a criminal case on circumstantial evidence when there are no witnesses to the crime itself. So they argue that the defendant was seen in the area just before the crime, that the recovered shells match a gun that he owns and which was found at the scene bearing his fingerprints, that he had recently expressed his hatred of the victim, that the victim had told friends that the defendant had threatened to kill him, that the defendant would have had to leave work an hour early to get to the scene on time, and that he told his boss he was feeling ill and in fact did leave an hour early, and so on. In short, the prosecution constructs a "theory of the crime" in which the defendant is the perpetrator, and tries to show that no other theory is, by comparison, nearly as plausible. If the circumstantial case is a good one, the jury, in effect, will conclude that it is "beyond a reasonable doubt" that the prosecution's theory is true.

If someone is going to present a persuasive case for Platonism, it will have to be circumstantial, because these entities by their very nature can't be witnessed in any ordinary sense of the term. (Notice that, for example, a case for the existence of *quarks* would also have to be circumstantial.) So the success of the case comes down to this: Platonism helps us construct a *theory* that explains a variety of phenomena whose occurrence we do not question. These prominently include: the phenomena of similarity and difference between concrete things in the physical world; the fact that we are able to believe things about the world outside us; the related fact of the meaningfulness of human languages; and the related phenomenon of successful human communication about external facts and events. Such a case, in itself, cannot be absolutely conclusive. But if the alternative theories of these phenomena are decidedly less plausible, the case for Platonism can seem quite strong, perhaps even beyond reasonable doubt. We will now take a look at some of the main competing theories.

3.2   Alternatives to Platonism

We begin by considering accounts that accept the existence of properties (etc.) but deny that they have one or another of the essential features that the Platonist claims they have.

What about the physicalist idea that properties (etc.) are somehow *concrete*? It may seem plausible to think that at least some properties, like *redness* or *being a table*, are actual physical parts of the things that have them, and hence are concrete because they're located in spacetime. But a closer examination shows this particular *in re* theory cannot really be right. The property of *being a table* cannot literally be a physical *part* of a table. For suppose we have two tables in front of us. If *being a table* were a physical part of *one* of them, then the *other* wouldn't be a table since it doesn't share any parts with the first. (What is critical, of course, is that it doesn't share the part that happens to be the property of *being a table*.) But of course it is a table. One of the crucial features of the property of *being a table* – however it is ultimately understood ontologically – is that distinct, nonoverlapping things are capable of instantiating it simultaneously. Of course, most properties have this feature of possible multiple instantiation (and for this reason they are sometimes called "universals"). So the idea that such properties are literal parts of their instances is untenable.

"literal"? or "physical"?

But there may be another way to locate these properties in spacetime, "where" their instances are located. Is California located where San Francisco is? Well, not *all* of it. But when you're in San Francisco, you're in California. Some of California is located there. So, in a not-quite-literal sense, California is. Suppose you have a pain in your hand, say in the palm near the top knuckle of your index finger. If you say "My hand hurts," you are not saying something that is false, even though other parts of your hand don't hurt. In a not-quite-literal sense, your hand is where the hurting is occurring. Following these leads, we might modify the physicalist view by making a similar departure from the literal. To do this, we identify the property of *being a table* with the "scattered totality" of all tables existing anywhere in spacetime. Now, this totality is simply a disconnected array of specific physical stuff, of which every actual table happens to be a (literal) part. Let's call this array of stuff "T." According to the revised theory, then, to instantiate the property of *being a table* is to be an appropriate part of T. (Notice that lots of parts of T aren't tables; for example, the parts that are the tables' legs aren't tables.) Now, on this account, the property of *being a table*, that is, T, is located where any given table is located in the same not-quite-literal sense in which California is located where San Francisco is located (and your hand is located where the pain is located). This revised theory is therefore not literally an *in re* theory like the original, but it is certainly *in re* in spirit.

But the theory has a tragic flaw: It cannot accommodate various ways in which things could have been different from how they actually are. For example, the world might not have contained the physical stuff T at all, and yet it might have included *tables*. These tables would then have been made entirely of stuff not included in T. So, in that circumstance, there would be things instantiating the property *being a table*, but none of these things would be parts of T. Since the theory says that to be a table *is* to be an appropriate part of T, it must be wrong. {**Exercise: Explain why it would be circular to hold that the tables existing in the imagined circumstance would collectively constitute T.**}

Now let's turn to the case of propositions. It is tempting to think that at least some propositions are concrete – that they are actual physical parts of the physical world. For instance, the proposition *that the dog is in the yard* (where the context fixes a specific dog and yard) might be thought to be that part of the world that contains the yard, along with the dog. But there are two major problems with this idea. First of all, if there really are propositions, then some of them are true and some of them are false. If the

46

dog really is in the yard, then what part of the world would be the proposition *that the dog isn't in the yard*? Obviously it can't be any part of the world that includes both the yard and the dog. But nor can it be a part of the world including all of the yard except for the part where the dog is. In short, there is no part of the world that can plausibly serve as the negation of a true proposition.

The second problem is this. Suppose the dog is lying down in the yard, and again suppose the proposition *that the dog is in the yard* is some physical part of the world including the yard and the dog. Then what part of the world is the proposition *that the dog is lying down in the yard*? The only remotely reasonable answer is that it's the part containing the yard and the recumbent dog. But this is precisely the same part as the part containing the yard and the dog! This means that the theory forces the proposition *that the dog is in the yard* to be the same as the proposition *that the dog is lying down in the yard*. But these are obviously different propositions, since the former could be true while the latter was false. So the theory should be rejected.

Now let's return to properties. We have seen two overtly concrete approaches fail for fairly simple reasons. but there is a more sophisticated *in re* theory that may not be so easy to dismiss. The central idea of any *in re* theory is that properties are somehow "in" their instances. The two we considered above got into trouble as soon as they got specific about how this was supposed to work. Maybe the best *in re* theory would avoid the trouble by not getting specific! The theory would claim that one and the same property can be "in" various disparate things that occupy various disparate locations (and that the existence of any property depends on its having instances), but it would refuse to say what "in" means or how this "multiple instantiation" works. The "in" relation holding between property and instance would be taken as a "primitive notion" of the theory.

Logically speaking, this is irreproachable. Every theory has to leave some of its central notions unanalyzed or else it will be involved in an infinite regress of analysis (or a vicious circle). For example, set theory takes the relation of set-theoretic "membership" as a primitive notion. The axioms and theorems of the theory tell us many things about membership, but they don't analyze it and they don't tell us how membership "works." Any understanding we might have of the inner nature of membership could only take place at an intuitive level.

Now, on the face of it, the idea that the world could contain an entity with the capacity of being located "in" different physical things (in different places) seems very mysterious. The mystery seems as deep as the more or less opposite religious mystery of the Trinity. Just as it is hard to make sense of the idea that three Gods can be "in" one God, it is hard to make sense of the idea that one "property" can be "in" more than one thing at once. A sophisticated *in re* theorist will not deny that there is an air of mystery here, but will claim that it is much more acceptable than the "myth" of a Platonic "heaven" outside of spacetime.

It appears, however, that there are two serious problems for the sophisticated *in re* view (which we will call S). The first problem takes the form of a double dilemma. S does not tell us about the nature of the "in" relation. That's fair enough, as we saw above. Still, the relation must have *some* essential nature, and there just aren't too many possibilities. If each possibility leads to trouble, then it looks like the sophisticated strategy of leaving the relation unexplained serves only to obscure the trouble.

Here is the major dilemma: Either "in" means *physically in* (that is, *part of*) or it doesn't. If it means physically in, then the property itself will have to be physical, and it looks like we're back to one of the two "concrete" theories that were rejected above. **[It's hard to think of an even remotely plausible theory other than these that makes the property be physical and "in" its instance. Exercise: Give it a try.]** On the other hand, if "in" *doesn't* mean physically in, then the properties won't themselves be physical entities and the "in" won't be literal, but just a figure of speech. That might be fine, but now we face a second dilemma: Do these nonphysical properties *occupy spacetime* or not? If they don't, then S evidently has "degenerated" into a covert version of Platonism. (After all, a Platonist is free to adopt a special, nonliteral sense of "in" according to which the claim that redness is "in" the rose merely means that the rose instantiates redness. Plato's heaven (and the Great Line of Being) are just vivid figures of speech anyway.) **[Another question worth thinking about is this: If the properties aren't in spacetime, then why are they dependent on their instances for their existence?]**

So suppose instead that S's properties *do* occupy spacetime. Then, to say that redness is "in" the rose would mean that redness – now a nonphysical entity – occupies the same spatiotemporal location that (part of) the rose occupies. So (assuming the above options are unsatisfactory, as suggested), we now have something that S was originally unwilling to provide, namely, an explanation of the nature of the "in" relation. The veil of sophistication has been lifted. But the result is that what appeared through the veil merely to be mysterious now seems downright absurd. S's properties, though nonphysical, are *nevertheless* spatiotemporal entities (and hence "concrete" as we are using that term). Certainly if a *spatiotemporal* entity occupies a specific region, R, at a certain time, then it does not occupy any region entirely separate from R at that same time. Of course, this does not deny the possibility that a spatiotemporal entity might have different *parts* occupying entirely separate regions, unconnected by other parts of the entity. But the present understanding of S is not one that says *part* of redness is here, part there. It says that *all* of redness is here and all of it is there. Since redness is now a *spatiotemporal* entity, this claim can only be understood literally. But taken literally, it seems absurd.

The second serious problem for S is this. We have an everyday conception of a property as something that a thing can gain or lose with the passage of time. But the *in re* conception makes the existence of a property dependent on its having instances. These two features fit together very awkwardly, at best. We can illustrate this with a little story.

Imagine that a primitive artisan, Tab, is making the world's first table. For simplicity, let's imagine that Tab and his friends speak English, and that they already have chairs. Tab says, "I want to make a thing that will have a reasonably flat surface, parallel to and about three feet above the floor of the cave. But I want most of the volume underneath the surface to be open, so we can pull chairs up close to it and sit down without smashing our knees against something. Then we can eat, play cards, set up our computers, and so on, and be more comfortable than we are now, trying to balance all this stuff on our knees and laps, or sitting sideways up against boulders. So I'm going to hew a fairly thin slab out of this huge dead tree trunk, and I'm going to put three or four narrow struts or "legs" of equal length near the edges, spaced equally apart, and perpendicular to the plane of the slab. The trick will be to get these legs attached rigidly and semi-permanently to the slab. Once I can figure out how to do that, I'll have what I want. In my own honor, I think I'll call it a *table*."

When Tab is at work on this project his friends sometimes ask him what he's up to. He replies by uttering the sentence

(3)   I'm trying to make a table.

If they ask what a table is, he tells them, using a variation on the above speech. Then the project finally succeeds and the first table exists. One of

Tab's friends, Fab, is fascinated by the table and decides to make one of his own. When people ask him what he's doing, he also replies with an utterance of (3).

Now several observations are in order. First, according to S, the property of *being a table* did not exist when Tab uttered (3). Yet (3) made perfectly good sense and Tab was able, in effect, to define the new word it contained perfectly well. Second, according to S, the property of *being a table* did exist when Fab uttered (3). And notice that Fab could explain this word in just the way that Tab did when someone didn't understand it. This leaves S in a bind. Does the word "table," when it occurs in Fab's utterance, express the property of *being a table* or not? Either choice seems to have bizarre consequences. First, if it *does* express that property, then Tab's utterance of (3) and Fab's utterance of (3) must have radically different meanings. This is extremely hard to defend in light of the fact that both Tab and Fab were able to explain what their utterances meant in exactly the same way. Moreover, it creates the severe problem of having to say just what Tab's utterance did mean. (Notice also that, in the case of properties that sometimes have instances and other times do not, off and on, the meanings of ordinary sentences will flip-flop depending on contingent facts that one would normally think were quite independent.)

On the other hand, if Fab's utterance *doesn't* express that property, then it's very hard to see what S needs properties for in the first place. Tab didn't need the property of *being a table* in order to make a table. And we don't need the property of *being a table* in order to make sense of sentences containing the word "table." Our normal conception of properties gives them the fundamental role of constituting things in various ways. And then, since we are able to talk about these ways, they inherit the role of serving as the meanings of words that we utter. Neither of these roles would need filling on the present option for S. So the present option is no more plausible than any of the others.

We have now considered and tried to dismiss several non-Platonist theories of properties that are more or less in the *in re* spirit. Now let's briefly consider the conceptualist view that properties and propositions are mental entities, products of human thought. There is one version of this view that is internally quite consistent but unfortunately very exotic and counterintuitive. It is the view that *everything* – including what seem to be independently existing physical objects – is really an *idea* (in the mental sense of the term). This theory might fit nicely with a kind of *in re* view, according to which properties were "in" things by being parts of them, and hence were themselves ideas. But there are many other possibilities for elaborating this "idealistic" position. Because there are so many, because they seem to have such an implausible core, and because we could not do an adequate job without probing the difficult and largely separate metaphysical issue of "idealism" proper, we will skip the effort.

So let's assume that there really are physical objects existing independently of us, and that (one way or another) these physical objects have lots of properties. Then the conceptualist view is that these properties are actually *mental* – the products of our perception of (and thinking about) these physical objects. What often leads people to this position is "too little of a good thing" when it comes to properties, along with a covert inclination to locate properties "in" things. If we think hard about our perception of objects in the external world, we come to realize that it has certain distinctive features. Say you're looking at a red rose. Now focus on your "inner," visual *experience* of the rose. It has certain special, "phenomenal" features. In particular, the part of your experience that represents the surfaces of the petals that you are seeing has a certain distinctive feature: a "color." When you think directly about *this*, it may seem that *the rose* could not conceivably have this property – this "redness" – independently of your experience. Many conceptualists accept this conclusion and then simply generalize it, holding that *all* of the properties of a thing are the products of mental activity.

This is too little of a good thing because it seems right that when we perceive things, our perceptions of them have various properties as a result. And "phenomenal redness" may be a good example of such a property. But why stop with these phenomenal properties? And why "project" phenomenal properties onto external things in the first place? The conceptualist is overlooking the possibility that the rose really *doesn't* have these phenomenal properties at all, but instead has *different*, nonphenomenal properties, quite independently of our perceptions, and that these properties are causally responsible for the fact that our perceptions have the various phenomenal properties. Furthermore, in projecting the phenomenal properties onto the external things, the conceptualist reveals the covert influence of the idea that properties are "in" their instances, a conception we have just now found seriously wanting.

So that's a diagnosis of a well-travelled road to conceptualism about properties. But it's also worth noting a couple of implausible consequences of the view. Recall that we have set idealism aside. So physical objects exist independently of us. Now, it certainly seems that lots of physical objects existed long before any people or other perceivers existed, for example, stars, asteroids, atoms and molecules, etc. These things had lots of properties even then. In fact, we seem – just now – to have admitted that some of the things that existed then had the property of being a star, others had the property of being an asteroid, etc. Also, each asteroid had a certain particular mass at each time, and so forth. It would be very far-fetched to think that there were no stars or asteroids prior to the appearance of intelligence in the universe, or to hold that these properties somehow retroactively came into being after intelligent life came on the scene. It is certainly true that we humans *think* about properties and give *names* to some of them. But it's an incredible stretch to think that the names *are* the properties or that we somehow *create* the properties merely by thinking about them.

A related problem concerns propositions. If there had never been any thinking beings, then no propositions would ever have been entertained, expressed, asserted, or believed. There would have been no thoughts or other mental entities at all. But even in those circumstances it seems that certain propositions would have been true. For example, in such circumstances the proposition *that there are no thinking beings* would be true, it would be true that $2 + 2 = 4$, and it might well be true that there are stars, and so forth. Innumerably many propositions would be true even though there would be no mental entities at all. The idea that propositions are mental entities is radically at odds with this common-sense view of things.

A final problem for conceptualism also concerns propositions. Somehow or other, it has to make room for the fact that you and I can "believe the same thing." We have seen how easily Platonism does this, and how doing so seems critical in accounting for successful communication. Now suppose a proposition is some (occurrent) mental event or configuration. Then it looks like it is impossible for you and I to believe the same proposition. The propositions you believe will be in your mind (or head), those that I believe will be in mine, and we'll never be able to have the same beliefs since what's in your head – automatically – isn't in mine. **[Exercise: Try to think of a plausible way to rescue conceptualism from this problem. In trying you may notice how easy it is to slip covertly into one or another form of Platonism.]**

We have now considered various non-Platonist accounts of properties and propositions, and have suggested that they do not succeed. So let's turn our attention to nominalism – the view that there are no such entities as properties or propositions in the first place. Nominalism typically starts with the following sensible-sounding thought about Platonism: Properties and propositions are held by Platonists to play the role of connecting what goes on in our minds and in our language with what goes on outside our minds and language. So they are "intermediaries" between us and the rest of the world. But if we can be connected to the external world *indirectly*, then why couldn't we be connected directly? Maybe the intermediary entities are entirely unnecessary for explaining how our beliefs and our linguistic behavior can be "about" the external world.

So a typical nominalist will try to follow up on this thought and produce an account that makes the right connection, but without appealing to properties and propositions. Let's take a look at one effort in this direction. We'll call it "linguistic" nominalism. Consider any simple subject-predicate sentence, say

(4)   Bill Clinton weighs over 200 pounds.

Platonists say the following six things about this sentence: First, the subject, "Bill Clinton," refers to a specific spatiotemporal entity. Second, the predicate, "weighs over 200 pounds," expresses the property of *weighing over 200 pounds*. Third, an utterance of (4) will express (and generally, assert) the proposition that the entity Bill Clinton instantiates the property of *weighing over 200 pounds*, that is, the proposition *that Bill Clinton weighs over 200 pounds*. Fourth, the proposition *that Bill Clinton weighs over 200 pounds* represents the world as being a certain way, namely as being such that Bill Clinton instantiates *weighing over 200 pounds*. Fifth, the proposition *that Bill Clinton weighs over 200 pounds is true* precisely because (let's assume) the entity in question really does instantiate the property in question. Sixth – and more will be said about this later on – we may regard sentence (4) as "true" in a *derivative* sense, because *utterances* of it express a proposition that is true in the *basic* sense. But it is propositions, not sentences, that are the fundamental "bearers" of truth-values.

A linguistic nominalist takes a very different position: First, it is agreed that the subject, "Bill Clinton," does refer to a specific spatiotemporal entity. But second, the predicate, "weighs over 200 pounds," is held not to express any property at all. (After all, there are no such things as properties.) Third, utterances of (4) do not express (much less assert) any proposition at all. (After all, there are no such things as propositions.) Fourth, utterances of sentence (4) already represent the world as being a certain way without benefit of intermediaries. Fifth, utterances of (4) are *true* because the entity Bill Clinton "satisfies" the predicate "weighs over 200 pounds." Sixth, we may regard sentence (4) as "true" in a *derivative* sense, because *utterances* of it are true in the *basic* sense. It is utterances of sentences, not sentences, that are the fundamental "bearers" of truth-values.

There is one problem for this view that we will only mention because there are much deeper problems that we want to discuss. It's this. How does the view account for the fact that people who don't speak English can believe "the same thing" we believe? To use our earlier example, how can they believe that snow is white? The Platonist says that the proposition *that snow is white* is expressed by various (utterances of various) sentences of all different languages, and that this single proposition is the object of everyone's belief. What can the nominalist say? That *sentences* are the objects of belief? Many have said this. But, so far, it doesn't answer the question, because (e.g.) the sentence "Snow is white" and the sentence "La nieve es blanca" are two different sentences! So believing one is quite independent of believing the other. (Similarly, it's *one* thing to satisfy the predicate "is white" and *another* thing to satisfy the predicate "es blanca" and yet *another* thing to satisfy the predicate "est blanche" . . .)

It should be pretty clear that the main weight of linguistic nominalism, as just described, is being borne by the notion of an entity "satisfying" a predicate. Needless to say, this is not an everyday notion that we already have some familiarity with. Instead it's a special "technical" notion. So the nominalist must either analyze it or else take it as primitive. Of course, if it is taken as primitive we should still be given an informal explanation of the idea since it isn't antecedently familiar to us.

Here's a presentation of an analysis of the notion of satisfaction that has sometimes been proposed. We'll state the analysis in the form of a definition of the technical term "satisfies":

(5)   An entity *satisfies* a predicate if and only if a majority of speakers of the language believe that (an utterance of) the declarative sentence composed of a name of the entity and the predicate, is true.

Now consider sentence (4). Suppose you're a Platonist and you're trying to decide whether (an utterance of) this sentence would be true. A natural first step would be to show up at the White House with a carefully calibrated scale. After all, you think the truth-value of the sentence depends on whether Bill Clinton *has a certain property*. So you're inclined to go find *him* and investigate. (Naturally there are many other ways of ascertaining this, some more indirect (and maybe less reliable): driver's license, medical records, maybe even just looking at him. Certainly this would work for "weighs over 5 pounds.")

But now suppose you're a linguistic nominalist and you're trying to decide whether an utterance of (4) would be true. Then the issue isn't whether Clinton has a certain property. It's whether Clinton *satisfies a certain predicate*. And (5) gives the definition of "satisfies." So it isn't going to help to show up at the White House. It might be very hard to get into the White House with a bulky package, even if the package only contains a scale. But it's going to be immeasurably harder to find out whether Clinton satisfies the predicate. For according to (5), you have to canvass at least a majority of English speakers – maybe even *all* – and find out whether they believe that the sentence is true.

Sounds hard, but it's even harder than it sounds at first. Mere legwork won't do the job. For, since this is your theory, the occurrence of the word "true" in (5) must mean what you, the linguistic nominalist, mean by it! So, imagine that in conducting your poll, you happen to be face to face with Hillary. You say, "Do you think the sentence 'Bill Clinton weighs over 200 pounds' is true?" She says, "Oh yeah! That's one of his less appealing features." You say, "Oh no, very sorry. That's not what I mean by 'true'." Then you explain how satisfying predicates is the basis for what you mean by "true," and you produce definition (5). But now Hillary says, "Look, I'm a busy lady here. If all you had wanted to know was whether Bill has that property, then I'd have been happy to cooperate. But I have no idea what the majority of English speakers *believe*, and I think it's pretty ridiculous for you to expect me to go traipsing around the world trying to find out. In fact, the more I think about it, the more it seems to me that a survey couldn't do any good. I mean, how is *anyone* going to be able to answer the question? I seem to remember something about circular definitions and definitions that produce infinite regress from my metaphysics course in college, and I think your (5) leads to an infinite regress. So your concept of truth can never be applied to any sentence whatever. Get lost! Go take Philosophy 101!"

Let's make the regress explicit because it's a little tricky. It will help to work with a schematic subject-predicate sentence, "x is P," and to abbreviate "if and only if" by "iff" and "satisfies" by "sat." Now, according to the theory, we have

(6) "x is P" is true iff x sat "is P"

Using definition (5), this means:

(7) "x is P" is true iff a majority believe that "x is P" is true.

But according to the theory, this means:

(8) "x is P" is true iff a majority believe that x sat "is P".

Again using definition (5), we obtain:

(9) "x is P" is true iff a majority believe that a majority believe that "x is P" is true.

So the theory generates a four-step cycle that will repeat *ad infinitum*. To find out whether a sentence is true is impossible because we would have to find out whether a majority believe that a majority believe that a majority believe that . . .

So the proposal doesn't work. A natural way to try to block the regress would be to change (5) to

(10) An entity *satisfies* a predicate if and only if a majority of speakers of the language would assent when asked the question, "Is the sentence [insert the declarative sentence composed of a name of the entity and the predicate, enclosed within quotation marks] true?" (Example: . . . when asked the question, "Is the sentence 'Bill Clinton weighs over 200 pounds' true?")

This would enable you to record Hillary as a *yes* even though she doesn't mean the same thing by "true" that you mean. So the problem *could* now be solved by extensive legwork. But the solution isn't very satisfying because "truth" is now determined by a majority vote of people not all of whom even mean the same thing by "true" – a term that makes a crucial appearance in the very question being asked. On the revised theory, lots of sentences like "There are ghosts" would wind up being "true" and lots of sentences like "William McKinley was once a U.S. president" would not wind up "true" (because a majority of speakers have never heard of him). Let's forget it. [Exercise: Suppose (5) is replaced by: (5*) An entity *satisfies* a predicate if and only if a majority of speakers of the language believe the declarative sentence composed of a name of the entity and the predicate. Would this block the regress? If so, does it have other difficulties?]

There are surely ways of analyzing satisfaction other than the two we have considered. But any analysis seems fated to move the question of the satisfaction of a predicate "too far away" from the entity satisfying it. One would think that whether Clinton satisfies "weighs over 200 pounds" should only really depend on *him*, that is, on *how he is*. But any effort to achieve *this* begins to look like Platonism in disguise. So the nominalist seems forced away from Clinton *himself* into the arena of English or English speakers. But the result of any such effort is likely to have consequences for the concept of *truth* as bizarre as those of the two we considered.

The idea of taking satisfaction as primitive is very unappealing for the following reason. Satisfaction is supposed to be a relation that can hold between a nonlinguistic entity and a predicate – a linguistic entity. It is terrifically implausible to think that *this* kind of relation could have taken hold independently of speakers of the language. If x satisfies "is P," this must be, at least in part, the result of some actual linguistic activity. It didn't just happen by nature alone. So the nominalist ought to be able to figure out the *kind* of linguistic activity that brought it about, and then ought to be able to exploit this knowledge to give an *analysis* of satisfaction. For this reason, and also because we have no everyday notion of satisfaction to rest on, let's set aside the primitive approach.

A final problem for linguistic nominalism is posed by its reliance on linguistic entities. What kind of entities are *they* in the first place? The nominalist had better have a pretty good answer. By sheer coincidence, we will now turn to this question quite independently of linguistic nominalism. We'll address it from the Platonist perspective.

3.3   Linguistic Entities

What kind of entities are the *sentences* we use to express (and assert) propositions? Surprisingly enough, this isn't an easy question to answer. But most linguists and philosophers hold that sentences are also abstract entities, that lots of them have never been uttered or written down (and probably never will be), and that there are infinitely many of them.

One reason for holding this view is that it is very compelling to think of human languages as governed by syntactic and semantic rules. Competent speakers will display a surprising amount of agreement as to whether a given sequence of words is or is not a grammatical sentence of the language. This leads directly to the idea that when we speak and understand our language, we are unconsciously applying rules of various kinds (and one of the fundamental goals of linguistics is to try to figure out exactly what these rules are). One of the basic kinds of syntactic rules separates legitimate sentences from ungrammatical strings of words. Here the idea is that sentences are "generated" from words in accordance with rules involving the "parts of speech" of the words. For a simple example, it might be a rule that any proper noun followed by any intransitive verb constitutes a grammatical sentence.

But now notice that it is extremely unlikely that every possible such combination has already been *spoken* or *written down* by someone. Yet (assuming there is such a rule) when a combination of this type occurs in speech or print for the very first time, we are still able to recognize "it" as a legitimate sentence. This suggests very strongly that the combination was somehow *already* a sentence, and that we are simply recognizing a concrete *representative* (or "token" or "instance") of it as such. The most natural way of allowing for previously "untokened" sentences is to hold that all sentences are Platonic entities, always distinct from their concrete tokens. The smoothest account along these lines holds that sentences are actually *properties*, properties that can only be instantiated by the concrete tokens of the sentences. Of course, on this account, the words comprising the sentence will also best be viewed as Platonic properties. [**Exercise: Using the idea that sentences are properties of their tokens, show how other natural syntactic rules would lead to the conclusion that there are infinitely many sentences of English.**]

But even apart from the matter of rules and sentence recognition, it should be clear that the (concrete) vibrations in the air that occur when we "utter a sentence," and the (concrete) marks on blackboards and paper that we make when we "write a sentence down" are certainly not *the sentence itself*. To hold that they are would generate an analogue of the infamous problem of "too many sevens" discussed in chapter 2.

Furthermore, the very same series of marks might represent different sentences in different languages. We can give a clear example of this at a simpler level – the level of words. If a word were just a physical sequence of marks (or vibrations), then surely the sequence

FORT

before your eyes would be a word. But what word? In English, the sequence would be taken as a noun for structures of a certain architectural type. But in French, it would be taken as an adjective meaning strong. There is nothing in the sequence *itself* that could possibly decide between these (and probably other) possibilities. So, in the absence of some further element, the physical sequence of marks isn't any particular word at all. It might be a little harder to find parallel examples of sentences from different languages, but even if they couldn't be found, it would still be *possible* that two different human languages contained sentences that looked (or sounded) exactly the same but had entirely different meanings. This is enough to show that the physical marks themselves could neither represent nor be a specific sentence unless some further ingredient were present.

So, let us call the concrete vibrations in the air (or marks on paper, etc.) that we make when we "utter (or write down) a sentence," *sentence-tokens*, and think of them as serving as representatives of the sentence itself. Then a plausible overall picture is this: It is the *physical characteristics* of a sequence of vibrations or marks (etc.) together with someone's *intention* to use (or regard, etc.) that sequence in a certain way that makes that sequence a particular sentence-token, that is, a representative of a particular (abstract) sentence (of a particular language).

But both ingredients are essential. We have just now seen that the physical sequence isn't any particular sentence-token unless an appropriate intention is present. But the right sort of intention, on its own, isn't enough either. For example, I may intend to use the physical sequence

TXRLL NNCOR LSQRR

to mean that there is life on Mars, and certainly I can do this if I wish. But that isn't enough to make it a sentence of *English* since it doesn't have the right physical characteristics. (It would take quite a lot of further evolution of English to bring it about that it did.)

So, on this picture, *sentences* (and *words*, *predicates*, etc.) are abstract entities, but there are concrete entities that, under certain "intentional" conditions, serve as *tokens* (or representatives) of sentences, but are not themselves sentences. In order to use a sentence to express a proposition, we simply create a token of that sentence in the normal intentional way. (And our intention also determines whether we thereby also assert the proposition we are expressing.) Properly speaking, then, it isn't the *sentence* that expresses the proposition, it's the *token* we produce – that is, the actual concrete utterance or inscription – that expresses the proposition.

This can be made a little more vivid if we consider a sentence like "I'm hungry." Certainly *it* doesn't express any proposition at all on its own (though of course it does have a meaning on its own). If the sentence did express a specific proposition on its own, then different people couldn't use it to express different propositions. But obviously they can, and, in fact, one and the same person can use it to express different propositions by uttering it at different times. If you utter it at 8 a.m., then you say something different from what you say when you utter it at noon. (After all, one utterance might be true, the other false.) **[Exercise: An actor in a play utters the line "I'm really hungry," when, in fact, he is not at all hungry. How can the present view accommodate this?]**

What determines the proposition expressed by an utterance of a sentence like "I'm hungry" is the meaning of that sentence – what its words mean when conjoined as they are – together with the "context" in which the sentence is uttered. In the example, the key aspects of the context are the identity of the speaker and the time of the utterance. So the meaning of the sentence is something like a mathematical function: It takes the speaker and the time as arguments, and supplies the proposition *that that speaker is hungry at that time* as the value of the function for those arguments.

Sentences like "I'm hungry" are called *nonunivocal* precisely because different tokens of them express different propositions. (The different tokens don't "have one voice" – they don't say the same thing.) In contrast, a *univocal* sentence is one any possible token of which would express the same proposition. Thus, for example, "US President Bill Clinton is hungry at 12 noon, Eastern Standard Time, on February 1st, 1995" appears to be univocal. No matter who utters it or writes it down, and no matter when and where the uttering or writing occur, the resulting token expresses exactly the same proposition. (Here we have to understand the verb as if it were "tenseless" – perhaps it would be better to replace "is" by "is, was, or will be.")

If S is a univocal sentence, then we may think of it as expressing a proposition "derivatively," in accordance with the following definition: S *expresses* (the proposition) P iff any token of S expresses (or would express) P. This definition is not circular even though the term "expresses" appears in the defining condition. The reason is that we already understand the occurrence in the defining condition – it expresses the concept of a *sentence-token's* expressing a proposition. What the definition does, in effect, is to analyze the concept of a *sentence's* expressing a proposition by appealing to the more fundamental concept of a sentence-token's expressing a proposition. To put it another way, the definition extends the range of applicability of the term "expresses" so that it now accommodates univocal sentences as well as sentence-tokens. It should be clear that we cannot make a similar extension in the case of nonunivocal sentences, since different tokens of them express different propositions.

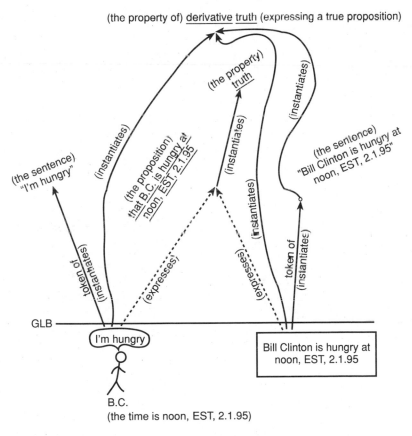

Figure 3.2

It is not hard to see that although the truth-values attach fundamentally to propositions, we may also apply them derivatively both to sentence-tokens and to univocal sentences, but not to nonunivocal sentences. This will have some importance in chapter 5. [**Exercise: Give the appropriate definitions.**]

We have now introduced five different sorts of entities that we'll make repeated use of in this book. Four of them are abstract (properties, relations, propositions, and sentences), and one is concrete (tokens of sentences, words, and other linguistic entities). So some *linguistic* entities are abstract and others are concrete. In the remainder of the book we'll assume without any further motivation that these various entities exist and that they are related among themselves in the ways described above. These relationships are depicted in the GLB diagram in figure 3.2.

4

Identity

The word "identity" has several senses in everyday English. Sometimes it has a psychological sense (as in "He had an identity crisis"); sometimes it has more of a cultural sense (as in "They tried to preserve their ethnic identity"); sometimes there are political overtones (as in "They saw it as a threat to their national identity"); and there are no doubt other senses as well. Many of these senses, including the ones just mentioned, have definite emotional dimensions. But when philosophers use the term, they usually mean nothing of the kind. They usually mean the *relation* of identity (mentioned in Section 3.1). It is difficult to think of any notion more devoid of emotional overtones than the relation of identity. Identity is the relation that, as a matter of necessity, every entity bears to itself, and no entity bears to anything other than itself. Despite its evident austerity and simplicity, this relation has caused an enormous amount of philosophical confusion and trouble, some of which we will explore and try to dispel in this chapter.

Not surprisingly, much of the confusion and trouble has its roots in language. One of the major sources is the English word "is," which is used in three remarkably different ways. (A similar phenomenon occurs in many other languages too.) One of these uses occurs when we attribute properties to things. A few examples: Snow is white; Sue is taller than Liz; What Joe said is true; Gold is denser than zinc; Superman is not human; and so forth. When "is" is used this way, we call it "the 'is' of predication," because it is the verb-part of the (grammatical) predicate of the sentence.

The second use of "is" appears in the following examples: Superman is Clark Kent; Sacramento is the capital of California; Eleven is the sum of six and five; Jane is the tallest player on the team; and so on. Here the "is" occurs between two so-called *singular terms* – expressions of the sort that are capable of *referring* to individual things. Singular terms include *(proper) names*, like "Superman," "Jane," "eleven," and "California." They also include what are called *definite descriptions*, like "the sum of six and five," "The capital of California," and "the tallest player on the team." When an "is" occurs between two singular terms it is called "the 'is' of identity," and the sentence is called an "identity sentence." In characterizing singular terms we said they are of the sort that are "capable" of referring to individual things. The example of "Superman" shows that they don't actually have to succeed. Superman, after all, does not exist. [**Exercise: Give other examples of "empty" singular terms, including definite descriptions.**]

The "is" of identity functions in exactly the same way as the sign of "equality" (also sometimes called "identity") in arithmetic (or mathematics generally). So, if "s" and "t" are any two singular terms, then the sentence "s is t" means precisely the same thing as the more mathematical-looking sentence "s = t." These sentences are true if and only if there happens to be *just one thing* that both "s" and "t" refer to. So, the sentence "Sacramento is the capital of California" is true because "Sacramento" refers to the very same thing that "the capital of California" refers to. The sentence "Palm Springs is the capital of California" is false because the terms "Palm Springs" and "the capital of California" refer to two (different) things, not to one and the same thing.

We will mention the third use of "is" in a moment. First we turn to two other seemingly simple words, closely related to "is," that get used in different ways, and thereby often create metaphysical confusion – confusion involving the notion of identity. One is the word "same," which can have two very different meanings. Not surprisingly, the same (!) is true of the word "different." It's very important to get clear about this.

Let's start with "same." Sometimes we use it to mean *very similar* or *similar in some (specific and important) way*. Suppose I have a turquoise-and-white 1955 Chevrolet Bel Air with a V-8 engine and standard transmission. My neighbor really admires the car and often says he wishes he had "the same" car. In fact, he even knows someone else who has "the same" car, and he admires it just as much. Now, in wishing he had the same car, my neighbor is not wishing he had *my* car – the specific car that I legally own – though certainly my car would do. But so would his other friend's, among many others. He's probably just wishing he had a turquoise-and-white 1955 Chevrolet Bel Air with a V-8 engine and standard transmission. Or maybe the engine and transmission don't really matter, just the color, year, make, and model. Or maybe just any '55 Chevrolet. *Exactly* what he's wishing doesn't matter – he may not even be all that clear about it himself. The point is that whatever it is, he's wishing he had a relevantly *similar* car, not that he have the very car that happens to be in my driveway. So sometimes "same" means (roughly) *appropriately similar*. But not always.

Now imagine that a ballistics expert is on the witness stand. She is shown two labelled exhibits. One is a pistol and the other is a spent cartridge. The prosecutor asks whether the pistol is "the same" pistol as the one that fired the cartridge. If it is, then the person whose fingerprints are on the pistol will have lots of explaining to do, not to mention an uncertain future. Here "the same" doesn't mean *similar* at all (no matter in what respect or degree). A *second* gun might be of exactly the same make and model, be indistinguishable by outward appearances, might even carry the defendant's prints, and yet not be "the same" pistol in the sense of the prosecutor's question. What the prosecutor wants to know is whether the pistol on display and the pistol that fired the cartridge are *one* pistol or *two* (pistols).

It might seem that we could put this last question in terms of the "is" of identity. The prosecutor wants to know whether the pistol on display *is* the pistol that fired the cartridge. Well, we can, but it's a *little* risky. For things are even more intricate with "is" than we originally thought. Not only do we have the "is" of predication and the "is" of identity, but the "is" of identity *itself* is ambiguous in just the way "same" has now been seen to be. That is, sometimes it expresses a *(relevant) similarity* relation. Here's an example of this third use of "is." You're in an automobile showroom looking at one of the most expensive Cadillacs. A salesperson sidles up to you and proudly announces, "This is the car that the president of General Motors drives." If you reply that you weren't interested in a used car, you've missed the point!

Here is a summary of what we have just seen. Suppose "X" and "Y" are singular terms. Then sometimes "X is the same as Y" means that X and Y are *similar* in some important way or ways. But other times it means that X and Y are *just one thing* (and not two similar things). Moreover, even "X is Y" may mean either of these two things.

Now consider the word "different." My imaginary neighbor might have said, "Sally has a '55 Chevy too, but it's different from yours." What he would have meant is that it's *dissimilar* in some important way, like maybe in color or model. He would *not* have meant merely that, between us, Sally and I own two '55 Chevys. But if the ballistics expert told the prosecutor, "This is a different gun," she would not have meant that it was dissimilar. In fact it need not have been very dissimilar at all. She would have meant that it and the gun that fired the cartridge were *two* guns, no matter how similar they might have been (even including configurations of fingerprints).

So we see that we need to be careful about whether a given use of "is" (or "are," etc.) is the "is" of identity or the "is" of predication. We also have to be careful about whether a given use of either "same" or "is" expresses *just-one-thing* identity or merely some form of similarity, and we see a parallel need for care in the case of "different." But our worries don't stop here because things do get a little worse. Even the word "identical" (and "identity") has two senses: They are exactly the same two senses – similarity versus just one thing – that we noticed in the case of "same" and "is." So my neighbor could say "Sally has the identical car," meaning a very similar car. And the witness could answer, "It's the identical gun," meaning there's just one gun under discussion.

In philosophy in general, and in this book, we try to minimize the potential confusion by reserving the word "identical" for the latter sort of case. So, if we say "X is identical with Y," we are saying that X and Y are just one thing, not that they are two very similar things. We will also confine our use of "X is Y" to just-one-thing cases. Sometimes we will emphasize this by saying that X and Y are *numerically* identical. (And if we say that X and Y are *qualitatively* identical, we mean that they have all the same qualities (i.e., properties), but leave it open whether they are in fact numerically identical.) So let us adopt it as a convention, now and forever (in this book), that "identical" and "X is Y" have only the just-one-thing meaning.

So far we have tried to clear up some common confusions about identity that are rooted in the ambiguities of certain important words. Now let's consider some more distinctly philosophical difficulties. Most philosophical problems about identity intimately involve a certain famous metaphysical principle. So we will state and discuss the principle, offer an argument in support of it, and then consider some arguments against it. The principle, often called "Leibniz' Law," is as follows:

The Principle of the Indiscernibility of Identicals: If A *is* B (i.e., if A = B), then whatever is true of A is true of B (and whatever is true of B is true of A). (Put a little differently: If A is B, then A and B have precisely the same properties.)

Notice that Leibniz' Law implies that if a thing A has a property that a thing B does not have, then A is *not* identical with B (i.e., A and B are two things, not one). Here are two examples. (1) Superman is Clark Kent, so (although Lois and Jimmy don't know it) Clark Kent is able to leap tall buildings in a single bound, comes from the planet Krypton, and so on. (Also, Superman is a reporter for a great metropolitan newspaper, often wears a business suit, etc.) (2) A defense attorney might argue in court as follows: "The murderer's blood type is A-positive but the defendant's is not. So the defendant is not the murderer."

Example (2) illustrates the way Leibniz' Law is typically used. Notice that this use is entirely ordinary and nonphilosophical. The lawyer making the argument has probably never even heard of Leibniz' Law. And the jury members will accept the argument without question or hesitation, provided they are convinced that the claims about the blood types are correct. [**Exercise: Think of other everyday cases where this form of reasoning is used.**] In fact, there is a diverse multitude of specific, ordinary cases like (2): They conform to the principle without explicitly appealing to it, and they are accepted without question as a matter of simple common sense.

Now, the principle is, in effect, just a generalization from these ordinary cases. So it is tempting to think that once it is understood, it should also be accepted (and seen to be a matter of common sense). Moreover, it even seems clear that denying it leads quickly to a contradiction. This is the standard argument in favor of Leibniz' Law. Suppose we have a case in which A is B, but A has a property, say P, that B doesn't have. Now notice that since A is B, A and B are just one thing. Hence we have a case in which there is just one thing that both has and does not have the property P. This is as clear a contradiction as one could ever hope to find. So Leibniz' Law is proved.

Despite this argument, and despite the mountain of ordinary evidence, the principle has sometimes been questioned. As an example of such a challenge, consider the following fascinating and difficult argument.

(1) Lois believes that Superman can fly.
(2) Lois believes that Clark Kent cannot fly. **Therefore:**

(3)   Superman has a property that Clark Kent doesn't have (namely, *being believed by Lois to be able to fly*). **So:**

(4)   If Leibniz' Law is correct, then Superman isn't Clark Kent. **But:**

(5)   Superman is Clark Kent. **Therefore:**

(6)   Leibniz' Law is not correct.

This argument raises interesting questions about the nature of *belief*, and this makes it more difficult to see that it is actually *invalid*. One way to expose the questions about belief is to expand the argument, as follows.

(1*)   Lois believes that Superman can fly. **Therefore:**

(2*)   Superman has the property of *being believed by Lois to be able to fly*.

(3*)   Lois believes that Clark Kent cannot fly. **Therefore:**

(4*)   Clark Kent has the property of *being believed by Lois to be unable to fly*. **So:**

(5*)   Clark Kent does not have the property of *being believed by Lois to be able to fly*. **Therefore:**

(6*)   Superman has a property that Clark Kent doesn't have (namely, *being believed by Lois to be able to fly*). **Hence:**

(7*)   If Leibniz' Law is correct, then Superman isn't Clark Kent. **But:**

(8*)   Superman is Clark Kent. **Therefore:**

(9*)   Leibniz' Law is not correct.

Now let's focus on the move from (1*) to (2*). (Exactly parallel remarks will apply to the move from (3*) to (4*). In (1*), it looks like *belief* is a ("two-place") relation that Lois bears to a proposition (the proposition *that Superman can fly*). But belief *apparently* functions very differently in (2*). In order for Superman to have the property of *being believed by Lois to be able to fly*, it must be true that:

(10)   Lois believes Superman to be able to fly.

Now, in (10), belief is seemingly *not* a two-place relation linking Lois to a proposition. For one thing, the phrase "Superman to be able to fly" doesn't express a proposition. For another, that phrase isn't even the direct object of the verb "believes" – the direct object is simply "Superman." (But notice that in (1*), "that Superman can fly" *is* the direct object.) So, in (10), it looks like belief is serving as a *three*-place relation linking Lois, an entity (Superman), and a property (*being able to fly*). (Certainly this must be the case if (10) is to support (2*).) But it isn't obvious that an instance in which the two-place relation holds guarantees that a coordinate instance of the three-place relation holds. So it isn't obvious that (2*) follows from (1*).

In fact, some philosophers deny that there actually *is* a belief phenomenon requiring any such three-place relation. Of course, if there is no such phenomenon, then there can be no such property as *being believed by Lois to be able to fly*. So (2*) would not follow from (1*), and the argument would be invalid. Philosophers who deny the three-place belief phenomenon would view (10) as a grammatically misleading paraphrase of (1*).

But suppose there really is such a three-place belief relation (in addition to the more familiar two-place relation). Then (10) is not just a paraphrase of (1*) and, in fact, (2*) cannot follow from (1*) unless (10) also follows. The Superman stories do suggest that (10) might be true. But whether it is true and whether it follows from (1*) are two different questions.

For a sentence like (10) to be true seems to require that the believer have very direct contact with the person or thing that the believing is "about." For this reason, sentences like (10) are often said to express "belief *de re*" — belief *of* (or *about*) *the thing*. In contrast, sentences like (1*) are said to express "belief *de dicto*" — belief *of the statement* (or *proposition*). So the substantive issue — the "problem of *de re* belief" — is whether a *de re* belief automatically follows from an appropriate *de dicto* belief and, if not, what further conditions must be met in order for it to follow. Most philosophers do not believe that *de re* beliefs automatically follow from *de dicto* beliefs. The reason is that we often do have *de dicto* beliefs in cases where we have no significant contact with the person or thing that the *de re* belief would be about, so that the needed three-place relation linking us, the entity, and the property cannot take hold.

As an extreme example, consider Ponce de Leon. It certainly seems likely that he believed that the Fountain of Youth was in Florida. So he stood in the two-place belief relation to a certain proposition. Fine. But surely he did not stand in the three-place belief relation with the entity the Fountain of Youth, and the property *being in Florida*, for the simple reason that such an entity does not (and never did) exist. [Exercise: Try to find a convincing example of a *de dicto* belief with no corresponding *de re* belief, but one where the entity that the *de re* belief *would* be about really does exist.]

We won't try to solve the problem of *de re* belief here. Instead we'll draw the modest conclusion that it seems very likely that the argument is invalid — specifically, because (2*) doesn't follow from (1*), and (4*) doesn't follow from (3*). But now imagine that whatever additional premises might be needed have been supplied and accepted, so that we now have both (2*) and (4*). Unfortunately, there is still a severe problem, because (5*) doesn't follow from (4*).

It is certainly true that no entity can be both able to fly and unable to fly. That would be a contradiction. But there is no contradiction in saying that Lois *believes* some entity to be able to fly and also believes *that same entity* to be unable to fly. Of course, Lois, if she is rational, could not *realize* that she has such a pair of beliefs and would not put them together in this stark fashion. Some mechanism or other would be operating so as to prevent her from making the connection. And if she were made aware that she held such a pair of beliefs, she would soon abandon one or the other. (Presumably, in the present case, if she were made aware that Superman is Clark Kent, then she would abandon the belief, about him, that he is unable to fly.)

It's important to see that a Superman-type case could easily arise in everyday life. All that's required is that you have fairly close and regular contact with a certain individual in two different sorts of circumstances, that you be unaware that there's just one person in both circumstances, and that the different circumstances have ingredients that lead you to form a pair of beliefs that could not both be correct. These ingredients needn't be nearly as exotic as those of the Superman story. **[Exercise: Construct such a case.]**

There is another way to see that (5*) doesn't follow from (4*). In accordance with the above discussion of *de re* belief, the truth of (2*) depended solely on Lois's standing in a three-place belief relation with a certain *entity* (Superman) and a certain property (*being able to fly*). It had nothing to do with any *names* that this entity might have. And "Clark Kent" is simply another name for the entity in question. So (2*) cannot be true, on this account, unless

(11)   Clark Kent has the property of *being believed by Lois to be able to fly*

is also true (and vice versa). After all, there's only *one* entity in question here, and either it has the property or it doesn't. If it has the property, then it shouldn't make any difference which of its *names* we use in reporting that fact. But (11) is inconsistent with (5*) — in fact, it's the "negation" of (5*).

So, if (5*) really followed from (4*), then (4*) would be inconsistent with (2*)!

So the Superman argument against Leibniz' Law is invalid. Still, there is a good deal more that could be said about the concepts involved. But that would take us deeper into philosophy of language and epistemology than we ought to go here. So, instead, we will look at a rather parallel, but importantly different, argument that has sometimes been made against Leibniz' Law. This argument has nothing to do with the elusive concept of belief. Instead it has to do with the elusive concept of necessity (which we will consider in some detail in chapter 8).

(12) Nine is necessarily greater than seven.

(13) The number of planets is not necessarily greater than seven. **Therefore:**

(14) Nine has a property that the number of planets doesn't have (namely, *being necessarily greater than seven*). **So:**

(15) If Leibniz' Law is correct, then nine is distinct from the number of planets. **But in fact:**

(16) Nine is the number of planets. **Therefore:**

(17) Leibniz' Law is not correct.

Here is a quick structural analysis of the argument: The crucial feature is that the second premise, (13), is ambiguous. It could express either of two different propositions. One of these propositions is false and the other, though true, doesn't entitle us to infer (14). So either way, the argument is unsound — either it has a false premise, or else it's invalid.

Here is one of the two possible readings of (13):

(13a) It isn't necessarily true that the number of planets is greater than seven.

That is, it isn't necessarily true that there are more than seven planets. (13a) is evidently true. If the development of the universe had been different in certain ways, then there would have been fewer than seven planets. (For example, there might have been no planets at all.)

The other reading of (13) is:

(13b) The number that is, *in fact*, the number of the planets, is not necessarily greater than seven.

That is, there is a certain number that, the way things worked out, happens to be the number of the planets, and *it* is not necessarily greater than seven. Well, just as surely as (13a) was true, (13b) is false. It happens that *nine* is the number of the planets, and *that very entity* certainly is necessarily greater than seven. So, if (13) is interpreted as (13b), then the argument is unsound because it has a false premise.

Suppose instead that (13) is interpreted as the true (13a). Then it doesn't follow that nine has a property that the number of planets doesn't have, because (13a) simply doesn't say that the number of planets – that entity – isn't necessarily greater than seven. That's what (13b) says, and we just saw that (13b) was false. So, if we interpret (13) as (13a), then we can no longer validly infer (14).

We have seen what seems to be a compelling argument in favor of Leibniz' Law and we have noted that ordinary, everyday reasoning often appears to depend on it (though it is not ordinarily explicitly invoked). Furthermore, we have seen fatal flaws in two well-known philosophical arguments against the principle. So let us finally accept Leibniz' Law and turn to a metaphysical problem in which it plays an important role. This problem may at first seem simpler than the above arguments, because it doesn't involve tricky concepts like belief or necessity.

Our ordinary way of thinking about physical objects like houses has the following two features. Feature I: A house is capable of having ordinary properties like *being white* or *having shutters*. Feature II: A house is a three-dimensional object that is entirely present at different times – it "persists" through time. But it's difficult to see how these views can be reconciled with Leibniz' Law.

Suppose that, on Monday, your house doesn't have shutters, but on Tuesday you install some. Then on Wednesday your house has shutters. Now remember that one and the same house is supposed to be entirely present on both occasions. So the very thing that is present on Monday is also present on Wednesday. But since the thing that is present on Monday doesn't have shutters, and the thing that is present on Wednesday does have shutters, Leibniz' Law seems to imply that they are two things, not one.

Using "M" as a name for the house that is present on Monday, and "W" as a name for the house that is present on Wednesday, we can condense this problem into the following four propositions.

(18)   M has the property of *not having shutters*. (By hypothesis, *via* Feature I.)

(19) W has the property of *having shutters*. (Similarly.)

(20) M is distinct from W. (Follows from (18) and (19), using Leibniz' Law.)

(21) M is W. (By hypothesis, *via* Feature II.)

Since (20) and (21) are inconsistent, something has to give.

There are three interestingly different ways to deal with the problem. We'll only consider them briefly here, because the topic will be treated in greater detail in chapter 9. One solution – probably the least satisfactory – goes like this: There really are no ordinary properties like *having shutters*. Instead, where we used to think there was this one simple property, there are – in its place – infinitely many properties, each of the form *having shutters at t*, where *t* is a possible time. On this account, your house has the property of *having shutters on Wednesday* and the property of *not having shutters on Monday*. But, unlike *having shutters* and *not having shutters*, these fancier, "time-indexed" properties do not conflict, so there is no problem with the supposition that one single thing has both. (Thus (18) and (19) are replaced by propositions that do not support an application of Leibniz' Law. So (20) doesn't follow.) Notice that, on this account, if a thing has a property like *not having shutters on Monday*, it doesn't just have it on Monday. It *always* has that property. So the properties of a thing never literally *change*. This solution abandons Feature I and, with it, our ordinary understanding of properties.

The second approach is to give up Feature II – the idea that houses are three-dimensional objects that persist through time. Instead they are held to be *four-dimensional* objects, different *parts* of which exist at different times. (It helps to understand this view if we picture ordinary objects as "spacetime worms.") Then the Monday-part of your house and the Wednesday-part of your house are two distinct, nonoverlapping entities. One of them has shutters (actually, shutter-parts) and the other does not. So, on this approach, the inconsistency of (20) and (21) disappears because (21) itself disappears. Your house is an entity some parts of which have shutters, other parts of which do not. When we say "Her house has shutters," we're speaking loosely. We really mean that *the current part* of her house has shutters. So, ordinary properties survive, but the three-dimensional account of ordinary things does not, and we are forced to reinterpret lots of things that we ordinarily say.

The third solution saves both ordinary properties and three-dimensionality. It holds that the entity that is present on Monday and the entity that is present on Wednesday are two distinct entities but, unlike the second approach, it leaves open the possibility that they have parts in common. The crucial idea is that when we say "M is the same house as W" – or even "M is W" – we are not expressing *identity*, but rather a special *similarity* relation. We can call this relation the *same-house-as* relation as long as we are clear that it isn't *identity*. So, what are literally distinct entities can bear the *same-house-as* relation to each other. Since this relation isn't *identity*, (21) no longer *expresses* identity and hence no longer conflicts with (20). In some ways this is an elegant solution, but it does leave an important question unanswered: We still need a general account of the *same-house-as* relation. That is, we need to know under what circumstances an entity X (existing at a time *t*) and a (possibly) distinct entity Y (existing at a later time *t**) stand in the relation.

The differences of the three approaches may be brought out sharply if we suppose that, on Wednesday, we say, "This house didn't have shutters on Monday." On the first solution, this means that this house (now) has the property of *not having shutters on Monday*. On the second, it means that the Monday-part of this house had the property of *not having shutters*. And on the third, it means that the thing that had the property of *being this house*, on Monday, also had the property of *not having shutters*, on Monday. So the third view may appear to pay a price in added complexity for retaining both ordinary properties and three-dimensionality. (There are undoubtedly other ways of treating this problem in addition to the three we have considered.)

Now notice that the problem of the house seemed at the outset to be a deep puzzle about the concept of identity. But in each of the three solutions we mentioned, the concept of identity survives as a simple relation, holding necessarily between each entity and itself (and never in any other case), and subject to Leibniz' Law. So none of the solutions involved any modification of our original, "naive" notion of identity, as characterized in the first paragraph of this chapter. Instead, the first solution involved a modification of our naive notion of *properties*, the second featured a modification of our naive notion of an ordinary *thing*, and the third exploited an ambiguity in the words "is" and "same" that we had already noticed on independent grounds.

A "solution" we did not consider would be to deny Leibniz' Law. Then (20) wouldn't follow from (18) and (19) and there would be no explicit contradiction of (21). The trouble is that even in the absence of (20) the situation *still* seems impossible. So denying Leibniz' Law wouldn't really

74

solve the problem. We would still need an explanation of how this seemingly impossible state of affairs could actually be possible.

Furthermore, any such explanation would evidently require tinkering with the concept of identity. Here we are, on Wednesday, admiring your house, W, which is identical with M. ("What lovely shutters!") We can see the shutters, touch them, smell the fresh paint. So the explanation will have to accomplish either one or the other of two very unenviable tasks. Either it must explain how M, which lacks shutters, is *not* before us, even though all agree that W is identical with M and W *is* before us. Or else it must explain how things that are before us can systematically appear to have (or lack) some of the properties they actually lack (or have). Now this is some serious tinkering with the notion of identity. It will have to involve transforming what seems to stand up very nicely as a simple (i.e., unanalyzable) relation into a very complex one.

Now, given that there really are relations, as we have conceived them, then certainly there is a relation, say R, that holds necessarily between each thing and itself (and never otherwise). When we think about this R, two things emerge. First, it must be a matter of *logical* necessity that if A bears R to B, then any property that A has is also had by B (and vice versa). This is so because every case of any A bearing R to any B is a case of a thing bearing a relation to *itself*. Since everything must have all of its properties and no others, it must be that any property had by A is also had by B (and vice versa). That is, if we rewrite Leibniz' Law for the relation *R*, then it must be true as a matter of mere *logic*. Second, R is inevitably *primitive*, or *simple*. We cannot imagine any *simpler* notions in terms of which R might be analyzed. To put it another way, anything that exists must bear R to itself automatically, without meeting any further conditions. That is surely the hallmark of an unanalyzable relation.

Since "Leibniz' Law" automatically holds for *R*, it follows that to deny Leibniz' Law (for *identity*) is, in effect, to deny that the identity relation and R are just one relation. In other words, it is to reserve the term "identity" for some relation other than R. Of course, someone who denies Leibniz' Law need not be aware of this. Now, we have already seen that "is," "same," and even "identical" are often used in everyday talk to express relations other than R — "similarity" relations of one kind or another. But it also seems clear that they are just as often used to express R and, in fact, we have made it a convention that (in effect) they will be reserved for expressing R when we use them in this book.

But now notice this. In the original puzzle, (21) was simply a result of our ordinary conception of things like houses, which takes them to be three-dimensional entities that persist through time. As applied to our story, this means that it is M *itself* that is present on Wednesday. So "is" in (21) can only be *properly* understood as expressing the relation that is, in fact, R. Since "Leibniz' Law" *automatically* holds for R, any effort to relieve the problem by denying (the literal) Leibniz' Law would therefore be based on a misunderstanding of the puzzle. The denial of Leibniz' Law is not even a logically possible solution to the puzzle.

The three solutions we considered are, of course, genuine logical possibilities. And we saw that none of them involved tinkering with identity. There may be a moral here: Because of its logical simplicity, it is hard to see how there could really be any genuine philosophical problems about identity (that is, R) itself. Of course many philosophers have often claimed that there are such problems and have devoted considerable energy to solving them. Could it be that they were working on genuine philosophical problems *involving* identity, but that identity was not the problematic element, or that they were working on problematic relations other than identity but which they *mistook* for identity? If we consider the problem of the house and the three proposed solutions, it certainly looks like the *problem* lies not with identity, but with some other concept or concepts, such as: *things and their parts*, the *properties* of things, *change over time*, or the like.

Let's make it a general policy to be suspicious about supposed philosophical problems about identity. At least, let's approach them with the initial methodological assumption that they are not really problems about identity, but rather problems about some other philosophical concept or concepts. That way we can attack them with a pure and simple notion of identity at our disposal, and see if we can figure out a solution that keeps identity pure and simple. If we can't make any headway under this policy – if we can't even convince ourselves that the problem really does lie with some concept other than identity – then that would be the time to start worrying about identity.

5

Is Truth "Relative?"

5.1 Two Concepts of Truth?

Philosophers have proposed many different analyses and characterizations of "the concept of truth." Interestingly, these tend to be of one or the other of two dramatically different sorts, often called "epistemic" and "metaphysical." The sharpness of their divergence raises a serious methodological issue that has, in fact, already been lurking in the background. Now is a good time to deal with it explicitly.

What are we doing when we try to analyze a philosophical concept? This is clearly a difficult, sophisticated question. In chapters 1 and 3 we presented a certain view of what concepts and analyses are, but where do the philosophical concepts come from in the first place? We have to get *some* kind of grip on a concept before we can attempt to analyze it. So how does this happen? The answer to this question has a significant bearing on whether there really are two very different (sorts of) analyses of "the concept of truth."

Philosophical concepts may be thought of as either "everyday" or "technical," and the latter concepts usually play a role in discussions of the former. The everyday philosophical concepts are those that arise in everyday life and are expressed by terms of ordinary language (knowledge, belief, justification, existence, cause, intention, responsibility, goodness, etc.). These concepts are the backbone of the discipline of philosophy. So philosophy is, in essence, the study of certain very difficult but nevertheless perfectly ordinary concepts. Because we are speakers of the language, we already have some grasp of these concepts, but our grasp is usually imper-

77

fect. We are generally much more adept at identifying their instances than we are at analyzing them (or defining the terms that express them).

One of the central tasks of philosophy is to enhance our understanding of these important concepts by analyzing them or otherwise characterizing them in ways that extend or deepen our ordinary understanding. This effort can have a variety of different outcomes. Let's mention just three. (1) We might find a plausible analysis or an enlightening characterization. (An example you are likely to encounter if you do more advanced work in philosophy is Bertrand Russell's account of the meaningfulness of nondenoting definite descriptions.) (2) It might be concluded that although the ordinary use of the relevant term seems inconsistent, it actually isn't, because the term is *ambiguous* (and each of its different senses is used consistently). Then the effort at analysis could be directed toward one or more of the different senses. (Example: the nonsubjective and subjective senses of the term "concept," as discussed in Section 1.2.) Or it might be concluded that there is genuine inconsistency, but only "at the fringes" of the term's use, with the result that although the term isn't ambiguous, there are fairly systematic mistakes in applying it, and these produce the inconsistencies. So analysis and clarification could proceed. **[Exercise: Explain why the term "cause" may provide a good example.]** (3) The term might prove to be unambiguous, but too *vague* to support a specific analysis. (Here a good example may be "love.")

Technical philosophical concepts aren't encountered directly in everyday life, even if they figure in the analysis of concepts that are. For example, suppose we are in case (3), and we conclude that a certain ordinary philosophical term is vague, but not ambiguous. Then there will generally be many different, reasonable ways of resolving the vagueness. Because (by hypothesis) these are not reflected in the ordinary use of the term, to decide to use it in accordance with one or another of them would be to adopt a convention giving that term a "technical" sense. Often several technical terms with different senses will arise from such a case.

But by far the most important area where we encounter technicality is case (1). Any plausible *analysis* of an ordinary philosophical notion is almost inevitably technical, involving philosophical concepts that are not explicitly considered in ordinary life. We saw an example of this in chapter 4 when we considered the notion of belief. Belief is an ordinary concept, deeply embedded in everyday life. But the discussion there made it pretty evident that any ultimate analysis or characterization of this concept would have to come to terms with the technical notions of belief *de dicto* and *de re*.

Truth is as clear a case of an everyday philosophical concept as one could hope to find. We begin learning about truth as soon as we begin learning to speak and to understand what others say. (For example, very early on, we are told that we should always "tell the truth.") Now, the fact that two dramatically different sorts of "analyses of truth" have been defended might suggest that this ordinary term is ambiguous, sometimes expressing one concept, sometimes another, and that the two different sorts of analysis apply to the two different senses. But the *ordinary* use of the term "true" does not actually seem to be ambiguous in the relevant way! Furthermore, the proponents of the different sorts of analyses often see themselves as *disagreeing* about "the nature of truth." (Of course, if the analyses were of different senses of the term, then they wouldn't be in conflict.) So what's really going on here?

Epistemic analyses of "truth" are those that make essential use of epistemic notions (like belief and justification). Metaphysical analyses are those that do not. So the issue – if it really is an issue – is whether "the concept of truth" is or is not epistemic in nature. (Epistemic analyses are typically favored by the American "pragmatists" and their intellectual heirs, and by many recent and contemporary continental philosophers. They seem to fit naturally with skeptical or anti-realist views about "the external world." Metaphysical analyses are usually favored by analytic philosophers and by linguists concerned with the semantics of natural language. They fit naturally with realism about the external world.)

On the metaphysical view, as elaborated in the Platonist terms of chapter 3, truth is a *property* that, properly speaking, can only be instantiated by *propositions*. When we say that a *sentence* or a *sentence-token* is true – as we often do – we are using the term "true" in an extended sense, one that ultimately depends on some *proposition*'s being true (in the *fundamental* sense). The true propositions are those that correctly (or accurately) represent the world (as being some way or other). So truth is, in fact, a *relational* property of the propositions that instantiate it. It will become clear later that this does *not* entail that truth is relative. (See Section 3.1 for the notion of a relational property.) Because propositions are mind-independent entities, and because the world is, in general, independent of our minds, whether a given proposition is true has nothing to do with whether anyone knows it, believes it, has any evidence for it, or any justification for believing it or asserting it, etc. In other words, this notion of truth has no epistemic content whatever. It's strictly a matter between the proposition and the world.

Of course, some propositions do concern epistemic matters, for example, the proposition *that Joe has an unwarranted belief that Sue knows that Ellen forgot*. This proposition is loaded with epistemic content. But its *truth* (or falsity) has nothing to do with whether anyone knows or believes *it* or has evidence (etc.) *for it*. Its truth or falsity depends only on whether it correctly represents (or "corresponds to") the way things stand in these epistemic (and other) respects with Joe and Sue and Ellen. (Metaphysical theories of truth are often called *correspondence* theories.)

On some epistemic views, truth may also be seen as a property, but not a property of propositions. Instead, it would be a property of sentences or, on some accounts, sentence-tokens. Other epistemic views are best understood as treating truth as a relation between sentences (or sentence-tokens) and some other entities. Exactly *what* property or relation varies substantially from account to account, and we aren't going to do a careful survey here. But it always has essential epistemic content. So, for example, some views claim that a sentence is true iff an "ideal observer" would be justified in asserting it. A variation would be that truth is a relation between sentences and possible conditions of justification. Or: . . . iff it "coheres" with other sentences of the language that are generally accepted. A relational version of this view is also a possibility. (Such views are called *coherence* theories of truth.) Or: . . . iff, if human inquiry were to continue forever, it would converge toward acceptance of the sentence. (Notice that this view rests on what seems to be an empirical claim.) Or even: . . . iff a majority of qualified speakers of the language in fact do accept the sentence. (A variation: truth is a relation between sentences and groups of speakers of the language. So a sentence may be true relative to one group, false relative to another.) When we considered linguistic nominalism in Section 3.2, we looked at two specific versions of this last sort of theory – versions that happened also to be nominalistic about properties. (Both were found defective.)

If we think about how we actually use the words "true" and "truth" (and "false," etc.) in everyday life, it is very clear that we use them overwhelmingly in accordance with the metaphysical conception, not the epistemic. In our practical affairs, unless we are confused, we always separate questions of truth from questions of belief or justification or acceptance (etc.), whether by majorities, "ideal observers," future generations, or what have you. **[Exercise: Read a newspaper or magazine, looking for the word "true" (and "false," etc.). Try to find even a single case where the use of the term seems more in conformity with an epistemic reading than with the metaphysical.]** This suggests very strongly that the ordinary terms are really *not* ambiguous, and hence that the ordinary philosophical concept is (unambiguously) the metaphysical one.

Many proponents of "epistemic accounts" do not hesitate to acknowledge this fact about the ordinary term. They see themselves as *reformers* who are trying to *replace* the ordinary notion of truth, not analyze it. They hold that the ordinary notion of truth is – one way or another – *bad*. Some reformers say it's useless, others say it's counterproductive, others say it's unattainable. Still others say it's an impediment to human progress or otherwise not in the interests of "the people." (Etc.) So, for one reason or another, they don't like it, and they want to replace it by what they see as a more useful, productive, attainable, progressive, revolutionary, or whatever, concept. They are therefore recommending that we start using the word "truth" for a concept other than the one presently expressed by the word. In other words – still in terms that a consistent reformer should accept – they are recommending that we start using the word "truth" for a concept other than the concept of truth.

Leaving aside the question of its advisability or attainability, there is nothing incoherent about this recommendation. The meanings of words *are* determined by the linguistic activity of speakers, and these meanings often do shift and evolve over time. We could start applying the term "dog" exclusively to cats and applying the term "cat" exclusively to dogs if we wished. If this became the standard usage, then the *sentence* "All dogs are felines" would be true (in the derivative sense). It would be true because its tokens would express the true proposition *that all cats are felines*.

It is very important to see clearly that if the term "dog" did come to apply exclusively to cats, that would *not* be a change in the (nonsubjective) *concept* of dog. It would be a change in the meaning of the word "dog" (and the subjective concepts we associate with the word "dog" would also change accordingly). Nonsubjective concepts are nonlinguistic, mind-independent entities. The concept of dog doesn't care whether it ever gets expressed or, if it does, what words are used to express it. (Notice that the notion of "conceptual change" – if it is to be coherent and literal – must therefore mean change *from* one concept *to* another, not change *within* a single concept.)

81

It is vital to recognize something that is conceded by the epistemic reformers of "truth" and, in fact, ought to be accepted by all parties to the discussion. It is simply that the metaphysical concept (assuming it is coherent) is a genuine concept, and each of the various epistemic concepts (if coherent) is a genuine concept, no matter how (or whether) we wind up using the word "true." None of these several concepts is going to go away. (Concepts don't do that since they exist independently of our mental activity.)

So let's not swim against the prevailing (and overwhelming) linguistic current. Let's continue to use "truth" to mean truth, that is, to express the ordinary philosophical concept of truth, and let's pay all of the various epistemic concepts whatever respect they might prove to merit, introducing new terms for them if we wish. There is just one concept of truth – the ordinary philosophical one – and there are several different, possibly important epistemic concepts (that may or may not be related to truth in significant ways). But none of these epistemic concepts can possibly be a correct analysis of the concept of truth, because that concept is non-epistemic at its everyday source.

Now, the central question of this chapter is whether truth is relative. And, as a matter of fact, it is beyond question that certain of the epistemic concepts we've been discussing *are* relative. So suppose a reformer whose specific concept *is* relative announces, "Truth is relative." What should we make of this? What proposition does it express? Well, it is clear what proposition the reformer *intends* to express (and that proposition is – by hypothesis and in the ordinary sense – true). But remember, the proposed reform is not yet in place. (In fact it isn't remotely near to being in place and the odds are very heavily against it.) The meaning of the ordinary word "truth" is out of the reformer's hands and, like it or not, it *isn't* the meaning intended. So the reformer can only be using the word in a special, *technical* sense. If the context makes this clear, then the pronouncement expresses a true proposition, but not a proposition about truth. If it does not make this clear, then, despite the speaker's intentions, "truth" has its ordinary meaning, and the utterance really does express the proposition *that truth is relative*. **[Exercise: Think about this in connection with the dog/cat case.]**

In the rest of this chapter we will confine our attention to the claim that truth is relative, where the term "truth" is understood in its ordinary, metaphysical sense.

5.2 Relativity and Truth

In everyday life, we might very well utter any of the following three sentences:

(1)   That proposition is true.
(2)   [While pointing at a written sentence-token]: That's true.
(3)   The sentence "Snow is white" is true.

So in everyday life we regularly apply the term "true" (and "false") to entities of all three categories. But we have already seen that it is only propositions that are *fundamentally* (or literally) true, not sentences or sentence-tokens. When sentences or sentence-tokens are appropriately called true, the term is being used in a *derivative* sense – one that depends on the truth of appropriate background propositions. It follows that in discussing truth itself, we really only have to worry about the notion as it applies to propositions. If we can settle this question, then the question of truth as it applies to sentences or sentence-tokens (when it does) will automatically fall into place. So we may now give the following statement of the doctrine of "relativism:"

> **Relativism:** No proposition is *absolutely* true (or absolutely false). A proposition can only be *relatively* true (or relatively false). Every proposition is true *relative to* (or *with respect to*, etc.) some perspective and false relative to others.

What does this mean? Perhaps we can gain some insight by considering a more familiar, but analogous, claim. Remarkably enough, the more familiar claim comes from the realm of physics:

> No object is *absolutely* at rest (or absolutely in motion). An object can only be *relatively* at rest (or relatively in motion). Every object is at rest *relative to* (or *with respect to*, etc.) some reference frames and in motion relative to others.

This is the doctrine of the relativity of rest and motion, accepted alike by Newton, Einstein, and informed common sense. It certainly sounds right. But what does it really mean? It means this: *Being at rest* and *being in motion*

83

are not *properties* of things at all, despite superficial linguistic appearances. Instead, the concepts of rest and motion are best seen as (two-place) *relations* that hold between objects and references frames. When we say "The ball is at rest," it may sound like we're just attributing a simple property to it, as when we say "The ball is spherical." But what's really going on is that we're taking a certain reference frame for granted, and saying that the relation of *being at rest* holds between the ball and it. (Or, what amounts to the same thing, we are attributing to the ball the relational property of *being at rest with respect to the earth*.) To say that the concepts of rest and motion are *relative* is merely to say that they are really *relations* between certain sorts of things rather than *properties* of things.

It's no different with truth, or with any other concept that is claimed to be "relative." When we say that a given proposition *is true*, it sounds like we're just saying that a certain thing, the proposition, has a certain property, the property of *being true*. But relativism is the view that being true isn't really a property at all, but rather is a relation that holds between the proposition and something else, usually something like a person, a culture, a conceptual scheme, or whatever. So relativists sometimes say things like "That may be true *for you*, but it isn't true *for me*," or "That's not true *for us*, but it is true *for culture* X." In statements like these, the supposed relativity is made explicit. By contrast, *absolutism* (about truth) is the doctrine that any proposition is either just plain true or just plain false, that is, that being true is just a property that a proposition either has or doesn't have, and that it isn't a relation between the proposition and a person or culture (or whatever).

So the dispute between the relativist and the absolutist is at bottom merely a "logical" dispute – a dispute about the logical status (or function) of a certain concept: Is truth a *property* or is it a *relation*? This makes it seem very odd that the dispute is often carried on with a great deal of emotional intensity. Certainly no dispute merely concerning the logical status of a concept – however philosophically important it might be – should have these effects on people. I think that the emotional overtones we sometimes find in these disputes are always the result of confusions, generally one or another of three specific confusions.

The first was discussed at some length in Section 5.1. Epistemic "concepts of truth" are often genuinely relativistic. But when a proponent of the epistemic concept says "Truth is relative," and a proponent of the metaphysical says "Truth is not relative," they are *not* expressing incompatible propositions, since only one of them is actually about the concept of truth. The only real dispute here is whether the concept of truth should somehow be replaced by the epistemic notion in order to foster some independent goal. Of course it would not be surprising if *this* turned out to be an emotional issue. But it's a confusion to think that this is the issue of whether the concept of truth is relative or absolute.

A confusion about the doctrine of absolutism can easily arise because the terms "absolute" and "absolutely" are ambiguous. We often use these terms to convey certainty or to claim knowledge. For example, when we say, "That's absolutely true," we usually intend the adverb to add a special kind of emphasis, suggesting that we feel certain about the truth of the proposition. But this use of the term has nothing to do with the doctrine of absolutism we are now discussing. That doctrine, again, is merely the claim that truth is a property of propositions rather than a relation between propositions and other things. It has nothing at all to do with knowledge, belief, conviction, or certainty. Unfortunately, many people have rejected absolutism on the basis of just this sort of misunderstanding. They think the proponents of absolutism are arrogant snobs claiming special powers of knowledge, and they feel it's important to oppose such a potentially dangerous view. It isn't surprising that emotions can run high here. But let's avoid this misunderstanding. If absolutism is wrong, it isn't because it claims knowledge or certainty where it should be more cautious. If it's wrong, it's simply because truth is a relation rather than a property.

The third possible source of emotion is a common confusion about the doctrine of relativism. We'll discuss this confusion after discussing relativism itself. What can be said in favor of relativism? The most common arguments depend on examples in which people of different cultures behave differently or react differently to certain sorts of behavior. Here is one version:

The Argument from Cultural Diversity
1   In society X, belching (or whatever) is impolite.
2   In society Y, belching is not impolite. **Therefore:**
3   The proposition *that belching is impolite* is only relatively true; it's true relative to some cultures, false relative to others.

Now, of course, cultural variations like the one reported in premises 1 and 2 really do occur. No one questions that. The question is whether this is enough to show that truth is relative. An absolutist thinks it isn't. Here is how an absolutist might reply to the argument.

Different tokens of the sentence "Belching is impolite" actually express different propositions. A token uttered by someone in society X (normally) says something about the social conventions of society X. But a token uttered in society Y (normally) says something entirely different – something about the conventions of society Y. Now, since "Belching is impolite" has this feature, it doesn't – on its own – express *any* proposition.

In Section 3.3 we emphasized that a *sentence* can express a proposition only "derivatively," and then only if all possible tokens of it express the same proposition. Such sentences were called *univocal*. So "Belching is impolite" is a nonunivocal sentence, like "I'm hungry." But the phrase "the proposition *that belching is impolite*" occurs in the conclusion of the argument! Because "Belching is impolite" is nonunivocal, there *is* no proposition *that belching is impolite*, and the conclusion of the argument is therefore incoherent. The relativist wanted to provide a specific example of a proposition that was only relatively true (and relatively false). But no such proposition has been found, so the argument offers no support for the doctrine of relativism.

Notice that if the conclusion of the argument had instead been, "Some possible tokens of 'Belching is impolite' are true and some are false," then it would not only be coherent, it would also be true. But it would still offer no support for relativism because tokens with differing truth-values would be expressing different propositions.

Nonunivocal sentences like "Belching is impolite" are sometimes called *context-sensitive* because the proposition that a token of the sentence expresses depends on the context in which it occurs. Context-sensitivity is a very common phenomenon in human languages. It promotes linguistic "efficiency" because it lets us take many things for granted in everyday speech. This makes our sentences shorter and easier to grasp. But it is crucial to keep in mind that context-sensitive sentences simply do not express any propositions *on their own*. They need the help of a specific context. This is really just another way of saying that it isn't the sentence that expresses a proposition, it's the specific sentence-token (which cannot help but occur in some specific context or other).

So the argument from cultural diversity rests on the mistake of confusing the (actual) context-sensitivity of a *sentence* with the (imagined) relativity of truth of a *proposition*. The sentence "Belching is impolite" is indeed context-sensitive. But there simply is no proposition that belching is impolite, and thus no proposition has yet been found that suffers from relativity of truth. Relativism about truth is in no way supported by the (undoubted) phenomenon of cultural diversity.

Now we turn to a pair of arguments *against* relativism. First, let's notice that a relativist isn't entitled to say, for example, "That's true," *unless* it is understood to be an *abbreviation* of the more complicated statement "That's true with respect to P," where P is some appropriate "perspective" (that is, some person, culture, society, or whatever). This is no different from the case of rest and motion. When we say "The ball is at rest," this is an abbreviation of something like "The ball is at rest with respect to the earth." (Otherwise it would be incoherent – analogous to "Sue is shorter than" or "Chicago is west of.") Of course, absolutists think that truth is a *property* of propositions, and thus think statements like "That's true" are *not* abbreviations and are perfectly coherent as they stand. Sometimes we will emphasize this by referring to the (alleged) property of *being true* as "just-plain" truth. In these terms, relativism may be thought of as the rejection of the notion of just-plain truth. Here is an argument that tries to show that relativism is contradictory.

The Iteration Argument

1 Let S be any specific proposition.
2 No proposition is absolutely true or absolutely false; any proposition is true from some perspectives, false from others. (This is just the statement of relativism with which we began. We'll call it "Rel.") **Therefore:**
3 S is neither absolutely true nor absolutely false; it is true from some perspectives and false from others. **Thus we may:**
4 Let P be any specific perspective from which S is true. **Then:**
5 The proposition *that S is true from perspective P* is true. **But then:**
6 At least one proposition is just-plain true. **Therefore:**
7 Rel is contradictory (since line 6 contradicts line 2).

In order to answer this argument a relativist would have to find a way to block line 6. But line 6 clearly follows from line 5 *unless* line 5 is an abbreviation of a statement involving a further perspective. So a relativist can only escape the argument by claiming that 5 is an abbreviation. But then a similar claim would have to hold for line 4. And ultimately, a relativist must maintain that Rel itself – the claim *that any proposition is true from some perspectives and false from others* – is not being asserted as a just-plain true proposition. It too must be regarded as including an implicit relativization to some further perspective. This raises the question of whether Rel is really a genuine *claim*, or *assertion*, in the first place. Does relativism actually have any *content*? The suspicion that it does not is made explicit in the following argument.

The No-Theory Argument

1   Any *theory* (about anything) includes a set of assertions – no assertions, no theory.

2   If S is any specific proposition, then to *assert* S is to claim that S is true. In particular, to assert Rel is to claim that Rel is true. **But:**

3   Relativists cannot claim that Rel is *just-plain* true without contradicting themselves, for they deny that anything is just-plain true. **Thus:**

4   Relativists can only be consistent if they are asserting implicitly that Rel is true relative to some perspective, say P1. **But:**

5   Then they are asserting *that Rel is true relative to P1*, i.e., they are claiming that the proposition *that Rel is true relative to P1* is true. **But:**

6   Once again, they cannot consistently mean *just-plain* true. So:

7   Relativists must be asserting implicitly that the proposition that Rel is true relative to P1 is true relative to some perspective, say P2. **But then:**

8   They are asserting that the proposition *that the proposition that Rel is true relative to P1 is true relative to P2* is true. **But:**

9   They still can't mean *just-plain* true. They owe us yet another relativization. (Notice that it doesn't matter whether the new relativization is to a new *perspective*. For example, the perspective in the relativization owed from line 8 might again be P2.) We can repeat the same pattern of reasoning as often as we like and we will never arrive at a genuine assertion, since there will always be the question "From what perspective is that supposed to be true?" **Hence:**

10   Either relativists contradict themselves by asserting that Rel is just-plain true (or by asserting *that Rel is true relative to P1* is just-plain true, etc.), or else they never actually arrive at any assertion at all, and so they have no theory.

The point of this argument may be summarized as follows: Either relativism is a genuine theory in which a real assertion is made, or else it isn't. But any attempt to assert relativism *without* relying on just-plain truth would inevitably fail, because it would generate an infinite regress. And, of course, any assertion of relativism that *does* rely on just-plain truth would be self-defeating. So it looks like any *apparent* assertion of Rel is either self-defeating or else is not a real assertion, but something more like an empty slogan.

The no-theory argument leans very heavily – see the first two premises – on two aspects of the concept of *assertion*: first, on the idea that theories consist (at least in part) of assertions, and second, on the idea that an assertion is a claim of truth. Now, it is beyond serious doubt that the *everyday* concept of assertion takes assertions to be claims of truth. So the argument may be thought of as concluding that the everyday concept of assertion is incompatible with a relativist conception of truth: it requires, or, better, *involves* the absolutist conception – just-plain truth. It is also beyond serious doubt that "proponents" of relativism generally take themselves to be making an assertion – that is, a claim of truth – concerning the nature of truth. So the argument may also be seen as concluding that any such assertion would have to be false.

It might be possible, at this point, for a relativist to adopt a reformist position concerning the "concept of assertion" (much as the epistemic theorists of Section 5.1 adopted a reformist view of the "concept of truth"). This would be to concede that the *everyday* concept of assertion incorporates the concept of just-plain truth, and to try to develop and foster a use of the terms "assertion" and "truth" for *some other concepts*, ones that would be immune to the no theory argument. But it is very hard to see what this new "concept of assertion" would be like. (Here it's important to keep in mind that an assertion like "That's true from perspective P" – as we would ordinarily understand it – doesn't fill the bill because, despite the fancy addition of the perspective, it's still just an *ordinary* assertion, a claim that the proposition *that that's true from perspective P is just-plain true*.)

Now let's pretend for a moment that relativism *is* a real theory, with a real assertion. Then that assertion is the denial of the doctrine that some propositions are just-plain true (and some are just-plain false) – a doctrine we'll call "weak absolutism." So, if relativism is refuted by the no-theory argument, then weak absolutism is thereby established, and there is no need for any further argument in its favor. (If any assertion turns out to be false, then its denial must be true.) On the other hand, if relativism is not a real theory, lacks genuine propositional content, then there is no competitor to the doctrine that some propositions are (just-plain) true, so again there is no need for argumentation in its favor.

Let's assume now that the arguments really do refute relativism, so that weak absolutism is established. Then some propositions are just-plain true (and others are just-plain false). But could it be that while *some* propositions are just-plain true (or false), *others* are only *relatively* true (or false)? Some might initially see this as a very attractive position. For example, it would leave room to regard any "merely factual" proposition as either absolutely true or absolutely false, but to deny that this species of truth applies to propositions of morality or esthetics, etc. Relative truth and falsity would be reserved for such "normative" propositions. In this way we might even be able to salvage something from the phenomenon of cultural diversity. Can we have our cake and eat it too?

Not really. Recall that relativism is the doctrine that truth is a relation, not a property. If this doctrine is refuted, then truth must be a property, not a relation. So, *for any proposition you like*, it makes sense to ask whether or not it has this property of being true. If it doesn't, then it must have the property of being false (and vice versa). There is no room for holding that a *proposition* might have no truth-value. (Though of course nonunivocal *sentences* generally lack truth-value.) Propositions represent the world as being one way or another, and the world either cooperates or it does not. So, a philosopher who initially wanted to reserve "relative truth" for "normative propositions" would be much better off holding that sentence-tokens that *appear* to assert normative propositions really do not assert propositions at all, but instead perform some other kind of linguistic task (such as expressing approval or disapproval).

We mentioned earlier that a confusion about the doctrine of relativism could help explain why people sometimes invest the discussion with unreasonable emotion. The confusion is to take "relativism" to be a certain doctrine that is actually quite independent of relativism. We'll call this independent position *The Doctrine of Free Belief* (*DFB*). DFB is somewhat vague, and it is best to see it as covering a variety of different views that are similar in certain important ways.

The central idea of DFB is that people (or cultures, etc.) are entitled to *believe* whatever they like. Closely connected to this idea is that it is wrong for one person (culture etc.) to impose his (or her) beliefs on someone else (some other culture, etc.). Further, DFB tends to include the idea that it is somehow wrong to feel very certain about one's own beliefs, and especially wrong to think they are superior to someone else's. So DFB combines a number of elements that many people find very appealing: (1) a "human right of free belief"; (2) a certain "anti-imperialism" about belief; (3) caution (or even skepticism) about one's own beliefs; and (4) humility about one's own beliefs.

Because this doctrine holds that beliefs that are actually incompatible are nevertheless, in a certain sense, on an equal footing, it is very easy and natural to think of it as a form of *relativism*, or to call it "relativism." But it isn't the doctrine of relativism about *truth* that we have been discussing in this chapter. Instead it's a doctrine about *belief*. DFB does not imply that truth is relative. It is simply a view about how we should regard and treat people who believe things we don't believe. So it's a "normative" doctrine, while relativism about truth is merely "descriptive." It might be very reasonable to accept some form of DFB. But it is not reasonable to confuse DFB with relativism about truth.

Absolutism about truth does not deny people's right to believe whatever they want. It doesn't say we should impose our beliefs on others. And it doesn't recommend confidence, arrogance, or dogmatism about what we believe. It doesn't concern our behavior or attitudes at all. Absolutism about truth is entirely consistent with DFB. But many people are motivated to *say* that they believe "truth is relative" because they hold some form of DFB, and they mistakenly think that this normative position is incompatible with absolutism about truth.

[Exercises: (1) There are lots of "height" properties: *being 4 feet tall, being 5 feet, 9 inches tall*; etc. "Height" is not a relative notion since each of the possible heights is a *property*. Explain, then, how it is that *being tall* is relative. (2) How can a property be relational yet not be relative?]

91

6

Color

For almost all of us, everyday waking life is (usually) flooded with visual experience, and this experience almost always includes the experience of color. But we will soon see that *color* (like many other notions we normally take for granted) constitutes a major metaphysical mystery.

The source of the mystery is an apparent conflict that is embedded in our common-sense view of the world. Most of the time, in everyday talk of color, we attribute what seem to be various color-properties to physical things outside us. Grass is green, tomatoes are red, and so on. This makes it sound like the color-properties are intrinsic features of things existing quite independently of us. But on other occasions we seem to be attributing the color-properties to things that are not independent of us, things that depend on, or are part of, our "private experience." Here are two examples.

(1) You tell a friend about a dream in which you are riding a beautiful horse. Your friend – a student of psychoanalysis – asks what color it was. You reply with no hesitation that it was white. Now, here you seem to be attributing a color to some thing, a thing that was "in" your dream. But that thing certainly wasn't a real, flesh-and-blood horse, because real horses don't (literally) occur in dreams. (Even if you dream about a real horse, say a horse you've actually ridden, that horse isn't *literally* in your dream. After all, your dream is some kind of personal experience made up of "images" and other "mental" components. It isn't made up of things like actual horses.) When you were dreaming, your eyes were shut, you were in a very dark room containing no horses whatever, and yet something went on that you are very inclined to say included some *white* thing. But what thing? A "visual image" is the usual answer.

(2)   It is nearly dark. You have forgotten to remove your sunglasses. It is also rather foggy. And you have been drinking champagne. You are walking through an apple orchard, one that you know includes trees bearing red apples and trees bearing green apples. Your friend – a metaphysics student – points to an apple on a tree and asks, "Quick, what color would you say that apple is?" You look and immediately reply, "Red." The dialogue continues:

Friend: Ah. Then it *looked* red to you?
You: Well, uh, not exactly. It looked sort of dark brownish, almost black.
Friend: So there really was nothing *red* in your actual experience?
You: Right. The color I actually experienced was dark-brown-to-black. So I figured the apple had to be red since a green apple wouldn't look that dark under these conditions.

Here, as in the dream, you seem to be attributing a color (dark-brown-to-black) to something that is part of your private experience, *not* part of the external physical world, like the apple. (Note that you are *also* attributing a different color, red, to the apple, on the basis of the experience.) It is very tempting in this case to say, as in case (1), that the thing that has the relevant color-property is a mental entity, a "visual image." For the moment we'll set aside the question whether mental entities, like thoughts, pains, dreams, and images, are in fact themselves physical entities (events or states in the brain) or nonphysical entities (events or states in a nonmaterial mind). So we'll try to use the term "mental" in a way that is neutral between these very different conceptions.

Our everyday willingness to attribute colors both to independently existing physical objects and to mental entities whose existence depends on us is really very strange. For now imagine that you are looking at a red apple in good light, you are not wearing tinted glasses, you are fully conscious and alert, etc., and you're concentrating on the color of the apple. It looks red to you. But notice that our dual usage of the color-terms apparently commits us to the view that the example actually includes *two* red things: an apple and a visual image (of that very apple).

But these two entities are very different in nature (even if it turns out that they're both physical). How can it be that they both have a property like *being red*? The redness of the apple seems to be an intrinsic property of its surface, a property having something to do with the potential reflection of light in a certain range of wavelengths. But the redness of the visual image doesn't seem to have anything to do with the potential reflection of light. The visual image doesn't even seem like the sort of entity that can reflect light (even if it's some sort of electrochemical event in your brain)! The redness of the image seems "experiential" in nature. But the redness of the apple's surface seems to have nothing to do with experience. (It would have been red whether anyone had ever experienced it or not.) So it looks like the two "rednesses" can't both really be one and the same property. They can't both really be *the color red*. But then which one really is? In a nutshell, this is the main metaphysical mystery of color. We will look at four possible solutions. The first two are standard philosophical positions about color. The last two are not as frequently encountered. We'll discuss the two standard positions first.

(i)   *Objectivism* is the view that the only things that really have color-properties are relatively large physical entities in the mind-independent, physical world: things like apples, cars, grains of sand, planets, clouds, lakes, and so on. Objectivism is the position that fits best with common sense and most of our everyday talk about color. Colors are features of things that they would have even if no one were around to perceive them, and even if no light were around to be reflected by them (or to pass through them or otherwise illuminate them).

The linguistic evidence that seems to favor objectivism is massive and, at least initially, compelling. It is clear that we attribute colors to external physical objects all the time. We do not take our color reports to be reports concerning our private visual experience, even though our evidence for those reports is very often given by visual experience. We very often question our own eyes: "Is that really green, or is there something funny about the light?" If we were talking about our visual images, and not about external things, then it would be hard to see how there could be any question about whether it was green. We also frequently question other persons' color reports: "No, it isn't really green – if you look from this angle you'll see it's really blue." If the other person's report were not about the external thing, but rather about a private visual experience, this sort of reaction would apparently be absurd.

There is also brute experiential evidence that may seem to favor objectivism. Colors look to us to be out there on the surfaces of external physical objects (etc.). They don't somehow look "internal" to us. They seem to be intrinsic properties of external things, very much like their sizes and shapes. Suppose you are looking at the Washington Monument. It's about 555 feet, five and one-eighth inches tall, and (we would ordinarily say) it's white (or very light gray). As you look at the monument, you have a visual image of it, and this visual image of course has features that are correlated with the height and color of the monument. Now, it would certainly be ridiculous to say your visual image was over 555 feet tall (even if we think that visual images are themselves physical entities – nothing in your brain is anywhere near 555 feet tall). And according to the color objectivist, it would be just as wrong to say your visual image was white. Your visual image has a certain "phenomenal" property that correlates with the whiteness of the monument, but this phenomenal property isn't whiteness itself. If we wish, we may call it "phenomenal whiteness" or "perceptual whiteness" or the like.

A related point is this. Suppose you and I look at something and agree that it's dark green. How do I know that your visual experience is anything "like" mine? If I'm looking at a giant green wall (say in Fenway Park), then I am able to notice a striking similarity between certain pairs of parts of my occurrent visual experience and, assuming I'm also seeing the sky above the wall, striking differences between other pairs of such parts. (E.g., the left part of the visual image of the wall is similar "in color" to the right part, but the "wall" part of the visual image is different "in color" from the "sky" part.) So it makes sense for me to compare (parts of) visual images, as long as they're *my* visual images. But I have no way of comparing your visual images with mine. I have no visual access to your visual images. **[Exercise: Think about this last claim. Is it right? What if there were a daring experiment in which our brains were surgically connected with a special tubular membrane, and then each of us started reporting a kind of "split screen" effect in our visual fields, with good correlations to the perspectives of our respective eyes? Try to argue that this still wouldn't be good enough for me to compare my visual images with yours.]**

Perhaps your experience is utterly different from (or essentially incomparable with) mine. But even if it is, we still seem to be able to agree that the wall is green. When you say the wall is green, it certainly seems like you're asserting the very same proposition that I assert when I say it's green. It seems like we're attributing the very same property to some one thing. If, instead, we're attributing properties to two different things (our respective, private visual images), then we have no way of knowing that our respective uses of the term "dark green" express the same property. But even if they *do* express the same property, there is still no way for us to disagree! If you say "The wall is dark green," and I say "The wall is not dark green," our statements are not in conflict since your statement is not about the same thing that mine is about. So both could be true.

All of this suggests strongly that the color-properties are properties in physical things that exist independently of our minds. It seems very clear that if we ultimately reject this objectivist conception, then we will have to make dramatic revisions in the way we ordinarily think about color.

(ii) *Subjectivism* is just such a dramatically revisionist position. According to this view, colors are entirely mind-dependent. They are not the sort of properties that external physical objects could possibly have. They are properties that can only be instantiated in private, mental experience. So, when you say that the wall is dark green, you are not literally attributing a color-property to the wall. Instead, you are saying (roughly) that *something* about the wall is producing a visual image in you that *is* (literally) dark green. But whatever it is about the wall that does this trick is not *itself* a color-property. It is probably some complex textural feature of the wall's surface.

This position is analogous to the Platonic account of *truth*. Strictly speaking, it's only propositions that instantiate truth. When we say that a sentence or sentence-token is true, we're using the term in a "derivative" sense, one that depends on the strict sense. The subjectivist view about color-properties is that when we say the wall is green, we're using the term in a similar derivative sense: "That wall is green" means only that the wall tends to produce visual images that are (nonderivatively) green. (Just as "That utterance is true" means only that the utterance expresses a proposition that is (nonderivatively) true.)

Before we consider this view in any more detail, a comment about the words "subjective" and "objective" is in order. (See Section 1.1 for a more detailed discussion of various senses of these terms.) Sometimes these words are used with the connotation that what is subjective is not real, and that only what is objective is real. This is emphatically not intended in the present use of the words. For the color-subjectivist, colors are just as real as they are for the color-objectivist. The disagreement is not about the reality of color, but rather about the nature of color and the things that have it. If the objectivist is right, colors are instantiated by (physical) *objects*. If the subjectivist is right, colors are instantiated by parts of the experiences of (perceiving) *subjects*.

We have already seen that most of our everyday color-talk favors objectivism, but we have also seen that some of it favors subjectivism. This makes our overall use of the color terms extremely curious, perhaps even contradictory. It creates the impulse to think that some of our everyday talk must be wrong, and should be reformed. The subjectivist is in the slightly uncomfortable position of recommending that the great majority of it be reformed. But the fact that the position is uncomfortable certainly isn't enough to show that it's wrong. So let's try to see what there is to recommend it.

Consider again the case of a "veridical" (that is, accurate) seeing of a red apple. We saw that if we take both the objective and the subjective trends in our ordinary color-talk seriously, then we are in the very awkward position of having to say there are two red things: the apple and the visual image. Both subjectivism and objectivism try to relieve the awkwardness by refusing to attribute genuine redness to one or the other of the two things.

So the objectivist says: "Look, our everyday talk is philosophically untenable if we take all of it literally. We have to reconstrue at least some of it in order to restore metaphysical coherence. So let's pick the easiest way: take the preponderance of everyday color-talk, the 'objectivist' part, literally. Then reconstrue the rest, the 'subjectivist' part, in some nonliteral way. Accordingly, we should understand the color words so that they apply literally only to mind-independent physical entities. Then visual images simply don't have colors at all. That doesn't mean they don't have proper-ties that *correlate* with colors of external things; indeed they do. If we like, we may say they have 'phenomenal colors' or 'experienced colors' or what-ever. A visual image has the property of phenomenal redness iff it has the feature that is normally present when (genuinely) red things are presented to the subject in normal light, the subject is conscious, alert, is looking in the right direction, and so on." End of story.

Subjectivists don't think the matter is this simple. They agree that it might be a good rule of thumb that when an everyday term is used in philosophically incompatible ways, we should take the dominant use liter-ally, and reconstrue the less common use in some suitable nonliteral way. But they think this would be a bad mistake in the present case. The reason is that subjectivists think one of the crucial facts the objectivist relies on actually counts *against* that view. This is the fact that colors seem to be "out there" on the surfaces of things. This was supposed to support objec-tivism. But now the subjectivist points out that the very properties that seem to be instantiated by (e.g.) the surfaces of things, in fact *clearly* are not. The properties that *seem* to be instantiated by surfaces are, after all, the very ones the objectivist wants us to call "phenomenal redness" and the like. Both parties ought to agree that *these* properties are "experiential," and so are not actually instantiated by physical surfaces. The properties that are instantiated by surfaces instead are complicated textural features that affect light in various ways so as to alter its wavelength, etc. But surfaces in the external world seem (e.g.) *red*, in the very same *phenomenal* way, regardless of whether one knows anything about the effect of textural properties on light wavelengths (etc.).

There is a further, related point that appears to support subjectivism: We *learn* the color terms as a result of their repeated association with the so-called phenomenal properties, not as a result of association with microscopic (or worse) physical characteristics of surfaces (etc.). As a matter of fact, this point may be made more effectively if we notice that it is not just surfaces reflecting light that produces sensations of color in us. Light itself may have perceptible color, and so may translucent media, like water, glass, smog, and so forth. Perceptions of red may arise from a myriad of very different physical causes. Yet when a child learns the word "red," the learning is entirely insensitive to differences in the intrinsic physical features of the presented examples of redness. The child is keying on the sameness of the recurrent phenomenal property, not on the diverse underlying physical causes.

So the subjectivist is prepared to insist that even though our color-talk mostly seems to attribute color to things external to our sensations, it is really to certain contents of our visual experience that these terms genuinely apply. Philosophical coherence is thus better obtained by taking attributions of color to visual images as literally correct, and reconstruing the talk that locates colors in the external world. So, when we say that the apple is red, this will be understood as meaning that the apple has some physical feature that, under normal viewing conditions, tends to produce red visual images in normal viewers. Thus the apple isn't literally red, but typical visual images of it are.

Both objectivism and subjectivism have problems. Let's look briefly at a few of the problems and then turn to two other positions on the issue.

(iii)   *A problem for objectivism.* Consider a red stoplight. It's basically a translucent piece of plastic or glass coupled with a light bulb. When the light bulb is on, the plastic filters out all but a narrow range of visible light. The visible light that is allowed to pass through the plastic falls solidly in the "red" wavelength range. When the light bulb is off, the plastic or glass may or may not even look red, depending on the surrounding lighting conditions. When the light bulb is on, the stoplight generally looks red, but its luminosity may vary quite a bit, depending on how dirty the filter is, the time of day, and the quality of the air. Now consider a life-size, hyper-realistic painting of a stoplight. It is certainly possible for the relevant red portion of such a painting to be indistinguishable in color from that of an actual, illuminated red stoplight under certain viewing conditions. A normal viewer will report that both are red, but will be unable to tell which is the real stoplight and which is the painting. Now let's call whatever property the real stoplight has that causes the subject's experience of red, P. And let's call the parallel property in the painting, Q. It is very clear that P and Q are *different* properties, because Q is a property of the surface of an opaque object, while P is one involving the internal structure of a translucent object together with the fact that light is passing through it. But the (shade of) redness in question is supposed to be a *single* property. It would be arbitrary and unreasonable to say either that redness is P rather than Q, or that it is Q rather than P. Furthermore, there may be many other properties that would produce experiences of redness (in normal viewers) that were qualitatively indistinguishable from those produced by P or Q.

Objectivists can make two different sorts of replies to this problem. One is to say that color-properties are "disjunctive." (The term is unfortunate because it isn't really clear what a disjunctive property is, but we won't worry about this.) So redness (of the appropriate shade) in this case is the property "P or Q" (and there may be other "disjuncts" as well). Of course anything that has P automatically has "P or Q," so, on this account, anything that instantiates P will also instantiate *redness*. (Similarly for Q.) One problem with this response is that it seems rather *ad hoc*. Another is that it is at least arguable that there really are no "disjunctive" properties. Is, say, *living in Kuwait or owning a parrot* really a *single property* that some people have?) [Exercise: How does the principle of predication bear on this issue? (See Section 3.1.)]

The second response is to claim that being red (of that shade) is a "dispositional" property. It isn't P, it isn't Q, and it isn't some funny "disjunctive" property. Rather, it is like the property of *being soluble (in water)*. For a substance to be soluble is for it to be – *one way or another* – such that it would dissolve if it were placed in water (under normal circumstances). Salt is soluble and sugar is soluble. Both are soluble because they have certain internal structural features, but the exact feature that makes salt soluble is different from the one that makes sugar soluble. So these two exact features aren't *solubility itself*, but rather are two different mechanisms that account for or "underlie" the solubility of the two substances. Some objectivists have claimed that color-properties are dispositional in essentially the same way. For a thing to be red is for it to be (any old way) such that it would cause visual sensations of a certain specific sort in normal viewers if it were viewed under normal circumstances. The stoplight is (a certain shade of) red and so is (the relevant part of) the painting. The stoplight has this property because it instantiates P, the painting has it because it instantiates Q. And other things might have it as a result of still different properties.

Subjectivists have often charged that "dispositional objectivism" is either *circular* or else is *covert subjectivism*, because an appeal to "redness" must be made in characterizing the types of visual sensations that the supposedly dispositional property would cause under the right circumstances. Let's look at these possibilities a little more closely.

Circularity: Dispositional objectivism says that "X is *red*" means that if a normal perceiver were to view X in normal circumstances, X would look red. Thinking of this as a definition of the term "red," it is understandable how one might suspect circularity. For it certainly has a classic symptom: The term being defined occurs in the very clause that states the defining condition. So it looks like we would already have to understand the term in order to understand the definition of the term, and there would be no way to get started. But an occurrence of the same term in the defining condition doesn't always guarantee circularity. We have already seen noncircular examples. For instance, we defined "true," as it applies to *sentence-tokens*, in terms of "true," as it applies to *propositions*. This is noncircular because the sense the term acquires as a result of meeting the defining condition is different from the sense the term has as it occurs in the defining condition, and the latter is a sense that we already understand. A dispositional objectivist may claim that this is what's going on with "red." The term "red," as it will apply to physical entities, is being defined in terms of the notion of "looking red," and the notion of redness involved here applies only to visual images. Since we are already familiar with this notion of looking red, from our own private experience, there is no circularity. [**Exercise: Evaluate this response to the charge of circularity.**]

Covert subjectivism: Even if it is agreed, on the above basis, that dispositional objectivism is noncircular, it may still be thought that something is seriously wrong. The defense against the charge of circularity depended on noting that the notion of *looking red* involved a different notion of redness from the one being analyzed in the theory. But, it may be claimed, the notion of redness that is involved in *looking red* is precisely the *subjectivist's* notion of redness. So dispositional objectivism would merely be subjectivism in disguise. The dispositional objectivist would have successfully defined the term "red," for application to physical entities, in terms of subjective redness. But notice that this is something a subjectivist can also do! The central claim of subjectivism is that the property *redness* is fundamentally a feature of subjective experience, not a feature of external physical entities. If we decide to call external things "red" we are free to do so as long as we are clear that they don't literally have redness. And the dispositional objectivist's definition, it would be claimed, does make this clear by defining "red" in terms of literal (that is, subjective) redness. (Of course, subjectivists would prefer to apply a term like "causally red" to the external things, suggesting that they have a property which, under proper circumstances, causes other things to be literally red.)

A thoughtful dispositional objectivist might reply as follows. When we look at things that we ordinarily call "red" (in normal conditions), we have a certain distinctive sort of subjective experience. Subjectivists say that the key feature of this sort of experience is genuine redness. Objectivists say that it is not genuine redness, and prefer to call it "phenomenal redness." But there is no disagreement as to whether our subjective experience really includes such a feature. The disagreement is over whether that feature is genuine redness. So let us step back from the dispute and call the property of our experience by some *neutral* name, say "phredness" (which might or might not turn out to be another name for *redness*). Then dispositional objectivism is merely the theory that "X is red" means that the viewing of X under normal conditions by normal observers (normally) results in phred visual images. Since this definition can evidently be made without presupposing that phredness is redness, there is no covert appeal to subjectivism in dispositional objectivism. [Exercise: **Suppose that these replies to the above charges of circularity and covert subjectivism are accepted. Does there nevertheless remain a problem about the appeal to "normal" perceivers and viewing circumstances?**]

(iv) *A problem for subjectivism.* Recall that we agreed to speak of "mental" entities in a way that would be neutral on the question of the ultimate nature of minds. But can one be a subjectivist about color and really maintain this neutrality? Certainly it seemed that one could at the outset.

But here is an argument that one cannot. It aims to show that materialism about the mind is incompatible with subjectivism about color. It takes the form of a *reductio ad absurdum*. Suppose that materialism is true. Then all of our sensations, visual and otherwise, are just events in or states of our brains. Now consider the case of a veridical perception of a chartreuse Cadillac. According to subjectivism, the subject has a *literally* chartreuse visual image. But nothing in one's brain is literally chartreuse. The brain's colors range from off-white to pink to brown over its various parts. So the visual image of the Cadillac isn't a part of the subject's brain. Furthermore, it isn't an *event* or *process* or *state* in the subject's brain either, for these aren't the sorts of things that can naturally be said to have colors in the first place. (And if we insist that they do have colors, then it seems they would have to be the colors of the brain's parts as described above.) So visual images cannot be parts of, or events in, or processes in, or states of the subject's brain. Assuming there are no other plausible "material" candidates, visual images must be nonmaterial. But this means that materialism about the mind cannot be correct.

If this argument is right, then it shows that subjectivism about color is coherent only in company with dualism – the view that our minds are nonmaterial entities over and above our brains. Of course this would not be a devastating problem for subjectivism unless one insisted on materialism about the mind. [Exercise: **Try to show that subjectivism and materialism may be compatible after all. This might consist in finding a problem with the argument, or it might involve tinkering with materialism so as to avoid the difficulty.**]

We now turn to a pair of less common theories about color.

(v) *Color-property Illusionism.* According to this position, there are no such things as color-*properties* at all. But this is not to say that there is no such thing as color-*experience*. It is just to say that in color-experience, there are no things that literally have colors. Color-experience incorporates the illusion that things have color-properties.

Let's return to (what we would normally call) the veridical seeing of the red apple. An illusionist will deny that there is a *property*, redness, that is instantiated either by the apple or by any entity that is literally a part of the subject's visual experience. Despite this, an illusionist will agree that the subject's experience is such that the apple seems to be red. So the crucial claim will be that the subject's experience can have *this* property – *being such that the apple seems to be red* – without any part or aspect of the subject's experience actually being red. (In fact, without there actually being any such thing as a property of redness.)

The subject's experience *represents* the apple as being red. It is tempting to think that this means that the experience contains an entity that represents the apple, and that said experiential entity is red. The illusionist denies this, holding that the visual experience (whether physical or not) is a complex event that may not intelligibly be broken into discrete parts, some one of which both represents the apple and is red. Instead, the entire event must be regarded as having the property of *representing the apple as being red*, and *this* property may not even admit of any further analysis.

An analogy may help make this position seem more plausible. Sometimes we test knives for sharpness by carefully feeling their edges with a finger. Sometimes they "feel sharp" and sometimes they don't. So sometimes it is correct to say that our tactile experience *represents the knife as being sharp*. But certainly it doesn't do this by containing an entity that actually *is* sharp. It's just that the experience has a feature that is reliably associated with sharpness in knives. And when a knife is dull, the tactile experience is reliably very different, but no more includes an entity that is actually dull than does the competing experience include something sharp. This analogy should help convince us that it is at least sometimes possible for our experience to *represent something as being* X without including a part that actually *is* X.

What is not clear is whether the case of color really is analogous in this respect to the case of sharpness. Perhaps the fundamental problem with color-property illusionism is that when we reflect on an actual color-experience, it really does seem to include entities that really are colored, embedded right there in the private experience itself, and this is at least arguably different from the case of sharpness. [Exercise: Is it really right that the knife-test experience doesn't seem to include anything that's really sharp? Remember, it's the *experience* we're talking about, so you can't say it's the *knife*.]

It may be tempting to reject the present theory because it threatens to drain color out of the world entirely. (Unfortunately, the name *illusionism* may encourage this idea.) It is important to see that this is a mistake, and that if we reject the theory it should be for better reasons. The theory does not deny that there is color in the world. It merely denies that colors are *properties*. At first this seems very counterintuitive (and of course it conflicts with both objectivism and subjectivism). But notice this. Most of us, no matter how sophisticated, cannot help *perceiving* motion as a property of things. But on reflection, we know better. It isn't a property at all, it's a relation between things. So to deny that motion is a property is not in itself to deny that there is motion. The same goes for color. The color-property illusionist, however, is not claiming that color is a relation (though a view along these lines might be defensible). The claim is instead that color enters our experience because parts of our experience represent things outside us as if they had color-properties (even though there are no color-properties). But of course the things outside us in fact do not have color-properties and, moreover, the representing somehow gets done without any parts of our experience having color-properties either. For the illusionist, properties like *representing X as red* are real properties that may be instantiated by parts of our experience. Having color-experience is nothing more nor less than having parts of our experience instantiate such properties. None of the vividness is lost just because this does not involve anything actually instantiating redness. We do see the world as if there were color-properties and things instantiating them. We cannot help it – that's just the way we are. (Or maybe we can help it, but so far we haven't succeeded.)

For a color-property illusionist, when we say that X is red, this means that X has properties such that, if it were viewed under normal conditions by normal viewers, those viewers would have visual experiences that instantiated the property of *representing X as red*. And further, for an illusionist, when we say (as in the orchard of example (2)) that our image of the apple was dark-brown-to-black, this means that our visual experience instantiated the property of *representing the apple as dark-brown-to-black*.

We may summarize the effects of the three theories we have now considered on our ordinary notions of color, as follows: Objectivism takes our attributions of color to external entities literally, and reinterprets the remaining attributions; subjectivism does precisely the reverse; and illusionism reinterprets them all. We now turn to our fourth and final theory. In a certain way, this theory manages to accept all of our normal color attributions without reinterpretation.

(vi) *Independent Ambiguism*: We noted in Section 5.1 that the effort to analyze an ordinary philosophical concept sometimes leads to the conclusion that what initially appeared to be a single incoherent concept was really two or more concepts, because the term in question was ambiguous, and that each of these concepts might be fully coherent.

Let's begin by considering an uncontroversially ambiguous term. The common noun "temple" is such a term. Sometimes it applies to buildings or other structures used for religious purposes. Other times it applies to a flat area on the sides of certain mammals' foreheads. In some sentences it might be quite unclear which sense was intended. ("The rabbi noticed his temple in the rear-view mirror – it glistened with moisture.") But it would be virtually nonsensical to maintain that one of these senses of the term was somehow its "real meaning" and the other was not. (Note that the question of which sense entered the language first is, of course, a real question. So is the question whether the two senses are etymologically related. But the answers to these questions – whatever they might be – would not entail that one of the senses was the real, literal meaning and the other wasn't.)

This kind of dispute can only really take hold when the senses of the ambiguous term are closely related, where one sense might depend on the other in some important way. We saw such a case with the word "true," where we concluded that it applied literally only to propositions, and then only derivatively to sentence-tokens and (sometimes) sentences. We may think of this as a case of "dependent ambiguity:" The term is ambiguous, but one of its senses is fundamental, and the others are dependent on this fundamental sense. Are the color-terms like this?

According to the present view, they are not, and so we call that view *independent ambiguism.* The color-terms are ambiguous, and their different senses are definitely (and systematically) related, but it is not true that there is any natural dependency in their relatedness that renders one sense more fundamental than another. The best defense of independent ambiguism probably consists in a consideration of what goes on when we perceive colors.

So we return for a final time to the veridical seeing of the red apple. Let's describe it using some contrived, neutral terms. You see the apple veridically and have a certain visual image. One of the key properties of your visual image has already earned the neutral term "phredness" – your visual image is phred. Now, the apple's surface has a certain textural property that has a profound effect on the light rays it reflects toward your eyes – it reflects rays preponderantly in a fairly narrow band of wavelengths. Let's call this property of the apple's surface "kredness." Then, if we like, we can say that light whose wavelength falls in that agreed-upon range has the property "skredness." So kred objects tend to reflect preponderantly skred light, and skred light tends to be causally efficacious in producing phred visual sensations. (We may also say that anything that has *any* property that – like kredness – results in the propagation of skred light, has the dispositional property of "smredness" – then anything that is smred, whether because it is kred or for some other reason, tends to propagate skred light, which, in turn, tends to produce phred images.)

Now notice that all of these several properties are real properties of actually existing things, regardless of how they might be further analyzed. More important, notice that, in all relevant ways, they are independent of each other. (1) You can have phred visual images even though you are not interacting causally with anything that is skred, kred (or otherwise smred). (2) Light can be skred even though nothing interacting with it is phred, kred (or otherwise smred). (3) Something can be kred even though nothing interacting with it is either phred or skred. (Of course, anything kred is automatically smred.) (4) Things can be smred without interacting with anything that is either phred or skred (though of course one way to be smred is to be kred).

According to independent ambiguism, because there is no (relevant) ontological dependency among the supposed competitors for being the "real" color properties, there is no serious philosophical content in the supposed dispute between, say, objectivism and subjectivism. (Assuming the subjectivist is a realist about the external world – if not, of course, then the real dispute is only peripherally about color.) What the participants take to be a profound philosophical disagreement turns out, on this view, just to be a "verbal dispute." It doesn't matter whether we decide, say by convention, to use "red" for smredness or for phredness (or for one of the others), or to continue to use it ambiguously for all of them. Since we use it ambiguously in everyday life, and there's no philosophically significant reason to change this practice, we might as well leave it alone.

Sometimes the result of a philosophical inquiry is the dissolution of an apparent philosophical problem, and one way this may occur is by seeing that it was merely a verbal dispute. This is in no way trivial. It is a significant form of philosophical progress. **{Exercise: Has the independent ambiguist really dissolved the problem?}**

7

Determinism, Freedom, and Fatalism

7.1 Causation

Determinism, as we will soon see, is a doctrine that depends on the notion of *cause*. In everyday life we are accustomed to thinking that events are caused by prior events (in a sense in which the prior events "produce" or "bring about" the subsequent ones). To put it a little more philosophically, we think of causation as a relation between events in which the event that is the "cause" precedes the event that is its "effect." But the exact nature of the causal relation has long been the subject of vigorous metaphysical debate. In fact, it has sometimes been claimed that there really is no such relation intrinsic to events in the world, and that our ordinary conviction to the contrary merely reflects a psychological fact, a fact about how we conceptualize what we perceive (and how we generalize the conceptualization).

This position is not as silly as it might first seem. To see this, think of a case in which we are normally convinced that causation is operating. Say a moving billiard ball, A, strikes a stationary, unconstrained ball, B, we hear a "click," and we immediately see B moving (and A continuing to move, perhaps in a different direction and at a different rate). We want to say that A's hitting B caused B to move. Putting this in terms of events, we believe that the event (say C) consisting of *A's striking B* caused the event (say E) consisting of *B's beginning to move*. But notice that we don't perceive the "causation." What we perceive is simply C being followed by E. This is not because we cannot perceive things as standing in relations to each other. Indeed, we certainly see (at first) A *approaching* B and (later) A *hitting* B, and we also perceive C *being prior to* E. But relations like *hitting* and *being prior to* aren't the relation of *causing*, and in fact there doesn't seem to be anything that we see (or hear, etc.) in this case that deserves to be called "causing."

A good way to see this is to notice that we can easily imagine C occurring without being followed by E: A moves toward B, makes contact, and then simply changes direction while B remains in the same position (even though it isn't glued to the spot or otherwise rigged to thwart the occurrence of E). The fact that we can imagine this reveals that we don't perceive *in C* anything like a "causal impetus" that guarantees the occurrence of E. For if we had perceived such an impetus in C, we wouldn't be able to imagine C without E.

The occurrence of C without E is evidently incompatible with physical laws that we accept. But that is very much beside the present point. There are two reasonable ways to understand the "laws of physics." According to one, they are a general codification of the present state of our understanding of causal relations in the physical realm. According to the other, they are a general codification of "regularities" that we have so far observed to occur in nature. The laws themselves, which after all are usually stated using abstract, mathematical formulas utterly devoid of terms like "cause," are entirely neutral between these two interpretations. So they don't require an interpretation involving causation. That events of type X are always immediately followed by events of type Y does not imply that events of type X *cause* events of type Y (in the "bring about" sense). Thus it appears that the world might look no different from how it actually looks (etc.), and the laws of physics might be no different from what they actually are, even though there is no such thing as genuine causation between events. To put it in a slightly different way, it seems that we can conceive of two possible worlds, each perceptually indiscernible from the other, but in one of which all of the regularities are purely accidental, with no event ever causing any other event, while in the other genuine causation is operating full time. In both worlds the same "laws of nature" would apply. [Exercise: Assuming the two worlds just described really are possible, could there also be "mixed" worlds – worlds that are perceptually indiscernible from these two, but in which causation only operates part of the time?]

Let us set these thoughts aside and assume that genuine causation really does operate in our world at least some of the time, despite our inability to perceive it at work. Then what must this relation be like? We can work toward at least a partial answer if we divide the problem into two parts, one corresponding to the notion that causes *precede* their effects, and the other to the notion that causes are *efficacious* – they "bring about" their effects.

(1) *Temporal priority*. In our ordinary talk about causation, we treat the causal relation as if it were "transitive" – that is, when we believe both that X caused Y and that Y caused Z, we generally do not hesitate to say that X caused Z. For example, suppose you're heading out the door on your way to work when the telephone rings. It's an important call and it takes ten minutes. After the call, you ride your bike along the usual route to work and it takes the usual amount of time. But you're ten minutes late. It's very natural to say that an important call caused your late arrival. But there is something metaphysically suspect about this, because the call might easily have occurred just as it did *without* your being late for work. Events that might have occurred after you hung up could have resulted in a timely arrival (a lucky ride with a neighbor who was heading that way), or even in the last-minute cancellation of the work day (a power failure at the office).

Furthermore, the assumption that causation is transitive leaves us with much stranger cases than this. For we can imagine "causal chains" of such length that the original cause and the ultimate effect are very far removed from each other in both space and time. In cases like these, the ultimate effect may actually be very unlikely to occur, even given that the original event occurs. It's at least very awkward to think that an event X is the cause of an event Y when the probability of Y, given X, is very low. **[Exercise: Think of a good example of this phenomenon.]**

So let's abandon the idea that the causal relation is transitive. In fact, let's require that there be no spatiotemporal gaps between causes and their effects, since gaps were at the root of the present problem. In denying transitivity we are, of course, not denying the existence of "causal chains." It will still be true that the beginning and end of a causal chain are causally *linked*. So we can refer to the beginning event as a *causal antecedent* of the terminal event even though we deny that it *caused* that event. Our philosophical use of the term "cause" thus now takes on a party technical dimension, since a good deal of ordinary usage of the term seems to presuppose transitivity.

A Brief Mathematical Note. Let's use the terms "instant" and "moment" to indicate segments of time that have no duration. (The term "point of time" is also sometimes used). Let's also assume that of any two instants, one and only one of them is (temporally) prior to (or "before") the other (which, in turn, is "after" the prior instant). (It could be that there are other temporal realms, not connected in this way to ours, but we are, in effect, confining our attention to our own temporal realm.) So all of the instants of time fall into a temporal "order." Unlike causation, temporal priority is a transitive relation. If x is before y, and y is before z, then x is before z. [**Exercise: Prove that on the present assumptions, given any three instants, one of them lies "between" the other two (in the sense that one of the other two is before it, and the other one is after it).**]

It is usually assumed that the temporal ordering of the instants of time is mimicked by the (natural) ordering of the "real" numbers. Another way to say this is that time is "continuous" – the instants of time form a "continuum." We do not need to know very much about these matters for our present purposes. But we do need one central fact, namely, that between any two real numbers there lies a third. (This property, usually called the "betweenness" property, is shared by the "rational" numbers, which are a proper subset of the real numbers.) So we will be assuming that between any two moments of time there lies a third. The main consequence of this assumption is that no two moments of time are "next to" each other.

Now suppose that x and y are any two moments of time, with x before y. In ordinary life we sometimes think of x and y as determining an "interval" of time. An interval is a period of time of some duration but with no gaps. So every point between x and y must be included. But should x and y be included? Well, the answer is easy enough: It depends on whether we *want* to include them. There are really *four* distinct intervals determined by x and y. One includes them, another excludes them, one includes only x, and the other includes only y. These intervals are usually denoted by $[x,y]$, (x,y), $[x,y)$, and $(x,y]$ (respectively). Intervals that include their "endpoints" are called *closed* and intervals that exclude them are called *open*. (And, for example, the interval $[x,y)$ is "closed on the left, open on the right.") Notice that an open interval has no first or last moment: For any point in the interval, there are always both earlier and later moments in the interval. But note that this *doesn't* imply that the interval lasts or has lasted forever.

Now let's get back to the metaphysics of causation. We need to make a couple of terminological decisions. According to our ordinary conception, "events" take time and involve noticeable or significant change. This

110

means we see them as unfolding over intervals of time, and surely each of the above four patterns is exemplified by the intervals of many events. We also make everyday use of the concept of a "state of affairs." In contrast with events, we normally think of states of affairs as "static." One way a state of affairs can be static is for it to have no duration, that is, to be instantaneous. But another way is for it not to include any noticeable or significant change. We are going to depart from the ordinary senses of both of these terms here. We will reserve "state of affairs" for the instantaneous case, and we will allow "event" to cover cases in which no significant change occurs. Thus, suppose my pen has been lying on the table undisturbed for the past hour. Then there is an event which we may refer to as "my pen's lying undisturbed on the table for the past hour," and this event is *not* a state of affairs. On the other hand, "my pen's lying on the table at exactly 3 p.m.", refers to a state of affairs, not to an event. Furthermore, "my pen's lying on the table at exactly 3:01 p.m." refers to a *different* state of affairs. So, in our technical usage, events always take time, but don't require change, and states of affairs never take time, and so cannot include change. (But note that events are made up of states of affairs.)

Now, given what we have assumed about time, and given our requirement that there be no gap between cause and effect, it follows that if the interval of a cause is closed on the right, then the interval of the effect must be open on the left (and similarly if the causal interval is open on the right). In other words, if a cause has a last moment, then its effect must have no first moment (and similarly for the other possibility). We will soon see that this leads to a real puzzle about causal efficacy.

(2) *Efficacy.* What does it mean to say that causes "bring about" their effects? Maybe we can shed some light on this question by adapting the logicians' notion of a "sufficient condition" to the case of events and states of affairs. We can do this directly with a definition: An event (or state of affairs) A is a *sufficient condition* for an event (or state of affairs) B iff A cannot occur without B also occurring.

Two things should be noticed. First, there is no requirement here that A precede B. Thus, for example, a person's dying (at some time) is a sufficient condition for that person's living (at some earlier time). Second, any event A is a sufficient condition for any event that is part of A (including A itself). But we have already concluded that we want causes to precede their effects (with no gaps), and we also don't want to have events causing themselves (or parts of themselves). Hence only *certain* sufficient conditions for events can possibly count as causes. So let's consider the proposal that A *causes* B iff (1) A precedes B, (2) A is spatiotemporally continuous with B, and (3) A is a sufficient condition for B.

This is a very interesting proposal because it isn't obvious that there really are cases where A and B meet these conditions. Conditions (1) and (2) guarantee that A and B are entirely distinct, nonoverlapping events or states of affairs, and – at least in the billiard ball case – it seems that we are unable to observe anything in one such event that would make it sufficient for the occurrence of the other. But we needn't stop with the billiard balls. Take *any* events C and E that meet conditions (1) and (2), and suppose that the laws of nature predict that E occurs given that C occurs. It *still* seems that we can imagine that C occurs but E does not. One way is to imagine that the entire world ends at precisely the right time. (E.g., if C is closed on the right, then its last moment is the last moment of time.) Another way is to imagine that the relevant laws of nature *change* at just the right time, and that the new laws predict that C is followed by something incompatible with E. (E.g., gravitation might suddenly become a force of repulsion rather than attraction.)

This last possibility may contain a clue for how to proceed. The rough idea is to bring the prevailing laws of nature actively into the picture. We can do this with the following definition. Let's say that an event or state of affairs A is an *inductively sufficient condition* for an event or state of affairs B iff, given that the relevant laws of nature do not change during the time interval of A and continue to prevail for a sufficient interval thereafter, A could not occur without B also occurring. Then we can just insert "inductively" into condition (3) of the proposal, and the result evidently rules out the cases that frustrated the original proposal.

Let's try to summarize what we have done so far. First, we concluded that we couldn't perceive the causal relation operating in nature. The prospect of figuring out whether there really is causal efficacy looked very dim. But we noticed that we are able to think of the laws of nature either with or without the assumption that the phenomena to which they apply involve real efficacy. This enabled us to arrive at a proposal for a technical definition of "cause" that has the following key feature: It applies in the cases where we *normally* think causes are efficacious *whether they are efficacious or not*. In other words, if we would normally say that x caused y (given the refinement about transitivity and gaps), then it will also be true in the technical sense that x caused y. In effect, the technical notion is neutral on the question of efficacy. So let's adopt this notion for our future reflections.

112

Earlier we promised to mention a puzzle about efficacy. Now is a good moment for this since we have settled on a specific notion of cause. Suppose C causes E and that C has a last moment, t. Now, the part of C that occurs only at t is a state of affairs, say S. If C is efficacious in the occurrence of E, then it's very hard to see how any part of C other than S can be the source of the efficacy. The earlier parts seem irrelevant to the occurrence of E. Now notice that E itself has to be an event. If it were a state of affairs, then there would be a gap between S and E. So E stretches over an interval that is open on the left. (It's a "continuum" of states of affairs that occur after t.) Now pick *any* state of affairs S* that is part of E. Say S* occurs at t^*. Since S caused E, it must also be true that S caused S*. But there's a temporal gap between S and S* since there are times between t and t^*. So it looks like S didn't cause S*. The same reasoning will apply to any state of affairs whatsoever that is part of E. But this makes it seem that S didn't cause E after all. [Exercise: (1) **State the parallel puzzle for the case when C has no last moment. (2) Propose a resolution that preserves efficacy.**]

Notice that this puzzle disappears if we abandon the ordinary notion that causes are efficacious. For then the connection between C and E is just that they conform to a regular pattern whose generalization is accepted as a "law of nature." Since C and E fit the pattern and include S and S* as parts, S and S* automatically fit the pattern as well. So the idea that there is no such thing as genuine causal efficacy is looking more and more respectable.

We will conclude this section with a further remark about our ordinary notion of cause, and how it fits or doesn't fit with our technical metaphysical notion. In everyday life we often use the term "cause" loosely, for events or states of affairs that we know don't come close to sufficiency or efficaciousness. This is evident in everyday "causal explanations." For example, we say things like "The rain caused my shirt to get wet." And someone in a teasing mood may reply by saying: "The rain didn't cause it on its own – you could have stayed indoors." Of course this playful reply really does make a legitimate point – namely, that we only mentioned part of the real (or "total") cause of the shirt's getting wet – we gave only a "partial cause." In more metaphysical terms, we cited an event or state of affairs that was only a part of the larger event or state of affairs that was the (total) cause.

As a matter of fact it would border on the impossible to make sure we always give total causes when we give causal explanations. In the present example we took for granted the fact that we were outdoors, were wearing the shirt, had no umbrella, etc. As a rule, a satisfactory causal explanation only requires mention of the factors that the hearer didn't know about. Notice that this entails that the concept of a satisfactory causal explanation is *relative* – it's a relation, not a property. (See chapter 5 for more on the notion of relativity.) A given explanation can be satisfactory for you but not for me, simply because you know more about what was going on when the event to be explained occurred.

We should not infer from the fact that we only mention partial causes in causal explanations that partial causes are really *causes*. The little dialogue about the wet shirt ought to be enough to show that even in ordinary life we are aware of this. In any event, the metaphysical notion of cause we have so far developed does not allow for any event or state of affairs that isn't an inductively sufficient condition to count as a cause. In short, there are no "partial causes" of concern to us here.

7.2   Determinism and Freedom

Determinism is the doctrine that every event and state of affairs in the universe is caused by a prior event or state of affairs. So events that occur at any time, past, present, or future, are "determined" to occur before the time of their occurrence. Of course, since our official notion of cause is neutral on the question of efficacy, so must be the notion of determination. In effect, to say that an event is determined to occur merely means that it is appropriately linked to a prior event in accordance with the laws of nature. *Indeterminism* is the denial of determinism, that is, the claim that at least some events or states of affairs occur without having been caused by prior events or states of affairs.

It will simplify our thinking about determinism if we assume that the ultimate laws of nature – whether they record causal efficacy or not, and whether we will ever know them or not – do not change over time. This is a substantial assumption, worthy of serious discussion, but we will not enter into it here. Real progress on the issue of freedom and determinism, even under this assumption, would of course be quite substantial in its own right.

When we think in a common-sense way about the world around us, determinism seems obviously true. At least we find it hard to accept that a macroscopic physical event should occur without being caused by what went before. The idea of such uncaused events seems to undercut our ordinary belief that anything that happens can, in principle, be explained. It seems to require a kind of "incompleteness" in the laws of nature. To say the very least, even though uncaused events are indeed conceivable, we certainly proceed in ordinary and, mostly, in scientific life as if they do not occur. (It should be mentioned that it is widely believed that certain physical events at the subatomic level are not causally determined to occur by what precedes them, and that this is a consequence of quantum theory. We will not assess these beliefs here, but notice that even if they are correct, such indeterminacy is not obviously incompatible with determinism at the macroscopic level. We will return briefly to these matters below.)

But serious philosophical trouble now arises because we have another common-sense belief that seems to conflict with determinism. This is the belief that we possess "free will" – that our actions are, at least some of the time, "entirely up to us" and are not forced upon us by prior events in the world. The power of this ordinary belief is evident in many of our social, religious, and legal practices, where we hold people responsible for actions both taken and untaken, but generally not when we think they could not have done otherwise. (Thus the problem of free will and determinism is closely connected to another deep problem of philosophy: the nature (and existence) of moral responsibility.)

We have already seen that other philosophical problems arise in just this way: We have common-sense beliefs about fundamental concepts, and these beliefs appear to be in conflict. The problem is then to decide whether the conflict is genuine and, if it is, how best to resolve it. Some philosophers have argued that the apparent conflict in the present case is illusory. This position – often called *compatibilism* – would be the ideal solution to the problem simply because it would preserve both sets of common-sense beliefs. So we ought to consider compatibilism before turning to its less desirable alternatives.

The claim that we have free will apparently has the following three components: (1) We are capable of "willing" ourselves to perform actions. (2) At least normally, when we will to perform an action, the willing is followed by the willed action unless its performance is prevented by intervening circumstances. (But notice that the willing is generally not a cause of the action, though it is a causal antecedent. [**Exercise: Explain clearly why this is so.**] (3) At least normally, when we will to perform an action, it is within our power instead to will not to perform it, or to will

115

to perform some other action, or not to will anything at all. This picture of free will is neutral as to whether our acts of will are always, never, or sometimes "felt" by us, but the usual conception is that we sometimes experience our willings and other times do not.

But what is an act of will? Evidently it's a mental event of some kind. So we see that there is yet another deep philosophical problem that is closely connected to the problem of free will and determinism: the question of the nature of mind. Whether compatibilism is plausible may ultimately depend on our view of the mind and mental activity. Let's explore this by considering two very different conceptions of the mental. We'll consider a simple *materialist* view, which holds that mental events are just certain physical events occurring in our brains. Then we'll look at a *dualist* view, which takes mental events to be nonphysical events that occur in our minds, which the theory also takes to be nonphysical (and hence distinct from our brains). But first, we need to get a little clearer about the notion of an act of will.

Suppose you (consciously) decide to wiggle your toes, and immediately proceed to do so. This seems like a typical case in which you will to do something, but it isn't obvious that the *willing* is identical with the *deciding*. We often decide to do things well in advance of doing them, and in this sort of case it seems that the willing occurs later, just before we perform the action (or maybe just as we perform it). This may suggest that willing to do something is just *trying* to do it. Usually when we try to wiggle our toes, we succeed, but not always. We may fail if our toes are somehow prevented from moving by an outside force. But notice this. You may know that you cannot move your toes because they are impaired or bound or whatever. A doctor who also knows you can't move them may nevertheless ask you to *try* to move your toes in order to learn about something else, perhaps how your toes feel to you when you try to move them. In this sort of case, it doesn't seem right to say that you will to move your toes. Instead you will *to try* to move them, knowing that you cannot. So far, it seems that willing is a distinctive sort of mental activity, not to be identified with the likes of trying or deciding.

But another possibility is that it isn't an activity at all, but rather just a feature that accompanies certain of our activities. Sometimes we speak of doing things willingly or unwillingly. Maybe this is all there is to it, so that there aren't any distinctive acts of will, just two different kinds of actions. But this doesn't seem right either. Suppose someone issues a severe and credible threat in an effort to get you to wiggle your toes – something you do not want to do. You're no fool, so you wiggle them. Then here is a case where you wiggle them unwillingly. But it's also a case in which you will to wiggle your toes. So "unwillingly" doesn't mean *without will*. It means something more like *under duress* or *without desire*. [Exercise: **Is there a more plausible way of analyzing the notion of will as a property of the actions that we normally think of as the results of "acts of will"?**]

Let's follow the lead of this brief survey and conclude that there really are acts of will (sometimes conscious, sometimes not), and that they are not identical with other familiar sorts of actions, like deciding or trying. Then, if we really possess freedom, our free actions must be preceded by such distinctive mental acts. Now we will ask how compatibilism meshes with the two views of mind mentioned above.

Compatibilism and materialism. According to the variety of materialism we are considering, any act of will is a physical event in the brain. So suppose W is such an event, say a willing by oneself to perform action A. Then, according to determinism, there must be some prior event (or state of affairs) C that is a cause of W. Now, it would certainly be an unusual case if C were *itself* an act of will. It *might* be that we sometimes will to will to do something, but if this sort of willing ever occurs, it is very rare. Notice that it is far easier to conceive of wanting to want X than it is to conceive of willing to will X. This is because it's hard to see how someone could will to will X without *thereby* willing X. [Exercise: **Give a convincing case in which someone wants to want X but doesn't want X.**] Anyway, we certainly do not will to will to will to do something. So even in the highly unlikely event that C is a willing, it isn't caused by a willing. Thus it seems clear that we don't have to look very far in order to find a causal antecedent of W that isn't an act of will. In fact, it seems that we don't have to look very far to find a causal antecedent that isn't a mental act of any kind (even though it may be an event occurring entirely within the brain). So, for simplicity, let's just assume that C itself is not an act that we perform.

Now, since C caused W, and C wasn't even something that we did, it's hard to see how it could have been within our power not to will to do A, as required by component (3) of the ordinary conception of free will. To put it a little differently, the action A at first looks like it was done freely, because we willed to do it. But our willing to do it was caused by something not of our own doing, namely C. So how can it be that A was done freely? Isn't it clear under the circumstances that W is an "act of will" in name only?

117

It may seem that compatibilism must crumble in the face of questions like these. But not everyone agrees. One possible strategy is to argue that although C is not an action done by us, it has a causal antecedent that is. So C isn't something that just came out of nowhere. Instead it was brought about by something we did earlier. So if C caused our willing to do A, it doesn't follow that either the willing or the doing of A was not appropriately "our own." Compatibilists sometimes suggest that our acts of will flow from our character and our beliefs: from "who we are." A person's character is something like a complex set of dispositions that reflect that person's goals, motives, desires, sense of right and wrong, social experience, and the like. Of course if one's character is entirely determined by external causes, then appealing to character is unlikely to help with the present problem. So the idea is that we are, in part, the architects of our own characters, and that whatever willings result from character are therefore, at least in part, attributable to earlier choices and hence attributable to us. So if W was a causal result of our character as it responded to a specific situation (with C the penultimate such result), then W was still an action fully our own (even though C was not itself one of our actions).

This position, though some have found it promising, is vulnerable to the charge that it simply pushes the problem back in time. For consider the earlier "choices" that helped to form our character. Each must have been caused by events like C that were not among our actions. In particular, it seems that there must have been a first choice, a first act of will. Our character would not have been formed by that time, so the fact that the corresponding C is not something done by us now looks very damaging. The appeal to character in establishing our current choices as truly our own cannot also be made when it comes to the earliest choices involved in building our character. But then it can't be made when it comes to the next choices either. Nor to those that follow, and so, ultimately, not to any choices made during the development of one's character. We are thus left with the mystery of how character can be the wellspring of our free actions if we have no free choice in its development. And this mystery seems quite analogous to the mystery of how W can really be free – can really deserve the title "act of will" – if it is caused by a nonaction like C.

Compatibilism and dualism. Here the story gets a little more complicated. For one thing, it isn't clear how comfortably dualism and determinism fit together. Some people see determinism as a doctrine concerned only with the physical world, because they think the notion of cause only applies to physical events. On such a view, mental events (as dualists conceive them) would occur in a realm that is causally isolated from the physical world. So the events that we call "acts of will" would neither be caused by physical events nor capable of exerting causal influence on physical events. As a result, freedom of the will would evidently be illusory. We would indeed sometimes experience "willings," and these would certainly seem to us to be causally instrumental in our ordinary actions, but the willings would be such in name only because they would really be causally inert.

But this is truly a strange combination of views. Probably most philosophers who think causation is confined to the realm of the physical think this because they think there is no other realm. But someone who accepts both dualism and determinism is most likely to believe that mental events have causes just like physical events. Indeed, the official statement of determinism easily accommodates this, for it depends on a notion of cause that ultimately rests on the *laws of nature*, and these may not be limited to purely physical laws.

If dualism is true, then mental events are not physical events, but they are still a part of nature – they happen in the world. And if determinism is true, these events must have causes just like any other type of events. So they must be provided for in the ultimate laws of nature. Now, if the will is truly free, then it certainly seems that mental events must often be among the causal antecedents of physical events. (Otherwise our willings could not result in our doing things with our bodies.) For example, it seems this way in a case in which you will to throw a ball you are holding, there ensues a complex chain of electrochemical events in your body, and this results in visible bodily motions and the crisp release of the ball. As a result, if dualism is truly compatible with determinism, then evidently some of the laws of nature must be what have been called "psychophysical" laws – laws that connect the mental with the physical. (The causal connection, of course, must also run in the other direction, as when physical stimuli produce a mental event – a visual image, a feeling of fear, or whatever.)

But now the situation seems relevantly no different from the case of materialism. A willing, W, may be a causal antecedent of an action, A, and so A may seem to us to be a free action. But determinism demands that there be a cause of W, say C. As before, we may easily assume that C isn't an action of the subject's. So we are once again faced with the question of how A can truly be free if it is a causal result of C. The fact that W is nonphysical on the dualist account in no way loosens the grip of this question.

Compatibilists sometimes defend their position by appealing to the way we ordinarily use terms like "free" and "constrained." Suppose you are at home and you decide to take a ride on your bike just for the fun of it. You find your bike, wheel it outside, mount and ride. Later you return. We would ordinarily call this a free action. But now suppose you are being held hostage in your own home by desperados. You hear them plotting. They have arranged with outside confederates to concoct an innocent-looking signal that will trigger some nefarious and possibly deadly activity. The signal is to be your leaving the house with your bike and riding away in a certain direction. Of course you don't want any part of this, but they threaten you so severely (and believably) that you comply.

We would ordinarily say, in a case like this, that you did not act freely. We would also say that you performed the action against your will. We say your action here was constrained while, in the first case, it was unconstrained. And so forth. Compatibilists often argue that to act freely merely means to act in accordance with your will, or without external constraint. They reason that since, as a matter of empirical fact, we often do act without external constraint, it follows that we often act freely. Furthermore, this conclusion has been reached without even touching the subject of determinism, which is regarded as a separate and independent question. Therefore, it is often concluded, freedom and determinism are compatible. (A slightly different way to capture the idea behind this reasoning is as follows. The kinds of constraints that result in unfree actions are always "interventions" that are imposed locally. If nothing intervenes in the flow of your activity, it will automatically be free activity. At the very least, the actions that proceed from your willings will be free.)

Incompatibilists usually respond to this sort of argument by claiming that the compatibilist has begged the question. Ordinary life certainly does proceed on the assumption that we are usually free. But this assumption cannot be true merely as a consequence of the fact that we ordinarily make it. So it is an open question whether the activity we usually think of as free really is free. The compatibilist begs this question by taking "free" to mean, roughly, *without intervening external constraint*. Since this guarantees that lots of our actions will be "free," it's much too easy.

What happens when people act under constraint is that they are being caused to act by events external to them and not of their own choosing.

Sometimes the constraint is obvious, as when someone is forced to act at gunpoint. (It is this sort of case that compatibilists often rely on, because here the contrast with ordinary activity is most striking.) But other times it may be much less obvious, as when someone acts under the influence of an unnoticed and accidentally ingested drug. The crucial point, missed by this compatibilist argument, is that if all of our actions are caused by events external to us and not of our own choosing, then we are always acting under constraint, whether that constraint is obvious or not, and whether we would normally describe such an action as "free" or not.

Although we have not exhausted the inventory of strategies that might be used to defend compatibilism, it certainly has begun to look like the position is doubtful. At the very least, it appears that it would take a subtle and ingenious defense to make it seem plausible. For the remainder of this section, let us therefore assume that determinism and freedom are incompatible. Then what?

One thing we can say about determinism that cannot so easily be said about freedom is that it is fairly clear what the doctrine really is. The version we are considering depends only on the notion of an event (or state of affairs), and on a concept of cause that, in turn, rests on the idea of a law of nature (a notion that is neutral on the matter of efficacy). But we have not said (and will not say) precisely what is meant by a "law of nature," and this is an area in which philosophical differences could surface. Despite this, we have said enough about determinism to make it apparent that the question of its truth or falsity is at least partly empirical. This fact has two interesting consequences. First, it means that no purely philosophical argument is going to prove or disprove determinism. Second, it means that no purely philosophical argument is going to prove or disprove freedom, since we are assuming that these doctrines are incompatible.

If we were entirely settled about the concepts of event and law of nature, the question of determinism would evidently be entirely empirical. That does not, of course, mean it would be easy to settle. For one thing, it makes an assertion about all events, past, present, and future. It does not follow from the fact that the events we are able to observe are causally determined, that the ones we are unable to observe are as well. But what may be even more important is that it seems unlikely that we could ever be in a position to feel that we knew all the laws of nature. So an apparent violation of determinism might seem so only because we were unaware of some law in accordance with which it was determined.

121

Contemporary physics provides a case in point. Certain subatomic phenomena seem to occur randomly or spontaneously. For example, radioactive materials emit alpha- and beta-rays from time to time, but not in accordance with any precise pattern, and not as a clear result of any particular causal influence. Reliable statistical generalizations are known, but that is as far as it goes. Still, it seems rash to infer that this disproves determinism. That would overlook the possibility that what are now believed to be the relevant laws are really not, and that the correct laws – which we may or may not ever discover – account for the emissions in a deterministic manner. (This possibility remains open even if what are now thought to be the right laws entail that such phenomena are indeterministic – these "laws" may simply be wrong.)

These epistemic difficulties make it very unlikely that we will ever be justified in feeling confident about the truth or falsity of determinism. And so the same must be true for any version of freedom that is incompatible with determinism.

But just what is the doctrine of freedom? Let's agree that it's the view that humans have "free will," and then focus our worries on what this means. A natural idea is that it means that we are sometimes in situations in which we have the ability to do different (incompatible) things, and which thing we ultimately do is entirely "up to us." At a fork in the road, say, it can be up to us whether to go left or go right. We can will either option. If we will to go left, we go left; if we will to go right, we go right. Since we are assuming incompatibilism, whatever "up to us" means, it entails that if we (say) will to go left, then we are not caused to will this by some inappropriate event. But it isn't easy to say just what this rules in and what it rules out. Let's look at a couple of efforts in this direction.

The Theory of Spontaneous Freedom (SF): This theory is a special form of indeterminism. It holds that certain of our actions are uncaused, and it regards the uncaused actions as free. So, our willing to go left isn't caused by an inappropriate event, because it isn't caused *at all*. The main problem with SF is that it isn't a very plausible formulation of the ordinary conception of something's being up to us, where it is we who determine what these actions will be. If our acts of free will are uncaused, then it seems that they aren't determined at all, so it's very hard to see them as being up to us. Instead they just happen, spontaneously, whether we like it or not.

A more promising conception of freedom is provided by The Theory of

Free Agency (FA): This theory is also a form of indeterminism, but it does not deny that our actions are caused. It consists of the following three parts: (1) Every event in the universe has a prior cause. (2) Some events are not caused by prior events but rather by "free agents." A *free agent* is any entity that, first, is not an event occurring in the universe and, second, can cause events to occur that are not caused by prior events. (3) Human beings are free agents.

According to FA, our willing to go left doesn't just happen, but it isn't caused by some inappropriate event either. It has a cause, but that cause isn't an event at all, it's a *person*. So, according to FA, the causal relation sometimes links an event to another event, but on other occasions it links an agent to an event. We may thus see FA as an attempt to find a middle course between two unacceptable conceptions of our acts of will: on one hand, the idea that they are random occurrences that we do not control, and, on the other, the idea that they are determined by events that we do not control. The whole point is to put us back into control.

But it is very difficult to understand how an entity that isn't an event can bear the causal relation to an event. As we have been conceiving causation, it occurs in accordance with the laws of nature. But all the familiar (candidates for) laws of nature connect events to events. If FA is correct, and this idea of causation is on the right track, then there must also be laws connecting agents with events. How would such laws be formulated?

Suppose A is a free agent and E is some event that A causes, like willing to go left at the fork. Can there be a law that entails that if A exists, then E occurs? One serious problem is that all events occur at specific times. So suppose E begins to occur at time t. Since A caused E, A must have existed before t. But then what explains why E occurred *at t*? Why didn't A cause E earlier, since A existed earlier? The most natural answer is that "agent-event" laws are more general, and involve types of situations as well as types of agents and types of events. Roughly, such a law might have the form, "If an agent of type X is in a situation of type Y, then that agent will produce an action of type Z." Then the reason A caused E at t is, presumably, that A was of type X, was in a situation of type Y just prior to t, and E was of type Z. Let's try to fill in some plausible specifics and then ask whether the outcome is plausible.

So imagine that A comes to the fork in the road just before t. Suppose he knows that the left road leads to his house and the right road leads to his friend's house. A has vaguely promised his friend that he will drop by to see her in a day or two. But A happens to be tired and hungry, and knows he will have an opportunity to visit his friend tomorrow. Still, he considers making the visit as he approaches the fork. He thinks about how tired he would be after visiting, and what the chances of being offered some food at his friend's house might be. Then A wills to go left and proceeds to do so. His decision may have been a "close call," but he feels very much that he chose freely to go home.

The particulars of the case we have described are ingredients that go to make up A's being of type X (being hungry, etc.) and the situation's being of type Y (being at the fork, etc.). There are doubtless other ingredients that we haven't specified, like the exact degree of hunger, the closeness of the friendship, how recently the friends had visited, whether A's eyes are sore, just how far his friend's house is along the right road, and much more. But it is quite clear what being of type Z must be in this case: it must be the property of *being a willing to go home.*

This looks like a very plausible case. But it raises two major problems. First, it looks very much like A's being of type X and the situation's being of type Y add up to a certain complex *event*. The event has some of A's deliberation as a part, it has some of A's bodily sensations as a part, it has A's geographical location as a part, and so forth. Of course, the event also has A as a part (or, at least, the relevant temporal part of A as a part). So, the first problem is that it looks like the sort of case we would naturally think of in trying to understand free agency is one in which an *event* is doing the causing after all. The fact that the event involves the agent as a part no longer seems relevant.

The second problem is that it looks like the law has undermined A's freedom. If, whenever you give A the X-properties in a Y-type situation, he's going to head for home, his feeling of freedom is illusory. We can, perhaps, explain why he has this feeling of freedom. To put it crudely, it's because it was a close call. Tiny changes in the X- or Y-properties would have brought into play a different law, one that determined A to will to go right. For example, it is reasonable to think that hunger, thought of as a kind of bodily state, comes in degrees that are more refined than are reflected in our feelings of hunger. Suppose we feel, for example, "pretty hungry." Pretty hungry feels hungrier than a little hungry, but not as hungry as very hungry.

Now, it might be that A felt pretty hungry, but his bodily state bordered on (but didn't quite attain) a condition that would have made him feel very hungry. This means he had brain states rather different from those he would have had if he had felt pretty hungry, but had a bodily state that bordered on one that would have made him feel only a little hungry. Still, he would only have felt, in either case, that he was "pretty hungry," because he isn't sensitive to the finer gradations of bodily state. Despite this, the finer gradations are there, evidenced in the brain activity, and they might make all the difference at the fork in the road. Pretty hungry to a minimal degree could have resulted in a right turn. Oversimplifying a bit (by concentrating only on this one factor), it is very plausible to think that A's feeling of freedom rests on the fact that he could easily imagine himself feeling pretty hungry and choosing to go right. But what A wouldn't have been able to notice in such a situation is that he would have been less hungry in bodily state.

We have considered the idea of free agency only in company with a couple of assumptions. First, that there would have to be laws of nature to support agent–event causation just as they are needed to support event–event causation. Second, we have examined only one way of formulating agent–event laws. There may be other plausible ways of elaborating the notion of free agency. [**Exercise: Try to do so.**] But it must be said that these assumptions certainly looked reasonable at the outset, and certainly do leave freedom looking suspect. The success of science and the seeming regularities in everyday external events both give evidence in favor of determinism. Of course this evidence is quite inconclusive. The main evidence favoring freedom – also quite inconclusive – comes from within. We simply *feel* free. But our consideration of free agency also yielded a promising sketch of an explanation of this feeling, one that is perfectly compatible with determinism.

Our discussion has revealed that the doctrine of freedom faces a serious dilemma, which we may characterize briefly as follows. Either a "free action" occurs in accordance with laws, and hence is caused by what went before; or else it does not, and hence is random or spontaneous. But it is hard to see how the action can be genuinely free in either case. Freedom seems to require personal control, and in neither case do we seem to be in control. The ultimate success of the doctrine of freedom depends on a convincing response to this dilemma.

It would be a mistake to see the present difficulties for freedom as support for determinism. Unfortunately, discussions of freedom and determinism often seem to presuppose that one or the other doctrine must be true. As a result, doubts about one position are sometimes taken to favor the other. But both doctrines could easily be false. In fact, this should be clear from the dilemma. For if no events at all were determined to occur by what went before, so that determinism was dramatically false, then the doctrine of freedom would also be dramatically false. Everything would be random, so nothing would be determined and no one would ever be in control of anything. For a less radical example, suppose that there really are spontaneous events at the subatomic level. Then determinism would be false. But there is no evident connection between events of this sort and human mental activity and behavior. So all of our actions might be rigorously determined in accordance with natural laws.

7.3   Fatalism

We now turn to a doctrine that is sometimes confused with determinism. *Fatalism* is the view that whatever happens is "inevitable" (or "unavoidable"). The fatalist believes this holds of all events, past, present, and future. Fatalism is not a version of determinism, which is a theory about causation. Fatalism says nothing at all about causation. Although determinism appears to entail fatalism, the reverse does not hold. So one might be a fatalist without being a determinist. For example, fatalism would evidently be true if, as recently imagined, no events ever have causes, so that everything is random and undetermined. Under this radical supposition, nothing would be in anyone's control, so everything would be unavoidable.

There is an extremely elegant and beguiling argument in favor of fatalism that we will now consider. It depends only on the concept of truth.

1   Let E be any event that occurs in the future. **Then:**
2   The proposition that E will occur is true. **So:**
3   Nothing that anyone can do can bring it about that E does not occur. **That is:**
4   It is inevitable that E will occur. **So (since E is arbitrary):**
5   All future events are inevitable, that is, fatalism (about the future) is true.

It is important to notice two things about this argument. First, if it shows that fatalism about the future – from our current temporal perspective – is true, then it also shows that unrestricted fatalism is true, since the argument would apply just as effectively from any past temporal perspective as it does from the present perspective.

Second, it should be recalled that Platonic propositions are entities located outside of spacetime. As a result, it is impossible for any proposition to change its truth-value, since only entities that are located in time can undergo change. It is therefore impossible to block the argument from truth by claiming that although the proposition that E will occur may be true *now*, later events might *change* its truth-value, thereby providing logical room for someone to prevent the occurrence of E.

It is worth noting in this connection that propositions generally do not themselves contain elements corresponding to the tenses of verbs in the descriptions we use to refer to them. So, when we speak of "the proposition that E will occur," we are merely letting the context do part of the work of specifying the proposition. In particular, the context supplies the current moment of time as a hidden ingredient. The description "the proposition that E will occur," uttered at time *t*, therefore picks out the proposition *that E occurs after t*. Anyone (past, present, or future) may pick out this proposition "tenselessly" by using the description "the proposition that E occurs after *t*." Thus we may say that this latter description is *univocal*, whereas the original, future-tense description is not. That same description, uttered at a different time, would pick out a *different* proposition – say the proposition *that E occurs after t** (where *t** is different from *t*).

This argument (along with several historical variations, including theological ones) has convinced lots of people of the truth of fatalism. It's a very compelling argument. If it's really true that E is going to happen, then it can seem very convincing that there's nothing anyone can do about it, that it's inevitable. Perhaps we can somewhat undermine this appearance by looking at an analogous argument. (This argument is loosely inspired by W. Somerset Maugham's very short story "Appointment in Samarra.")

1   Let A be any person who is now in Baghdad. **Then:**
2   The proposition that A is now in Baghdad is true. **So:**
3   It cannot be that A is not now in Baghdad. **That is:**
4   It is a necessary truth that A is now in Baghdad. **So:**
5   All persons are wherever they are as a matter of necessity – it is impossible that anyone should be anywhere else.

This argument parallels the argument from truth, but it involves the concept of necessity instead of the concept of inevitability. It seems pretty clear that the move from 2 (via 3) to 4 in the argument is suspicious. Whatever our views about necessity may be, it shouldn't follow from the mere fact that something is true that it is *necessarily* true. It may *in fact* be that anything that is true is necessarily true, but the concept of necessary truth is still one that goes beyond the mere concept of truth. So it cannot just be a matter of logic that whatever is true is necessarily true. In other words, there is room to believe that the conclusion of the argument is true, but still to think that the argument is invalid. And if this argument is invalid, there is a good chance that the analogous argument from truth for fatalism is also invalid.

Someone rejecting the location argument on this basis might reject the fatalism argument by reasoning as follows. To say that E will occur is to say something short of saying that it is inevitable that E will occur. In other words, the concept of an *inevitable future event* is one that goes beyond the mere concept of a *future event*. This must be true even if it turns out that all future events really are inevitable. So it cannot just be a matter of logic that whatever will happen is also inevitable. The argument from truth is invalid, even if fatalism is true.

Here is a vivid way of making the same point. We invite a proponent of the argument to perform the following thought experiment with us. First, we pretend that some future events really aren't inevitable. The fatalist doesn't believe this, but still should be able to pretend it. So we pretend there is at least one possible future event – say E – such that (as of now) E can happen, but also "not-E" (the failure of E) can happen. Then neither E nor not-E is inevitable. Now consider the proposition *that E will occur but isn't inevitable* and the proposition *that not-E will occur but isn't inevitable*. Since it is a matter of logic that either E or not-E will occur, and since neither would be inevitable, one of these propositions is true (and the other is false). But if the argument from truth were valid, each proposition would have to be not only false, but actually *inconsistent*, since the argument purports to derive inevitability from mere truth. We have to conclude that the argument is invalid.

There is yet another way to reason that the argument is invalid, one that brings in the notion of free choice. Notice that the argument depends entirely on the simple premise stated on line 1. (Line 2 is supposed to follow from line 1; line 3 is supposed to follow from line 2; line 4 is supposed to be a restatement of line 3; and line 5 is supposed to follow from line 4.) So everything depends entirely on the premise that E is a future event. Of course, there will be future events whether or not we have genuine free choice. Now notice that having free choice – as long as the notion is logically coherent – is perfectly compatible with there being future events (and in fact requires that there be). If we do have genuine free choice, then there are some future events that it is within our control to prevent even though we will not choose to prevent them. That's what it means for an event to be "avoidable." So, genuine free choice is incompatible with fatalism. But then the argument from truth must be wrong. For its only premise is compatible with genuine free choice, but its conclusion is not. Somewhere along the way a mistake must have been made. (This reasoning depends on the logical principle that the conclusion of a valid argument cannot entail something that its premises (taken together) do not entail. In the present case, the conclusion entails that there is no genuine free choice, but the premise does not.)

It provides no ultimate solace to know that the argument from truth is invalid, since fatalism may still be true. If it is, then we do not have genuine free choice. Although we saw in Section 7.2 that it isn't really clear exactly what genuine free choice amounts to, it does seem safe to say that whatever it is, the conclusion that we don't have it would be momentous. So there may be a good philosophical lesson here: Beware of simple philosophical arguments with momentous conclusions.

8
Modality

8.1   The Metaphysical Concept

A theologian may say, "It's a *necessary* truth that God exists." A metaphysician (or a modal logician) may say, "If x is identical with y, then it's *necessary* that x is identical with y." A probability theorist (or a gambler) may say, "It's *possible* for 100 consecutive tosses of a fair coin to come up heads." And anyone might say, "It's *possible* that the world will end tomorrow."

The notions of possibility and necessity come as an "interanalyzable" pair. To see this, consider the claim that it's necessary that God exists. We may rephrase it by saying that it isn't possible that God does not exist. Similarly, for it to be possible that something will happen is simply for it not to be necessary that it won't happen. So we may "analyze" either concept in terms of the other. A consequence is that anything we may conclude concerning the notion of possibility will have immediate implications for the concept of necessity (and vice versa).

Unfortunately, there are many different notions of possibility (and necessity). In this chapter we are only concerned with one of them, a perfectly ordinary notion that we will call "metaphysical" possibility (and necessity). Despite its ordinary status, it isn't easy to characterize metaphysical possibility directly, without appealing to less familiar notions. But it will make matters a little easier if we first narrow the field by saying what this concept of possibility is not.

Sometimes we use "possible" to express a notion of physical capability. For example: "For a long time people thought it wasn't possible for a human to run a mile in under four minutes." It turned out that they were wrong. But consider the following much more guarded claim: "It's impossible for any person now living on Earth to run a mile in under 30 seconds." There is a legitimate notion of possibility according to which this claim is certainly true. Of course, the human species might ultimately evolve to the point where some individuals were capable of such a feat, but we aren't anywhere near that stage now. The "physical capability" notion of possibility is not the one we are concerned with here. It will soon become clear that it *is* metaphysically possible for contemporary people to run a mile in under 30 seconds.

A closely related concept is sometimes called "physical possibility." That something is physically possible means, roughly, that it's consistent with the laws of physics (or, perhaps, with the laws of *nature*). And to say that something is physically necessary means that the laws of physics imply that it will occur, given appropriate "initial conditions." In this sense, it's necessary that an initially stationary mass that is suddenly subject only to a gravitational force will accelerate along the path of action of that force. Although this is an important notion of necessity, it isn't metaphysical necessity. We will soon see that the laws of physics themselves are not metaphysically necessary. So, you might be standing (briefly) in an otherwise empty, perfect vacuum chamber, on the surface of the earth, holding a golf ball. It is metaphysically possible for you to release the ball and for it to maintain its position, or for it to rise, or for it to disappear, with a fluttering parakeet occupying its recent position.

Another occasion for the use of the terms "necessary" and "possible" is any activity or behavior that is governed by rules or laws, or other normative standards. What is "possible" is what the rules allow and what is "necessary" is what they require. It's *necessary* to file an income tax return if you earn more than a certain amount of money. It's *possible* to file late if you apply for an extension. And so on. The various "normative" notions of possibility (and necessity) are definitely not the metaphysical one.

Other uses of these terms are even further from the metaphysical concept. Here are some examples: (1) "Necessary," in the logicians' sense of a "necessary condition." (2) "Possible," as when a meteorologist says, "Rain is possible today." (It means that at least some of the available evidence favors rain, though maybe not very strongly.) (3) "Necessary," as it applies to what is needed or desired, as in "Water is necessary for human survival." (We also say it's a "necessity" of life.) Also: "Good balance is necessary for expert skiing."

There is another notion of possibility – so-called *logical* possibility – that is very close to the metaphysical one, perhaps even identical with it. Intuitively, something is logically possible if it can't be ruled out on the basis of logic alone. It may be a little better to restate this in terms of necessity: Something is logically necessary if its denial is contradictory. But this is a pretty crude characterization. For one thing, does it involve a formal system of logic? (If so, what system?) A related problem is that we haven't said what sorts of "somethings" are eligible for logical possibility or necessity. People who discuss the notion often seem to presuppose that the proper somethings are linguistic entities – *sentences* of some language or other. But metaphysical possibility and necessity are properly understood, at least in their primary roles, as *modes of truth*. (This is why, e.g., "It is necessary that . . ." and "It is necessarily true that . . ." are synonymous.) But, as we argued in Section 3.1, truth is fundamentally a property of *propositions*. Perhaps this seeming divergence can be reconciled easily, perhaps not. Probably there are several distinct notions of logical possibility. We will avoid the issue and simply leave it open whether the notion is ultimately coherent, and, if it is, what it has to do with metaphysical possibility. (Of course this will not prevent us from appealing to logic in discussing the metaphysical notion.)

We said that the metaphysical notions are modes of truth. In fact, they are sometimes called *alethic modalities*. ("Alethic" means having to do with truth.) This does not mean they are *kinds* of truth, since something that is *possible* (i.e., *possibly true*) need not be *true*. We may think of the modalities as complex concepts that involve truth as a component, but are not to be identified with truth itself. Like truth, they apply fundamentally to propositions, and they bear the following two invariable relations to truth: First, *necessary truth* entails *truth*, and second, *truth* entails *possible truth*. (Since the reverse entailments do not hold, the concept of truth is intermediate in logical strength between the concepts of necessity and possibility.)

We have said that metaphysical possibility is an ordinary concept, like truth. It is the broadest (or most inclusive) notion of possibility that we employ in thinking about how the world might have been. From now on, when we say "possible" (or "necessary") with no modification, we intend this metaphysical concept. The metaphysical notion of possibility may be illuminated as follows. Imagine that God truly exists and that, as traditionally conceived, he is "all-powerful." This means he can bring about any *possible* situation. He can cause a purple cow to come suddenly into being in the Oval Office of the White House. But he cannot cause any cow to be both entirely purple and entirely green. He can cause all physical matter or any fragment of physical matter to cease existing instantaneously. But he cannot cause a specific fragment of matter to be entirely located in separated places at the same time. He can create a perfect duplicate of our entire solar system, right down to every subatomic particle, somewhere in deep space, or even in some unconnected spacetime. But he cannot bring it about that *your duplicate* in that solar system is *you*.

The mere fact that we can conceive that God could, if he chose, produce these remarkable states of affairs, shows that we *already* think of them as, in an appropriate sense, *possible*. So their possibility does not actually depend on the existence of God, nor on any such possibility ever being actual. This familiar concept of possibility is the metaphysical one we have been seeking. Of course, as with any ordinary philosophical concept, our grasp of it is not so certain as to rule out disagreement over specific cases.

So far we have contrasted metaphysical possibility with several other senses of "possible" and we've looked at a few specific possibilities and impossibilities. None of this goes very far toward saying what it *means* to say that something is possible. It turns out that there are several very different positions on this question.

8.2   Understanding Possibility

Before considering any specific analysis or characterization of possibility (or necessity), let's consider the idea that the notion is *simple* (that is, unanalyzable), and that it should therefore be taken as primitive, like the relation of identity. Unfortunately, this idea is very difficult to sustain. Like truth, the modalities are properties of propositions. But truth is not simple. It's a complex relational property – roughly, the property of correctly representing the world as being one way or another. Since the *necessity* of a proposition entails its *truth*, it would be unreasonable to think that necessity is simple. [Exercise: There is a principle implicit in this claim. Try to state and evaluate it.] We already saw that necessity and possibility are interanalyzable. So, if either concept is simple, it ought to be possibility.

Thus consider an assertion that a certain proposition, P, is possible. If this merely says that P has some *simple* property, then it's hard to see how it can tell us anything about the reality that lies outside P itself. But certainly assertions of possibility are about this reality just as much as assertions of truth (or necessity). To learn that it is possible for 100 consecutive coin tosses all to come up heads is to learn something about the way the world is, not merely to learn something *nonrelational* about the Platonic *proposition*. For a proposition to be true is for it to stand in a certain relation to the world. For a proposition to be possible is also for it to stand in a certain relation to the world, but one that is apparently more complex. It cannot be that a *simple* property of propositions could have this "external" relational import.

Much of the contemporary discussion of modality has appealed to one or another concept of *possible worlds*. The idea of possible worlds may be traced back at least to Leibniz and it has had its ups and downs, but it enjoyed a marked resurgence during the second half of the twentieth century. Some philosophers have tried to analyze the modalities by appealing to (possible) worlds. Others, while recognizing that the modalities are complex, have declined to offer analyses but have nevertheless appealed to worlds in an effort to characterize or otherwise shed light on these important notions. The discussion of possible worlds and their deployment in treating modality (and other topics) is sometimes called "world theory."

The basic ideas behind world theory are these: (1) In addition to the *actual world*, there is a plenitude of other possible worlds. (2) Any possible world either *is*, or else somehow *represents*, a complete "way the world might have been." (3) Every way the world might have been is accommodated by one possible world or another. (The way the world actually is, is accommodated by the actual world.) (4) A proposition is possible (in other words, possibly true) iff it is true (or, on some accounts, represented as true) "in" some world or other. (5) A proposition is necessary iff it is true (or represented as true) in every possible world.

We already have a rather vague, everyday notion of a "possible situation," and this is where the idea of possible worlds takes root. Often when we consider (say) a proposed course of action, we imagine two possible situations: one in which the action is done and one in which it isn't. This sort of mental activity often helps us decide what to do. But the possible situations we think about in everyday life are usually very local and limited in what they include. Possible worlds are not. They are like everyday possible situations except for the crucial fact that they are global and "complete." So when you think about the possible situation in which you go to the movies tonight, you aren't imagining an entire possible world. A possible world must not only include whether you exist and go to the movies, but also exactly how much you weigh, where you were born, the precise population of Madrid, exactly how many grains of sand there are in Florida at every specific instant of time, how many carbon atoms there are in the universe, and so on. Since the world could be different in countless ways that have nothing to do with whether you go to the movies, there are countless different worlds in which you do go, and countless different worlds in which you don't go. A little reflection on these matters makes it clear that possible worlds would have to be very peculiar entities indeed. It cannot be obvious that any worlds exist other than the actual world we inhabit. So it shouldn't be surprising that the idea of worlds has produced a number of very different elaborations and reactions. We will now consider three of them.

(i)   *Concrete Worlds.* (The best-known proponent of this position is the American philosopher David Lewis. The current presentation will not follow his theory in every detail, but it will in spirit.) The *actual world* is the "concrete" spatiotemporal realm in which we find ourselves. But there exist innumerable other spatiotemporal realms that are, more or less, entities of the same sort as the actual world. Some of them contain stars, planets, people, plants, and animals. Others do not. Some of them are very similar to the actual world; others are hardly like it at all. All of these other worlds are physically inaccessible to each other. They never physically overlap each other, no signal can ever pass between any two of them, and no causal relations can hold between events in any two of them. Each of these worlds is "actual" from its own "point of view," and no world enjoys any privileged sort of actuality since all of the worlds are literally existing, spatiotemporal realms – parts of a single, scattered reality. The philosophers of other worlds are correct when they think of themselves and their worlds as actual. And we are correct when we think that these philosophers and their worlds are not actual. [Exercise: Give a definition of "actual" that makes it clear that the last two assertions really are consistent.]

As in any world theory, we will see that *possibility* depends on what is true in some world (or other), and that *necessity* depends on what is true in every world. But a most impressive feature of this particular theory is that it will permit us to regard the ultimate formulations as providing *analyses* of the concepts of possibility and necessity, analyses that appeal only to the notions of truth and possible worlds. Of course, any world theory will ultimately have to depend on an analysis of truth (and the general lines of one have already been suggested). But since, on this theory, the possible worlds are simply concrete parts of reality, there is no need to provide an analysis of the concept of a world. (Other world-theoretic analyses will not get off so lightly.) Despite this elegance, there are problems. We will look at three: (1) the problem of singular propositions; (2) the ontological problem; (3) the problem of relevance.

Problem (1). Consider the false proposition that snow is blue. Is it possibly true? Well, of course, the *theory* doesn't have to tell us. What it tells us is that it's possible iff there's a world in which snow is blue. Even if we cannot decide empirically whether there is such a world, we still understand the analyzing condition perfectly well. But the proposition that snow is blue is a so-called *general* proposition. It doesn't involve any specific individual entities. Things are not so straightforward with *singular* propositions – those that (supposedly) do involve specific entities.

So consider the proposition that the White House is blue. It's false, but certainly it might have been true, even for all of its history. (If the White House had been blue from the start, it's very unlikely that it would have been *named* "the White House," but even that seems *possible*, and anyway it isn't relevant.) If anything, we are even more certain that the White House might have been blue than we are that snow might have been blue. But our certainty here is not matched in the theory by a clear analyzing condition. It will not suffice to say that the proposition is possible iff there's a world in which it is true, that is, a world in which the White House is blue. The reason is simple: Since worlds don't overlap, there is no other possible world that contains the White House. So if we applied this straightforward condition, we would be forced to draw the unwanted conclusion that the White House could not have been blue.

It is undoubtedly true that if the present theory is right, then there are lots of worlds that contain blue buildings that (otherwise) look like the White House, are even called "the White House," are similarly situated, function in the same complex way that the White House functions in the actual world, and so forth. These worlds may also contain people who speak a language internally indistinguishable from English, and who say "The White House is blue." It is crucial to see that when they say this, they are expressing a true proposition, but *not* the proposition that we express when we utter the same words. Their propositions are simply not about the house that ours is about. So their worlds are not worlds in which the proposition *that the White House is blue* is true. What is true, in such a world, is a proposition to the effect that some other house, one that happens to be similar in many ways to the White House, is blue.

Proponents of concrete worlds address this problem by regarding entities in other worlds (like the houses just imagined) as "surrogates" or "counterparts" of the White House. These counterparts, collectively, manifest all of the nonactual possibilities for the White House. More generally, proponents hold that there is a two-place relation – the "counterpart" relation – that holds between every entity (in every world) and itself, and often holds between entities that occupy different worlds. Now suppose that x is any entity in any world, and P is any property. Then the (singular) proposition *that x has property P* is *possible* iff there exists an entity y such that y is a counterpart of x and the proposition *that y has property P* is true. (Notice that y may be identical with x, so that the singular propositions of this form that happen to be true conveniently wind up being possible.) We may state this a little less formally as follows: It's possible for a given entity to have a given property iff some counterpart of that entity has that property. [Exercise: **Give the appropriate analyzing condition for the** *necessity* **of the same singular proposition.**]

In order for this approach to be plausible, a concrete world theorist will have to say enough about the counterpart relation to give it some independent credibility. This is not an easy task, and we will not undertake it here. It is, however, closely related to our problems (2) and (3).

Problem (2). It is certainly conceivable that reality is composed of distinct concrete spatiotemporal realms, no two of which are physically accessible to each other. But there are many different ways in which this is conceivable. For example, it is conceivable that there be a total of two such realms. Or eleven. Or an infinitude. But if the concrete world theorist is right, then most of these seeming possibilities for reality are really not possible after all. At the very least, the finite ones are certainly not. The reason is that a mere finite number of such realms can't provide the ontological basis for all of the genuine possibilities that we normally acknowledge.

To see this, imagine that there are exactly n such detached realms. Then each one of them contains a certain total number of dogs (past, present, and future). Either they all contain infinitely many dogs, or at least one contains only finitely many dogs (allowing the possibility of zero). If they all contain infinitely many dogs, then there is no realm in which the proposition *that there are finitely many dogs* is true. But this conflicts with something we all accept: that it is possible that there be (only) finitely many dogs. Now suppose that at least one of the realms has only finitely many dogs. Since there are only finitely many realms with finitely many dogs, at least one of them must have at least as many dogs as every other such realm. Suppose that this maximal number is k. Then there is no realm in which the proposition *that there are exactly k + 1 dogs* is true. But surely this proposition is also possible. Therefore the supposition that there are only finitely many detached concrete realms is incompatible with concrete world theory and various simple possibilities that we normally accept. Ironically, one of these simple possibilities is that there be (only) finitely many detached concrete spatiotemporal realms.

The ontological problem for concrete world theory may be summarized as follows. Although the hypothesis of detached concrete realms seems perfectly conceivable, it is just as conceivable that the number of such realms could have been finite. But it cannot be finite if concrete world theory is to give a correct accounting of everyday possibility. So, paradoxically, concrete world theory must reject what seems a clear everyday possibility in the effort to capture everyday possibility. Something has to give. {**Exercise: It also seems possible that there should only be one (connected) spatiotemporal realm. Where would this leave concrete world theory?**}

Problem (3). Suppose there really are infinitely many detached realms, as the concrete world theorist imagines. Why should what goes on in the other realms have anything to do with what is possible for this realm? It's one thing to *call* these realms "possible worlds," but quite another for them to be relevant to actual possibilities. In fact, when we think about the pure ontological picture of all these realms (without the aid of special terminology), it seems *wrong* to regard one of them as the "actual world" and the rest as "other possible worlds." They are all simply detached parts of the one and only actual world. Certainly the world *could* be spatiotemporally scattered, but why should this have any bearing on what is locally possible?

Suppose the world were not scattered in this way, but that it contained a planet in another solar system that was very much like Earth and that included someone very much like you but who had a somewhat different array of talents. Say this person has the same name as you, looks just like you, lives in a town that looks like and has the same name as the town you live in, and so forth. But suppose this person is an excellent pianist (while you are not). Would the circumstance of there existing this person on this faraway planet have anything to do with the question of whether you might have been an excellent pianist? If it seems to have little or no relevance, then would its relevance be enhanced if the planet happened to exist in a spatiotemporally disconnected realm instead of merely far away? On the other hand, if it does seem to be relevant, then how much of its relevance stems from the fact that the person looks like you, has the same name, and so on? After all, this person *isn't* you. Maybe any relevance lies simply in the fact that it shows that human beings can be excellent pianists. But if this is all there is to it, then we don't need another planet in the first place, since we have already had Artur Rubinstein, Thelonious Monk, and legions of others right here at home.

The question of the relevance of the other realms to what is possible in this realm is not an easy one for the concrete world theorist to answer. It is important to see that introducing the "counterpart" relation does not constitute an answer, but rather presupposes that there is one. We need a plausible, independent account of why some blue house in some inaccessible realm deserves to be regarded as a counterpart of the White House. The fact that said house is very similar in many ways to the White House seems to fall short of a satisfactory answer.

(ii) *Abstract Worlds.* A number of different, but essentially similar, treatments of worlds as abstract entities have been proposed. Very roughly, the idea is that the possibilities for the actual world are adequately represented by actually existing abstract entities, like certain *propositions*, all of whose "constituents" actually exist. (This way of putting the matter raises the possibility of a paradox. How can an entity that is only a minor, abstract part of what exists adequately represent everything that exists, including itself? Since worlds are supposed to be "complete," wouldn't such an entity somehow have to be "bigger" than itself? We will not pursue this interesting but very technical question here.)

Here are the rudiments of one abstract treatment of worlds, compressed into three definitions. (1) A proposition is *consistent* iff it is possible for it to be true. (2) A proposition, P, is *maximal* iff for every proposition Q, either P entails Q or else P entails the negation of Q ("not-Q"). (3) A (*possible*) *world* is a proposition that is both consistent and maximal.

One thing to notice about this account is that there is something it cannot do that a concrete world theory can do, namely, *analyze* the modal notions. The reason is that definition (1) depends on the notion of possibility. As a result, abstract world theory can claim at most to offer an enlightening characterization of modality. Needless to say, that would be worthwhile. But it does leave open the question of analysis, and with it, the question of how we come to understand the modal notions.

A second thing to notice is a matter of pure logic. Certainly some propositions are consistent (for example, *that dogs exist*). And certainly some propositions are maximal, since inconsistent propositions entail every proposition. (To see this, notice that "P entails Q" means it is impossible for P to be true *and* Q to be false. Now, if P is inconsistent, then it is impossible for P to be true, period. So, no matter what proposition Q is, it is impossible for P to be true *and* Q to be false.) But it doesn't follow from the fact that some propositions are consistent and some propositions are maximal, that any propositions are both consistent and maximal. So it doesn't follow that there exist any "possible worlds." Thus, one task that an abstract world theorist must accomplish is to convince us that these worlds exist. Then a second task is to convince us that there are enough of them to capture the structure of genuine possibility.

The first task may be approached by trying to find a proposition that characterizes a very simple possibility for the entire world. Suppose we isolate a specific hydrogen atom and call it H. Now consider the proposition (O) *that only H exists*. It certainly seems consistent. And, at the intuitive level, it may seem to characterize a unique total way things might have been. But is it maximal? Probably not. There is, for example, a problem about causal generalizations whose antecedents cannot be realized in such a simple "world." More specifically, consider the claim (C) that immersion in water causes sugar to dissolve. C is certainly true, but it might have been false (say, if the laws of nature had been somewhat different). Moreover, in the "world" characterized by O, no sugar could ever get immersed in any water since neither substance exists. So it does not seem that O entails either C or not-C. But according to the theory, it must entail one or the other.

So it appears that any attempt to specify even a very simple consistent and maximal proposition will meet some significant resistance. (Note that the same sort of example evidently applies just as effectively in the case of an even simpler "world" – the one characterized by the proposition *that nothing exists*.) The hope of finding a proposition that characterizes a very complex world, like the one we inhabit, therefore appears extremely dim. Of course, it does not follow from our inability to specify a consistent and maximal proposition that no such propositions exist. But the burden of proof surely rests with the proponent of the abstract world theory. And even if it can be shown that some abstract worlds exist, it will not follow that enough exist to capture all of the possibilities that we normally acknowledge.

In fact, here is an effort to show that there cannot be enough such worlds. First, we all agree that there could have been entities other than the ones that actually exist, and that there are different possibilities for such "nonactual entities." For example, a certain childless couple ("A and B") might have had a daughter who studied philosophy, but who might not have studied philosophy. Now, some abstract worlds do entail the proposition that A and B have a daughter who studies philosophy. And other abstract worlds entail the proposition that A and B have a daughter who does not study philosophy. But how could any abstract world of the second sort insure that we are dealing with the same daughter? Since A and B never actually *do* have a daughter, there are no singular propositions about any daughter they might have had, the way there are about you and me. Aristotle studied philosophy, but he might not have. This possibility is captured in the abstract theory by any world that entails the proposition *that Aristotle didn't study philosophy*. No similar propositions exist that can cover the present case. [**Exercise: Why won't it suffice to say that some abstract worlds entail the proposition that A and B have a daughter who studies philosophy but who might not have studied philosophy?**]

There is another difficulty (hinted at above) that the abstract theory faces but that we will only mention in passing. Some philosophers have claimed that under certain reasonable and minimal assumptions about sets (or properties), abstract world theory may be shown to be inconsistent. Specifically, they argue that the assumption that there exists a consistent and maximal proposition leads to a contradiction. (The argument is tricky and technical.)

(iii) *Modality without Worlds: The Property-Theoretic Approach*. We have seen two quite different world-theoretic approaches to modality, both of which face some serious difficulties. We now turn to an approach that, like the concrete theory, offers an analysis of modal concepts, but, like the abstract theory, depends on Platonic entities (specifically, properties and relations). Despite these similarities, it may be more promising than either type of world theory.

The central idea behind the present theory is to take the claims of

Platonism about properties and relations very seriously and literally, specifically the claim that properties *constitute* things as being how they are. (It may be a good idea to look again at Section 3.1 before continuing.) Now, with this in mind, let's ask why it's *necessary* that anything that is green is colored. Is it because there are special entities called "possible worlds" (whether abstract or concrete), and that, "in" every such world, all things that instantiate *being green* happen also to instantiate *being colored*? On the face of it, that seems like a pretty roundabout, even unhelpful, answer. Fortunately, it appears that serious Platonists have the resources to reject it.

To be green is to instantiate the property *being green*. To be colored is to instantiate the property *being colored*. It is inconceivable that properties could have these constitutive roles if they were *simple* entities. They must be complex, and their complexity must – somehow or other – enable them to constitute. We will almost certainly never know just how this works since we can't directly observe properties and their internal structures. But if Platonism is correct, it *does* work, one way or another.

The reason it is necessary that everything green is colored is now pretty much staring us in the face. It is that when *being green* constitutes something as green, it *thereby* automatically constitutes it as colored. This might be, for example, because *being colored* is an integral part of *being green* – a "subcomplex." Or it might be for some other reason. At any rate, there is a special relation that holds between the property *being green* and the property *being colored*. We might as well call this relation "entailment" (though "inclusion" would be just as good). After all, even in everyday, nonphilosophical life people sometimes say, "Being green entails [or 'involves'] being colored." (Note that we might also say, "Part of what it is to be green is to be colored," or even, "Being green includes being colored.")

Because the constitutive role of properties is undoubtedly linked to their characteristic kind of inner complexity, the entailment relation is like the *shorter-than* relation – it depends only on *intrinsic properties* of the related entities. (And so we call it an *intrinsic relation*.) In the case of shorter than, A's being shorter than B depends only on the respective heights of A and B (which are, of course, intrinsic features of A and B). In the case of entailment, P's entailing Q depends in some way (whose exact nature we do not know) on intrinsic features of P and Q. Entailment is an intrinsic relation between properties.

Just as one property may entail (or include) another, other properties may be "incompatible with" (or "exclude") each other. For example, *being green* is incompatible with *being purple*. The structures of the two properties do not permit anything to instantiate both (entirely and at the same time). Of course, if P entails Q, then P must be "compatible with" Q. But many properties are compatible with each other even though neither entails the other, for instance *being green* and *being round*.

According to the present theory, the *necessity* that all green things be colored depends solely on the fact that the intrinsic relation of entailment holds between these two properties (in the right order). And the *possibility* that something be both round and green depends solely on the fact that the intrinsic relation of compatibility holds between the two properties. Thus the question arises whether all cases of necessity and possibility may be explained in this general way. Some contemporary property theorists think the answer is affirmative. If they are right, then the properties of necessity and possibility will have an analysis based on the primitive concepts of entailment and compatibility between properties (and, perhaps, generalizations of these notions to the case of relations).

There are two major problems confronting the property-theoretic approach. First, a plausible and rigorous theory of properties must be advanced and defended. Such a theory must evidently be, in effect, a new branch of mathematics, much like set theory. Several promising efforts in this direction have already been made, but so far nothing like a consensus has formed, even among Platonists. Modern property theory is truly in its infancy. The main impediment to consensus is not so much the mathematical difficulty of the project as it is the variety of different *philosophical conceptions of properties*. Property theorists need consensus here in order to know which conception to try to capture in their formal theorizing. At the same time, we already do know that several different mathematical projects along these lines are viable, and that the present approach to modality may be accommodated within more than one of them.

A second problem for this approach (as so far described) is that it is confined to so-called modality *de dicto* – necessity and possibility as properties of propositions. But many metaphysicians hold that there is a type of modality that is not reducible to the *de dicto* variety. This claimed species of modality is sometimes called *de re*, and we turn to it now. We will later ask whether *de re* modality creates a serious problem for the property-theoretic approach.

8.3 Essentialism

In *de dicto* modality, the modal concept applies to the statement or pro-position ("dictum"). But some philosophers claim that another type of modality applies, *via* properties and relations, to arbitrary *things* (hence the term *"de re:"* of the thing). (This purported distinction parallels the distinction between *de dicto* and *de re* belief discussed in chapter 4.) Thus, in addition to ordinary properties like *being red* and *being human*, there would be *modal* properties like *being possibly red* and *being necessarily human*. Things that actually instantiate *being green* may nevertheless also instantiate *being possibly red*; and things that actually instantiate *being human* may also instantiate the further, distinct property of *being necessarily human*.

The difference between *de dicto* and *de re* modality may be explained vividly by appealing to possible worlds in the following ontologically neutral, *metaphorical* way. Imagine that there are (perhaps in God's mind) innumerably many "possible worlds," that only one of them is actual (that is, only one corresponds to our spatiotemporal surroundings), but that entities existing in our world may also exist "in" other possible worlds. So, for example, there are worlds in which you exist but never read this sentence, there are worlds in which you exist but I do not (and vice versa), and so on. Finally, to say that a proposition is *possible* means that it is true in some world or other, and to say that it is *necessary* means that it is true in all worlds.

Now consider the following two claims:

(1) Necessarily, something exists;

(2) Something necessarily exists.

(1) evidently asserts that the proposition *that something exists* is necessary, that is, true in all possible worlds. So (1) conforms to the *de dicto* conception of modality. But (2) does not, or at least there is a reading on which it does not. On this *"de re"* reading, it says that something has the property of *necessary existence*: in other words, that some actually existing thing instan-tiates this modal property. So understood, (2) goes beyond (1), for (1) could be true even if all of the actually existing things were contingent entities, but (2) could not. The truth of (1) requires only that in each possible world, something or other exists. But the truth of (2) requires that some actually

existing thing also exist in all other possible worlds. (1) and (2) are therefore parallel to the following belief assertions.

(3)   Sally believes that some people are dishonest.

(4)   Some people are believed by Sally to be dishonest.

(3) can be true even if there is no specific person whose honesty Sally doubts, but (4) cannot be true under these circumstances.

Unfortunately, there is some confusion over the question of just how the modal properties behave. To illustrate this, first consider the property (S) of *being self-identical*. Of course everything has this nonmodal property. Now consider *being necessarily self-identical*. It is certainly necessary that everything instantiates S. That is, there are no worlds in which any entity fails to be self-identical. But this does not guarantee that everything is necessarily self-identical since, as we just saw, necessity *de re* does not automatically follow from necessity *de dicto*. But what does it mean to say that a thing *x* is necessarily self-identical in the first place? In particular, does it imply that *x* exists in every possible world? It may be possible to hear it in a way that carries this implication and also in a way that does not. Let's avoid this question by adopting a technical device. We'll say that *x* is *essentially self-identical* if *x* is self-identical in every world in which *x* exists. *Being essentially self-identical* is then a modal property that contingent entities may have. (It's identical with *being necessarily self-identical* on *one* of its readings, but not on the other.) Then, if we say that *being self-identical* is an "essential" property of *x*, this is just a loose way of saying that *x* has the modal property *being essentially self-identical*. (It does not mean that *being self-identical* is a modal property.) Notice that since it is necessary that everything is self-identical, it follows that everything is essentially self-identical.

Now, it is easy to believe that properties like *being self-identical* are essential to their instances because it is a truth of logic that everything is self-identical, and there are no possible worlds in which truths of logic are false. So *being self-identical* is a trivial essential property of its instances, in the sense that everything is guaranteed by mere logic to instantiate it. This raises the question whether things may also have *nontrivial* essential properties. The claim that they do is called *essentialism*. Aristotle was an early proponent of a form of essentialism, but for most of the twentieth century the doctrine has generally been considered absurd or, at least, clearly false.

145

Let's examine two claims about essentialism that led many philosophers to reject it.

First, it was held that the placement of the modal adverbs "necessarily" and "possibly" in typical English sentences had no effect on their meanings. For example, a sentence like (2) was claimed to be just a variation on (1), differing not at all in meaning. Since the only clear interpretation of (1) is the *de dicto*, that must also be the sense of (2). Proponents of this view bolstered their position with the claim that there simply was no way to associate a clear and different meaning with sentences featuring the "inner" placement of the modal terms. In other words, there was no clear way to make semantic sense of supposed *de re* modality.

But we just saw that, aided by the idea of possible worlds, we *are* able to draw a principled distinction between the propositions expressed by (1) and (2). It is true that our appeal to worlds was metaphorical, but it was also unnecessary. Developments in modal logic and its semantics (for example in the work of the American philosophers Ruth Barcan Marcus and Saul Kripke) showed in a precise and formal way that this criticism of *de re* modality was simply incorrect, and so gave new life to the question of essentialism. But even without these developments, and even without possible worlds of any sort, it should have been suspected that the meanings of (1) and (2) differ. The reason is that (2) evidently claims that some actually existing entity or other meets some specific condition, but (1) does not. (Here the parallel with (3) and (4) is also useful.)

The second (very influential) objection to essentialism began with a minor concession. It was held that it can sometimes make sense to attribute a modal property to a thing, but only when that thing is described or referred to in certain ways. It cannot make sense to attribute modal properties to things independently of description (or mode of reference). So, for example, consider Bill Clinton. He is the president (of the USA in 1996), and he is Hillary's husband. If we refer to Clinton as "the president," then he isn't necessarily married, but if we refer to him as "Hillary's husband," then he is. Such examples led some to conclude that any *absolute* attribution of a modal property to a thing must be absurd, since a thing may have a certain modal property "under one description" but not under another.

The proponents of essentialism claimed that the argument that is implicit here is either incoherent or invalid. Let's assume that it makes good sense to speak of an entity "having a property under a description." (Of course if it doesn't, then the premises won't make sense, and we won't

146

have a coherent argument.) Then the general form of the argument is as follows.

(5)   *x* has property P under description D;

(6)   *x* does not have property P under description D*; **Therefore:**

(7)   The idea that *x* could have P independently of any description is absurd (as is the idea that *x* could fail to have P).

Either every argument of this form is valid or every such argument is invalid, regardless of the nature of P (in particular, regardless of whether P happens to be a *modal* property). To see that the form is in fact invalid, let *x* be Bill Clinton, let D be the description "Hillary's husband," and let D* be the description "the president," but let P be the (nonmodal) property of *being married*. Then (5) and (6) would have to be true under any reasonable construal of having a property under a description, but (7) is clearly false. Certainly the individual entity, Bill Clinton, instantiates the property of *being married* regardless of how or even whether he is described (or referred to). The fact that he is married is in no relevant way linguistic in nature (though, of course, we cannot express it without using language, and becoming married may involve engaging in some linguistic activity). It simply does not depend on any descriptions of (or references to) Clinton now being made or even being available. And according to proponents of essentialism, switching to a modal property would not affect this conclusion at all. It makes just as much sense to claim that an entity has a modal property independently of descriptions as it does to claim that it has a nonmodal property.

So representative efforts to undermine modality *de re*, and hence essentialism, seem anything but conclusive. Moreover, proponents of essentialism, notably Kripke, began to make arguments in favor of the doctrine. These arguments were often accompanied by efforts to dispel confusions held to underlie resistance to the doctrine. Just as the second argument against *de re* modality seemed to involve the irrelevant introduction of linguistic considerations, Kripke would claim that initial resistance to specific examples of (nontrivial) essential properties often rested on similar confusions. Chief among these was the confusion of necessity with *analyticity*.

A true declarative sentence is called *analytic* if its truth depends only on the meanings (and arrangements) of the words it contains (and not upon nonlinguistic facts in the external world); otherwise it is called *synthetic*.

By this standard, "Hillary's husband is married" is analytic, but "The president is married" is synthetic. Analyticity is thus fundamentally a linguistic concept — it explicitly concerns the meanings of occurrences of words in sentences. But necessity is not. Necessity either attaches to a proposition or else to an entity by way of a property. (Of course, the occurrences of a given univocal sentence might express a necessary proposition, and this might lead us to call the sentence necessary in a derivative sense. But that wouldn't make the notion of necessity linguistic in nature.) So analyticity and necessity are two distinct concepts, fundamentally applying to different sorts of entities. But even philosophers sensitive to these distinctions often assumed, first, that a sentence (-token) expresses a necessary proposition only if it is analytic, and second, that an entity has a property essentially only if the sentence expressing the proposition that the thing has the property is analytic. Kripke urged that these assumptions were unwarranted and offered what he took to be everyday counterexamples.

As a counterexample to the first assumption, Kripke offered (for example) the proposition that all whales are mammals, which seems necessary even though the sentence "All whales are mammals" is certainly not analytic. (That the proposition is necessary is supported by the following thought experiment: Suppose we came upon a creature which, by all outward appearances, seemed to be a whale. We might very naturally assume it was a whale. But if we subsequently discovered it wasn't a mammal, we would not conclude that some whales are nonmammals, but rather that we had been wrong to think it was a whale in the first place.) But let us now turn to the *de re* case, which is of more immediate concern.

A frequently used example of Kripke's goes like this. Suppose we are in a room containing a table that is, in fact, made of wood. Then, according to Kripke and other essentialists, *being made of wood* is an essential property of that particular object. But if we point at the table and say "This table is made of wood," we certainly are not uttering an analytic sentence. Nor would we be if we said "T is made of wood," with "T" a proper name of the object.

But Kripke held that these failures of analyticity did not in any way undercut the essentialist claim. He proposed a thought experiment: Try to imagine a possible situation in which this very table would not have been made of wood. And he claimed that no matter how our imaginings proceed, if they ultimately involve a nonwooden table, then the situation is better described as one in which we are not considering this very table at all, but rather some other table. Many people who initially found essentialism absurd were convinced by this strategy, and concluded that they had rejected the doctrine hastily, usually on the basis of confusions like the one involving analyticity. Let's look at a few attempts at the thought experiment.

(1)   Imagine someone sneaked into the room the night before and replaced the table with a plastic table artfully (?) detailed so as to look and feel like the original. That's a situation in which we might have falsely said "This table is made of wood" (if we were fooled), or else truly said "This table is made of plastic." But it clearly isn't a case in which the original table would not have been made of wood. In fact, the very description of the case gives this away. The original table – the one claimed to have the essential property – has been replaced by another table. It's this *other* table that isn't made of wood, not the original.

(2)   Imagine that when the wooden components of the table were coming down the assembly line at the table factory, a worker stole them, substituting similar-looking plastic components. Then, at the end of the line, another worker assembled the plastic components into a table, which subsequently was shipped to the university and placed in this room. The thief used the wooden parts to build a rocking chair for his TV room. In this situation we again might (wrongly) say "This table is made of wood," or we might do a careful inspection and say "This table is made of plastic." But either way, we aren't talking about the original table. In this situation, the original table doesn't even exist, so it isn't a situation in which the original wooden table is made of something other than wood.

(3)   Here is a more difficult case. Suppose, prior to the thought experiment, that the original table is in fact a very old wooden table that has been in this room for over 400 years. (Say we're in Oxford.) Now comes the thought experiment. Imagine that beginning about 400 years ago, some elves began sneaking into this room at night and replacing matchstick-sized parts of the table with similar-looking and similar-feeling pieces of plastic. They conceived this as a long-term project designed to result in a total replacement of all of the wood in the table by plastic. They knew the table was in the Philosophy Department and took joy in the thought that some metaphysicians might ultimately be deceived. (By around the late

1950s the project was complete, and the elves contented themselves with listening in on classes to reap their harvest of mirth. They were not unrewarded.) Here, it might be thought, is at last a possible situation in which the original table really would not have been made of wood.

Now, it ought to be conceded by all that, without further argumentation, it really isn't absolutely clear that the ultimate plastic table is the same table as the one the elves started working on four centuries ago. (For one thing, it certainly doesn't seem to be the same physical object.) And if it isn't the same table as the one the elves started working on, then it isn't the table that's *actually* before us in the room either, since that table *is* (in fact, by hypothesis) the one the elves started working on. So, on this option, the thought experiment is another apparent failure.

But suppose we decide (for some philosophical reason or other) that, within the thought experiment, the ultimate plastic table really is the same table as the one the elves started working on. Then it looks like we have to concede that the original (actual) table might not have been made of wood *right now*. So, *being made of wood right now* wouldn't be an essential property of the (actually wooden) table. Fair enough. But an essentialist can reply that this just means we weren't quite careful enough in selecting our candidate for essentiality. We should have selected, say, *having been originally made of wood*. Then the thought experiment would fail, and we would still have a plausible example of a nontrivial essential property of an ordinary physical thing.

Thought experiments like the ones just described convinced many philosophers that the much maligned doctrine of essentialism was, after all, true. If nothing else, this provided a telling example of the dangers of philosophical complacency and the deceptive difficulty of some philosophical concepts. For not only were people changing their view on a very fundamental question, they were changing it from a view they had formerly held to be *obviously* true.

8.4   A Property-Theoretic Response

Can the property-theoretic account of modality deal adequately with necessity *de re*? A better question might be: Should it? In this brief section we will see (perhaps ironically) that the *de re* conclusions of the essentialists' thought experiments may actually be unwarranted. If this is right, then property-theoretic modality may not need any revision or extension.

Let's reconsider the thought experiment involving the elves (and also recall the options for dealing with the house that acquired shutters in chapter 4.) We already noted that the plastic object present in the room today did not seem to be the same *physical object* as the wooden object present four centuries ago. After all, the elves might have saved the wooden parts they removed and might have reassembled them in just the way they were originally related to one another. If so, it certainly seems that that object is a much better candidate for being the same physical object as the original wooden object than is the plastic one now present. But it may be one thing to be "the same physical object" and quite another thing to be "the same table."

It is very natural to think that a physical object, regardless of its nature, function, origin, etc., is really just an aggregate of parts, and that when any parts change, so does the object (though the new object may still have many parts in common with the old). Suppose we take this view seriously. (We will discuss it more fully in chapter 9.) Then, if you change the tires on your car, the result is a different physical object from the one you started with. But, of course, we don't want to say it's a different car. It's "the same car," but with different tires. What many metaphysicians haven't noticed is that there is no contradiction here at all. Saying it's a different object doesn't force us to say it's a different car.

What is it for a *car* or a *table* to exist? According to a property theorist, it's simply for an object to exist that instantiates the property *being a car* or the property *being a table*. And for each car (or table, etc.), there is also the property of *being that* (specific) *car* (etc.). What is crucial to see now is that there is nothing to prevent different *objects* from instantiating, say, the property of *being that car* at different times (or in different possible situations). Since it would be terribly inconvenient (with the Department of Motor Vehicles, etc.) to think that you have a new car every time you replace an old part, our concept of car provides very generous leeway for change of parts over time. (Exactly how much leeway is an interesting question, but one we won't consider.) Same for tables, human bodies, and so forth. From the present perspective, this means that the "same car as" relation is simply not the identity relation. Instead it is some kind of similarity relation. (See chapter 4.) To say that x is the same car as y is merely to say that there is a specific "car-property" that they both instantiate. They may or may not happen to be a single physical object.

And so our mischievous elves may not be quite as smart as they think. They have succeeded in replacing the original table with a distinct, in fact entirely nonoverlapping, physical object that is also a table. But on the present view it may nevertheless be "the same table." That is, it may instantiate the same (specific) table-property.

Now let's return to the thought experiments. They all have the same general shape. First, we consider an ordinary object, like a wooden table. Second, we convince ourselves that there is some nontrivial property (like *being originally made of wood*) that it has and that we cannot imagine its not having. Third, we infer that this property is "essential to that table." Fourth, we conclude that there are nontrivial cases of *de re* necessity, that is, we conclude that there are cases in which physical objects have nontrivial essential properties – that essentialism is true.

Now, I think that a careful property theorist can claim that two things have gone wrong here. (1) The fourth step doesn't follow from the third. We already have the means to see why. Property theorists can construe the third step as meaning that the nontrivial property in question is one that *any* object instantiating the relevant table-property would have to have. In other words, *being that table* (T) entails (say) *being originally made of wood* (W). But it doesn't follow from this that any physical object that happened to instantiate T would *itself* have any nontrivial essential properties at all.

Let's be careful to see that this is correct (on the present property-theoretic view). The first thing to notice is that the fact that T entails W supports (in the theory) the strictly *de dicto* claim that it is necessary that anything having T also has W. It doesn't support any *de re* claim at all. So, as a merely logical matter, step four doesn't follow from step three. The second thing to notice depends on the "aggregate-of-parts" conception of physical objects. On this view a given piece of wood – say the original instance of T – need not have been made of wood! The atoms in question might have been arranged in such a way that the object wasn't wood. Yet it would still be the same object. So, not only does step four not *follow* from step three, it even seems *false*.

Mistake (1) is the notion that the thought experiments support *de re* necessity. The property theorist has claimed that they don't because *de re* modality only appears in the invalid step four. But there is another problem with step four. (2) The very identification of essentialism with *de re* modality is suspect. Why is the (step-three) fact that W is entailed by T not *already* an "essentialist" claim? After all, it captures the core of the thought experiment: that nothing could be "this table" unless it had property W. This is precisely the sort of claim that the opponents of "essentialism" wanted to reject. The thought experiments seem to establish that these critics were wrong. But what they don't establish is that there is any nontrivial modality *de re*.

It therefore appears that there is room for a property-theoretic account of modality that accommodates essentialist "intuitions," but without making any appeal to nontrivial *de re* necessity.

9

Things and Their Parts

Ordinary things, like chairs, planets, and trees, apparently endure over intervals of time. During the time an ordinary thing exists, it undergoes changes. Sometimes these changes are comparatively small, but sometimes they are drastic. What is it that makes a thing at a given time be "the same thing" as a thing at a later time that may have very little or nothing in common with it? Is this a clear and unambiguous question? It looks like a question about the identity relation, but it is really? Why is it that things of certain kinds can tolerate major changes, but things of other kinds cannot? What is a *thing* in the first place? We have already touched on a couple of these questions, both in chapter 4 (with the house that acquired shutters) and in chapter 8 (with the table and the elves). In this chapter we will take a more comprehensive look at these questions and other closely related matters. For simplicity, we will confine our attention to purely physical things. The terms "thing," "object," and "entity" will be used interchangeably.

9.1   A General Conception of Things

People used to think that many visible objects like chunks of gold were "solid matter" or "solid stuff" – in other words, that they included no unoccupied regions of space within their outer boundaries. On this picture, if you were lucky enough to have an acorn-sized lump of pure gold, then every point within its boundaries would be occupied by "gold-stuff."

We now know that this is wrong, at least assuming that something approximating the atomic theory of matter is right. In fact, it's wrong for three different reasons. First, there is unoccupied space between adjacent gold atoms. Second, there is unoccupied space within individual gold atoms, for example between the nucleus and the electron "cloud." Third, no mere point within the boundary of the sample, even if it is occupied by stuff, is occupied by gold-stuff, because gold doesn't come in point-sized amounts. It takes an entire atom to count as gold, so occupied points within an atom are not occupied by stuff that is itself gold (though they are occupied by stuff that is part of some gold).

An important consequence is that ordinary things that are large enough to be seen with the naked eye are what philosophers call *scattered* (or discontinuous) objects, even though they don't look scattered. But these are not the only scattered objects. In everyday life we often regard what are visibly scattered arrays of things as constituting single objects. A good example is a disassembled bicycle. We do not think a bicycle goes out of existence when it is taken apart for repair. (If you know that your (sole) bike is presently disassembled in some repair shop, and someone asks whether you own a bicycle, you will reply that you do.) Of course the same story holds for any artifact that has component parts that can be readily disassembled. And we also seem to recognize visibly scattered natural objects, like flocks of geese, groves of trees, and galaxies. So it appears that visibly scattered objects are actually quite common in our everyday lives. (A scattered object is sometimes called a "mereological sum" – or just "sum" – of the objects that are its nonoverlapping parts. This terminology is convenient, but it is important to keep in mind that being a sum doesn't require any bringing together or attaching of the objects constituting the sum. *Mereology* is the theory of parts and wholes. We will be concerned with mereological sums throughout this chapter.)

Now, here is a radical-sounding philosophical idea. Just as the visibly scattered parts of your bicycle constitute a single thing, so do the members of *any* collection of things in spacetime. In other words, any collection of things has a sum. Call this theory Q. Let's try to ease into Q by starting with a very simple example. According to Q, your wristwatch (minus its strap) and the baseball that Henry Aaron hit for the home run that broke Babe Ruth's career home run record comprise a single thing. A likely reaction to this claim is: "C'mon, that's two things, not one!"

Well, it is certainly true that the watch and the ball are two things. Each of them completely fills up a very complex, scattered region of spacetime. But there is another complex, scattered region of spacetime that is also completely filled with material stuff: the region made up of all the spacetime points of both of these regions. On the present theory, the stuff that fills up this region constitutes just as legitimate a physical object as does the stuff that fills up either of the others.

The tendency to react this way is very natural. Its source is that we see the watch and the ball as too dissimilar and too unrelated to constitute a single thing. But this tendency generally fades away when we fully appreciate two features of the situation. First, the dissimilarity is really irrelevant. Many parts of your bike are also quite dissimilar from each other, for example, a tire (T) and the speedometer (S). **[Exercise: Think of other artifacts that can easily be taken apart and that have even more dramatically dissimilar components.]** The second point has to do with relatedness: There is nothing about T and S *in themselves* that relates them in *any* way that T is not *also* related to any other, indistinguishable speedometer (S*) that has never been part of a bike.

It's worth thinking about this more generally and in some detail. Sometimes things are related as a consequence of how they are *intrinsically*, that is, in themselves. For example, if A is shorter than B, then this is a consequence of intrinsic features of A and B, namely, their heights. Let's call relations with this feature *intrinsic*. Other relations between A and B depend on things external to them. For example, if A is the brother of B, then this depends on entities external to A and B, namely, their parents. Relations of this sort are called *extrinsic*. Using this terminology, we are saying that the intrinsic relations that hold between T and S also hold between T and S*. So any relation that holds between T and S but *not* between T and S* must be an extrinsic relation. Here are two examples: T and S are related by being parts of the same bike, but T and S* are not. Also, T and S are related by having the same owner, but T and S* (we may assume) are not.

Now let's go back to the watch (W) and the baseball (B). The reason we don't normally regard them as constituting a single physical object is simply that the extrinsic relations in which they stand are not of any particular interest to us. **[Exercise: Give examples of extrinsic relations between W and B.]** But it isn't hard to imagine that they might have had more interesting extrinsic relations, ones that could result in our acknowledging their sum.

For example, suppose W is a high-quality calendar watch that displays the day of the week and the date (including the year), as well as the time. Imagine that you were in the stands on the occasion of the record-breaking homer, and that you in fact caught the ball. When you gave the ball to

Aaron after the game, you told him that just after catching the ball you noticed the time on your watch, and that the total visual image of the ball in your hands and your watch on your wrist would stay with you forever because the moment was so magical. He asked to see your watch. When he saw it was a calendar model, an idea struck. He wanted to buy the watch, have a jeweler freeze its settings to reflect the exact moment when you caught the ball, and then have an artisan embed the watch symmetrically into the surface of the ball for display in the Hall of Fame. It would come to be known as "the watchball" (which would carry a double meaning since the period leading up to the great event had been known by baseball fans the world over as "the watch"). The watchball would, of course, be disassembled for cleaning from time to time by the curator of the Hall of Fame. (The watch-part would go to a jeweler for polishing.) But the watchball would not go out of existence during these episodes any more than your bike does while under repair.

Now, let's remind ourselves that we're striving for a general account of what it is to be a physical object. We have seen that being visibly scattered is no impediment. And we have seen that dissimilarity of detached parts doesn't matter. Also, a specific visibly scattered collection of things is sometimes regarded by us as a single thing while other, intrinsically indistinguishable collections are not. **[Exercise: Give clear examples of this.]**

It therefore seems that whether we *regard* a given collection as a single thing is entirely dependent on our interests and activities, and not at all on the physical natures of the things involved. It also seems that the property of *being a physical thing* is one that really shouldn't have anything to do with our interests, activities, or whether we happen to regard something as instantiating it. After all, it's a property that many things would have had even if we had never existed. It's hard to think of a clearer case of a property that ought to be *intrinsic* to its instances. So a metaphysically satisfactory account of physical things should not restrict them to those that we ordinarily count as things. At the very least (and in harmony with the above examples) such an account should include all sums of contemporaneous, visibly scattered things.

The theory Q includes all of these, but it also includes sums of things that are scattered temporally. Temporally scattered objects may be a little harder to accept at first, but this is really just another reflection of our interests and activities. And in fact there are some everyday examples that we evidently do accept. A good one is the polar ice cap. It periodically melts and "refreezes." There are also lakes and streams that dry up, only to refill later. These entities have a temporally discontinuous existence. We nevertheless regard them as single things because their temporally scattered parts are extrinsically related to each other in ways that figure importantly in our interests and activities. Now, it is true that in these cases there are important similarities among the temporally scattered parts, but we already saw that similarity isn't relevant in the case of contemporaneous sums. Nor should it be relevant here. [**Exercise: Try to give a case of a generally accepted, temporally scattered object, whose temporally continuous parts are not very similar to each other.**]

It may now seem that Q is a sensible theory of physical objects, even if it originally seemed excessive. But there is a problem. Q depends on a prior notion of "thing" since, in effect, all it tells us is that any bunch of *things* constitutes another thing (no matter where the original things happen to be in spacetime). This didn't cause trouble for the kinds of examples we considered above, but how *small* do things get? And how *brief*? Most people would probably say an atom is a thing, and that a proton is a thing, but what about the northern half of a proton? Or what about the part of a proton that exists only at a specific instant of time? Examples like these are more likely to produce bafflement than general accord.

One solution is to continue in our liberal ways, and simply admit all such things. This approach is very much in the spirit that led to accepting normally unacknowledged sums. The key idea there was that even though we might not have any use for them, these things are intrinsically no different from sums that we do have use for and, in fact, accept. The same seems to be true of the very small and the very brief. So let's agree to extend Q as far as possible in this direction, too. One nice consequence is that we may then state the theory very efficiently: Q now says simply that the stuff of any fully occupied region of spacetime constitutes a physical object (no matter how small, how large, how brief, how lengthy, how compact, how disconnected, how diffuse, etc., it may happen to be). After all, the stuff is physical stuff and it occupies a definite spatiotemporal region. Nothing else should matter.

Our theory is now completely general and no longer rests on a prior notion of "thing." It depends on the primitive notion of stuff and the primitive relation of occupancy between quantities of stuff and regions of spacetime. Q is undoubtedly somewhat idealized. It needs to be revised so as to conform with quantum theory and relativity theory (or whatever the ultimate physical theory might be). But there are two compelling reasons why we shouldn't worry about that now. One is that there is no general agreement on the proper interpretation of (for example) quantum theory, even among those who accept it. But the project of revising Q certainly cannot be done independently of settling on a clear interpretation. The second reason is that nothing that follows will depend on having an ultimate formulation of Q.

Q is in some ways a fairly "weak" theory. To see this, suppose that two nonoverlapping regions of space are both fully occupied by stuff at the instant t. Then, according to Q, there is a thing in each region (as well as a thing in the total region). Let's call them T and T*. It seems clear that T and T* are distinct – after all, they have to be constituted by different stuff (since the stuff that is here cannot also be there). But even if this is clearly true, nothing in Q guarantees it. Of course, if we like, we can easily extend Q so as to insure the distinctness of entities like T and T*. But now let's turn to a different case, one that isn't so obvious.

Suppose R is a region of space that is fully occupied by stuff at the instant t and also at the instant $t*$, later than t. Do we *automatically* have *two* entities in such a case? Many philosophers hold that the answer is no, claiming that "stuff can persist through time" (and hence – given Q – that objects can persist through time). But others claim the opposite. On the former view, time is like a river that is flowing past objects, with the result that the same object exists at different times. On the latter view, the passage of time is better represented by a movie, with the images on the screen playing the role of physical objects in the world. In a movie, new images keep appearing and replacing others, which then cease to exist. This is true even in a film of totally motionless and unchanging objects, where the new images are indistinguishable from the ones they replace. So, on this view, the stuff that comprises the universe is continuously being replaced by brand new stuff, sometimes indistinguishable from the stuff it replaces. The theory Q is designed to be neutral between wading in the river and going to the movies. But we could modify it so as to capture either metaphor.

In order to conform to the river image, we would modify Q as follows. First, since we want physical objects to be (at most) three-dimensional, Q can no longer hold that the stuff occupying *any* (fully occupied) spacetime region constitutes a thing. Instead, things are constituted by the stuff occupying (fully occupied) *instantaneous* spacetime regions. Second, we need a principle to the effect that things are "determined by" stuff, so that if a certain quantity of stuff persists over an interval of time, then a single physical object – the one determined by the stuff – persists over the same interval, and therefore exists at many different times. That's how we make room for the river effect. Now, this leaves a loose end, namely, all the other fully occupied spacetime regions. They're all fully occupied by physical stuff, so, if they aren't physical objects, what are they? One answer is that they are physical *events*. For example, consider the stuff existing in a certain region at time t. It constitutes an object, say x. Now suppose x persists until the later time t^*. Then there is a four-dimensional spacetime region, R, fully occupied by precisely the same stuff that constitutes x. It is easy to see that any temporal cross-section of this region is fully occupied by the same stuff as any other (and by the same stuff that fully occupies R itself). Then the event constituted by the stuff occupying R is the event of x's persisting from t to t^* (and perhaps changing its position, the arrangement of its parts, and other properties). Events constituted by discontinuous regions may seem somewhat less natural, but we do have the linguistic means to describe them. [**Exercise: Give an example. Also, argue by means of examples that we would not yet have an adequate theory of events because it would conflate what are intuitively distinct events.**]

It's a little easier to make Q conform to the movie idea. We retain the original conception of there being an object for every fully occupied region, but we add to it the principle that if the regions are different, then so must be the stuff and, therefore, the objects. Then, in addition to objects of zero, one, two, and three dimensions (all spatial), we also have temporally extended objects (of one, two, three, and four dimensions). For now, we will not make a choice between the river and the movie. Instead we will turn to a metaphysical position that seems to go nicely with Q under either modification.

9.2 Mereological Essentialism

The everyday examples we discussed earlier featured things – like bicycles – that have readily detachable parts. Certainly we often use the term "part" in such a way that only detachable components count. But, obviously, if we adopt a theory like Q, then things are going to have "parts" in a much more general sense. If an (appropriate) region R is fully occupied, and so contains a thing T, then any subregion of R must also be fully occupied and hence contain a thing. As long as the subregion is other than R itself, that thing

160

will be a part of T that is different from T itself – a *proper* part. In general, most of the parts of a thing will not be readily detachable components like what we normally think of as the parts of a bicycle.

Now let's consider a modal question. Suppose we accept some theory like Q. And suppose we have an arbitrary thing, T, constituted by some arbitrary stuff in an arbitrary (appropriate) region R. The question is: Could T have been constituted by different stuff? We are *not* asking whether R could have been fully occupied by different stuff. Surely it could have. And we are *not* asking whether T could have occupied some region other than R. Surely that is also possible. The question is whether there could have been a region containing stuff that constituted T, but which either included some stuff that isn't actually in R, or else excluded some stuff that actually is in R (or both).

Because Q sees things as constituted by stuff, and because the concept of part appropriate to Q is the very general one just mentioned, our question can be posed a little more simply: Could T have had different parts? That is, could T have had a part that it does not actually have, or lacked a part that it actually does have (or both)? There are two considerations that strongly favor a *negative* answer. In other words, they favor the view that any physical thing has all of its (actual) parts *essentially*, a view that is known as the principle of "mereological essentialism." **[Exercise: Argue that if *x* has all of its (actual) parts essentially, then it could not have had any parts in addition to its actual parts.]** The first consideration favoring this view is a two-part thought experiment.

Part One: Imagine that we have an arbitrary thing. We might as well stick with T because we haven't said anything about it that would compromise its arbitrariness. So we know nothing about the specific features of T: not what *kind* of object it is, whether it is visible, whether it is visibly scattered, temporally scattered, large, small, etc. But let's assume that T does have proper parts. Now let P be any proper part of T. Then there is also a third thing in the situation: the thing consisting of all of T except for the part P. Let's call this part D. (So T is the sum of P and D.) Now imagine a situation that is as much like this as possible, but from which P is entirely missing. This certainly seems like a situation in which D exists and T does not. It doesn't seem like a situation in which T still exists, but doesn't have the part P. (If we described it this way, would T be identical with D or would D be a different proper part of T?) It seems that we would need some special reason to think that T exists in this situation. But the ground rules of the thought experiment provide no such special reason.

The only natural conclusion is the one that first came to mind: We have described a situation in which D exists and T doesn't. Part One of the experiment therefore suggests strongly that an arbitrary thing could not have failed to have any of the parts it actually has.

Part Two: Start again with T arbitrary, and imagine there is a further (arbitrary) thing A that has no parts in common with T. Now try to imagine a situation that is as much like this as possible, but in which A is a part of T. This seems very hard to do. If we could do it, then why wouldn't the original situation *already* be one in which A is part of T? To put it a little differently, we're trying to imagine a situation in which we have an entity that has exactly the same parts as the original T, but nevertheless isn't T. It's only a proper part of T. Moreover, this situation is supposed to include another entity that has exactly the same parts as the original A. But now it's part of T. Of course the configurations of stuff in spacetime needn't have changed at all. (There doesn't seem to be any way of changing them that would matter! In fact, we don't even know what they are, apart from the fact that A and T have no parts in common in the original.) Now notice this. If there were such a possible situation, then it would violate Part One of the experiment. For the *original* situation would then be one in which a thing (T) failed to have a part that it had in another situation (namely, the part A).

This thought experiment makes it seem very unnatural to think that any thing could have had parts different from those it actually has. But many will object that the experiment was unfair because we weren't allowed to know what *kind* of thing T was. If we had known that T was, say, an automobile, then it would have been easy to imagine a situation in which T lacked a part it actually has (or had a part it actually lacked). This sets up the second consideration in favor of mereological essentialism.

Suppose we now know that T is your car, and suppose it has a rear bumper, B. Then it's easy to imagine a situation in which your car might have lacked the part B. Even though this didn't actually happen (we assume), it could have been that members of a ring of bumper thieves came late last night and removed B from your car. They took B away and hid it in a barn that already contained hundreds of bumpers stolen from other cars. If this had happened, then T would not now have B as a part. Right?

Wrong. Well, at least if something like Q is an adequate account of physical objects, then this is wrong. The reason is that T would still exist and have B as a part! T would not have lost any *parts*, but it would have lost a *property*: the property of *being your car*. Instead, the thing that is all of T

162

except for the part B (call it C) would have that property. [Exercise: Treat, in a parallel fashion, the possibility of your car's having a part that it actually lacks.] The crucial point here is that the natural temptation to say that T has lost a part is simply a reflection of our everyday failure to recognize most grossly scattered objects as legitimate physical objects. Once we overcome this failure and adopt a view like Q, we see that, in the imagined circumstance, the sum of C and B is still a perfectly legitimate physical object, even though it isn't a car. (A proper part of it, C, is a car.) So, even though "your car" would have lacked a part it actually has, there is no reason to think that T would have lacked a part it actually has.

Hence it would be very awkward to accept a liberal view of physical objects like Q while rejecting mereological essentialism. So we now officially adopt mereological essentialism. It is very important to notice that this does not commit us to any particular view about change of parts "over time." It's strictly a *modal* principle. The issue, therefore, was whether things could have had different parts, not whether things gain or lose parts. Intuitively, change of parts over time, if it occurs, is something that happens in the actual world. We don't have to imagine other "possible worlds" to think about it. But we do need other worlds in thinking about whether things could have had parts they don't actually have. Now, it would not be surprising if the modal and temporal questions proved to be closely related. But the present point is simply that they are different questions.

9.3 The River and the Movie

In Section 9.1 we claimed that the property of *being a physical thing* ought to be intrinsic to its instances, and shouldn't have anything to do with our everyday interests and activities. In other words, it shouldn't be a relational property that involves us. We are now going to consider an idea that may at first seem incompatible with this view. The idea is that the concept of a physical thing is nevertheless – to a certain extent – a matter of "convention."

It is a *convention* that we drive on the right side of the road in some countries. In others, we drive on the left. Different systems of measurement are also good examples of conventions. Nature does not determine that, say, its distances must be measured in meters. We can measure distance in yards or in meters or in light-years. Or we can invent an entirely new system with new units. These are examples of conventions that are – more or less – legislated, or otherwise explicitly put into effect. But other familiar notions are also conventional even if they just "evolve" into effect. For example, the meanings of the words of our languages. There is nothing in nature that *requires* the English noun "dog" to apply to dogs. It just worked out that way. It might have applied to cats, or to tables, etc. So our words have their meanings as a matter of convention, even when no explicit semantical conventions are actually adopted.

Now, let's try to focus on the question of the river and the movie in as clear and sharp a way as possible, while retaining our overall goal of a Q-like theory. So suppose a mere *point* P of spacetime is occupied by stuff of a certain kind, and that a later point P* is occupied by stuff of the exact same kind. Suppose further that there is a continuous curve in spacetime that connects P and P*, and that every point on this curve is occupied by stuff of the same kind that occupies P and P*. A final supposition is a little hard to state carefully, so we'll settle for a rough statement. Suppose that the events taking place in the vicinity of the curve connecting P and P* do not include what we might *ordinarily* think of as the *replacement* of the stuff occupying P by other stuff of the same kind at any point along the curve. (So there are no displacements, there is no "rolling" of any continuous and homogeneous sphere along the curve, etc.) To put it another way, we have a situation that we might "ordinarily" describe as containing a point-sized, single thing that floats along a curve in spacetime. (Of course, the actual laws of physics may require that it be closely accompanied by some other things tracing more-or-less parallel curves. But we shouldn't care about that, since we aren't worried about *physical* possibility anyway.)

Now suppose someone asks whether the stuff that occupies point P also occupies point P* (and the intervening points along the curve). If the answer is yes, then it looks like we have a case in which a physical object persists through time in accordance with the image of the river. If the answer is no, then the reason could only be that new stuff is continuously coming into being and "replacing" previous stuff, as captured in the movie analogy. Then physical objects would never persist through time, though many of them would be four-dimensional objects with different temporal parts.

But what if there is no "right answer?" What if the question itself is somehow not a "factual" question? One reason we might think it isn't a *purely* factual question is that there is no conceivable test we could perform – say on the stuff occupying P, and then later on the stuff occupying

P* – that would settle the question. We already have all the information that any empirical investigation could supply. So, if it isn't a purely factual question, then we ought to be able to regard it as a matter calling for *some* degree of conventional legislation, like the adoption of a specific system of measures. Any convention must, of course, fit the relevant facts. But the point is that it isn't fully determined by those facts. We would have some leeway for convention.

On the other hand, it may after all be a strictly factual question, but one we are powerless to answer. For example, it could be that God "sustains" the world in a certain way, a way that fits with the analogy of the river, or else does so in some *other* way that fits, instead, with the analogy of the movie. The specific way that God operates is, let's suppose, beyond our grasp (as a matter of principle), or at least beyond all (possible) evidence. But, precisely because it is inaccessible to us, there is an important way in which it shouldn't matter even though it is a genuine matter of fact. What is within our grasp is that the interplay of time and stuff either works like the river or else like the movie. So we ought to be able to develop a coherent view of the world under either assumption. If we happened to settle on the one that is factually incorrect, it wouldn't matter in any way that could ever be discovered or that could have any tangible effect on us.

In fact, it should be clear that either approach would "translate," in a systematic and easily definable way, directly into the other, much as one system of measurement translates, *via* familiar formulas, into any other. As a result we could even avoid the risk of factual error by adopting a kind of *conditional* convention. For example, we could opt for "the river," but agree to understand river formulations conditionally: as expressing river concepts if the world really is river-like, and as expressing their movie counterparts if the world is movie-like. The fact that we can never know which way the world is would not be relevant.

It thus appears that our question is either one calling for a pure convention, like a system of measurement, or else is one we are in no position to answer, but for which we can adopt a conditional convention without risk of error. So let's agree to this. We will adopt the following conditional convention. We will adopt *river* terminology, but understand it conditionally, as expressing river concepts if the world is really river-like *or* if the matter is purely conventional; and as expressing the appropriate movie concepts otherwise.

We are therefore proceeding *as if* we have concluded that stuff (sometimes) persists through time, and hence as if *things* (sometimes) persist

165

through time. Of course we haven't really concluded this. Our conditional convention keeps us off the hook if stuff really doesn't persist through time. But from now on everything will go more smoothly if we forget about conditionality and pretend that our conclusion is unconditional.

Accordingly, we are concluding that the entity that occupies P also occupies P*, and, in fact, also occupies every point on the continuous curve connecting P and P*. This thing, say T, is a 0-dimensional object (since it only takes up a point at a time) that persists through time. (There is also a 1-dimensional entity occupying the curve connecting P and P*. Even though that entity is composed of the very stuff that composes T, it isn't T. As suggested above, it's best viewed as a different sort of entity, perhaps as an *event* incorporating T's persisting over the relevant interval of time.) We can easily imagine that there are also 1-, 2-, and 3-dimensional objects that persist through time because all of the stuff that constitutes them at one time also exists at a later time (and at the times in between). (Notice that it is consistent with the present view that stuff can come into existence and go out of existence.)

It may at first seem that adopting the river convention fits best with our common-sense view of ordinary things like bicycles and human bodies. After all, we certainly speak and behave as if they persist through time. But when we think a little more carefully about this, we notice that this can't really be literally true. We don't think the 5-year-old child's body has persisted through time and is now present as the body of the 80-year-old adult. Even though most of the stuff that comprised the 5-year-old's body may still exist, it isn't present in the 80-year-old's body. That stuff is now scattered in various places around the world, and the 80-year-old's body is composed of largely, if not entirely, different stuff. So even if stuff, in general, does persist though time, ordinary things like organisms and bicycles do not. They undergo a more-or-less continuous turnover of the stuff that constitutes them, over time. In some cases the turnover is dramatic, and in others it may be quite minor, but the literal persistence of an *ordinary* thing over a significant period of time is certainly much more often the exception than the rule.

It's very important to be clear about the ramifications of this. Let's suppose that all of the stuff comprising the 5-year-old's body at a certain moment seventy-five years ago still exists. Then there is a physical object that has persisted through time for the past seventy-five years. But for most of this period it did not constitute *any* ordinary thing like a human body.

166

In fact, very soon after the moment in question, it did not constitute a human body. Instead, it constituted a scattered object that overlapped considerably, but not entirely, with an object that was a human body. On this picture, then, we do have persistence of objects over time, but we do not normally have persistence of "ordinary objects" over time. What we think of as ordinary objects are continually gaining and losing parts. As a result, it is seriously misleading to think of, say, a bicycle (or a human body) as a *single* thing in the first place. Different things constitute "your bicycle" (and your body) at different times. Over time, ordinary things are more-or-less continuous streams of *different* (three-dimensional) physical objects.

A certain mass of stuff constituted Plato's body, say B, at a certain moment in the past. It is conceivable that this stuff still exists, and always has existed in the interim, so that B has always existed. For most of this time, it is highly likely that B was a very scattered object. Parts of B may have been parts of various plants and animals at different times. Other parts may have simply floated around in the air or water, or lodged in the soil. But it is not inconceivable that all of this stuff has now come together again, and at this very moment happens to constitute a human body, say yours. That would mean that B once had the property of *being Plato's body* and now has the property of *being your body*. (Of course it would not mean that Plato has miraculously reappeared in our midst.) It is also conceivable that B now has the property of being a flock of geese. Much more likely, to be sure, is that B is now a very scattered object belonging to no *ordinary* category of objects. [**Exercise: Think through the possibilities discussed in the last two paragraphs from the movie perspective.**]

Let's return briefly to the topic of the river-or-movie convention. What creates the leeway for a convention is the *epistemic* fact that we have no way of knowing whether a specific parcel of stuff can exist at different times or not, or even whether this is a genuine factual question. We saw how to adopt a *conditional* approach to the convention that would avoid the possibility of error. But let's now set conditionality aside and pretend that the question is factual (even though we cannot know its answer). Let's also recall that, for independent metaphysical reasons, we have opted for a Q-like theory of things along with mereological essentialism. Now notice how the truth of the factual question affects the concepts of thinghood and identity. If the river image is right, then stuff really does persist through time, and we get a universe of things that includes the possibility of a thing that exists at one time being identical with a thing that exists at another time. But if the movie analogy is right, we get a somewhat different universe of things, and no thing that exists at one time can exist at any other time.

On the other hand, if the matter somehow *isn't* factual, however that might be, then we have an absolutely free (and risk-free) choice between the river and the movie. Our choice has the effect of tightening up a small amount of slack in the concepts of thinghood and identity. But it is important to see that, even then, *being a thing* is an intrinsic, purely physical feature of things, and *identity* is a simple and unanalyzable relation. A good way to see this is as follows. If there really is no fact as to whether stuff persists through time, then the universe simply contains lots of stuff in spacetime. The various parcels of stuff have many intrinsic, purely physical properties. Certain (instantaneous) parcels have an intrinsic property that we may think of as *river-thinghood* and yet another that we may think of as *movie-thinghood*. Other (temporally extended) parcels lack the former property but do have the latter property. The simple, unanalyzable relation of identity applies to things instantiating either of these properties. But the *extension* of the identity relation under the river conception will differ from its extension under the movie conception, reflecting their different views as to whether stuff persists through time. It is important to see that this does not mean that there are different identity relations, one applying in one case and the other in the other. Both candidates agree as to what makes for genuine identity: we have a case of identity when we have the same stuff.

To pick one of these concepts and call it "thinghood" is *not* to deny the existence of the other. It is merely to notice that we don't need both in order to give a physically satisfactory description of the universe, and then to choose one as our official way of doing business. The other would have done just as well. So, even if the matter *is* one of pure convention, that doesn't mean that thinghood (or identity) are concepts that we create or that involve us relationally as constituents.

9.4 Total Turnover

Let's try to apply our conclusions to the kinds of examples that raised perplexities in earlier chapters. The case of the house and the shutters (chapter 4) featured what we would *ordinarily* describe as a partial change of parts over time. The case of the table and the elves (chapter 8) featured what was *arguably* a complete change of parts (in a nonactual situation). Here we will offer two interestingly different versions of an often-discussed example (sometimes known as "The Ship of Theseus"). Consider first a simple short narrative, which we should imagine as given by a non-metaphysician.

The Neptune

Chapter I: The Fisherman.   A young fisherman, Billy, built a rowboat entirely of wood and named it *Neptune*. As each of the wooden planks, struts, pegs, and so forth began to wear, decay, or deteriorate, Billy would carefully replace it. Over the years, the *Neptune* acquired many new parts. In fact, one day Billy realized that his rowboat no longer had a single original part. He found this interesting, but he didn't doubt that his boat was still the *Neptune*. (Neither did the Registry of Oared Vehicles.)

Chapter II: The Beachcomber.   One day a young beachcomber, Sally, noticed Billy putting the finishing touches on a rowboat he had built and named *Neptune*. Sally had often wished she had a boat like that. Some time later she saw Billy replace a worn oarlock with a new one. He discarded the old one and Sally picked it up and put it in a special corner of a warehouse she happened to own. She kept an eye on Billy and, whenever an old part of the *Neptune* got discarded and replaced, she picked it up and put it with the other parts in her warehouse. Eventually, after some years had passed, Sally noticed that she had a complete set of parts for a rowboat. In fact, they were precisely the original parts of the *Neptune*. All of the parts were a little worn or a little dried out, but (thanks to Billy's compulsiveness) they were all still perfectly usable. Sally reassembled them and a smile crossed her face. She thought: "Not only do I now have a boat like the *Neptune*, I actually have *Neptune* itself! My friend Billy may think he still has *Neptune*, but he's wrong. He discarded it and now it belongs to me!" (The agents at the ROV politely suggested that she call her boat *Neptune II*.)

Who is right? Is there any real fact of the matter? What's going on? Maybe we can shed a little light on things if we consider a variation on the story.

169

The Neptune (Version II)

Chapter I: The Fisherman. [EXACTLY AS ABOVE]

Chapter II: The Beachcomber. One day a young beachcomber, Sally, noticed Billy putting the finishing touches on a rowboat he had built and named *Neptune*. Sally already had a boat – the *Poseidon* – built on the exact same plan as the *Neptune*, but it was very old and all of its parts were in very bad shape. Some time later she saw Billy replace a worn oarlock with a new one. He discarded the old one and Sally picked it up and used it to replace one of the *Poseidon*'s inferior oarlocks. She kept an eye on Billy and, whenever an old part of *Neptune* got discarded and replaced, she picked it up and used it to replace one of *Poseidon*'s decaying parts. One day Sally realized that her rowboat no longer had a single original part. She found this interesting, but she didn't doubt that her boat was still the *Poseidon*. (Neither did the ROV.)

Now, by the standards of riverized Q, there is nothing that prevents the physical object that Sally winds up with (at some final moment) from being the same in *both* stories. (Of course this would require that any interchangeable parts would ultimately occupy the same relative positions; also that, against all odds, the parts that languished in the warehouse did not display "changes" that the parts that saw nautical duty did not; and so forth.) So, in the interest of starkness, let's assume she does ultimately possess the same physical object in both versions. Then what is striking is that she is so certain she has the *Neptune* in the first version and so certain she doesn't in the second. (Furthermore, we may also assume that the physical object in Billy's final possession is the same in both versions. Then Sally's view of this object will again flip-flop between the two versions, though Billy's will not.)

These stories capture some important things about the way we *ordinarily* think about entities like boats. The first, already noted, is that we think they persist through time. The second is that we have two different, rough epistemic "criteria" that we often use in trying to decide whether a boat in our possession is "the same boat" as one that existed at some earlier time. Both of these criteria are rough, but both generally serve our ordinary purposes pretty well. One is that earlier boat A is "the same boat as" later boat B if there is a continuous curve in spacetime that connects (a point within) A to (a point within) B *and* every intermediate point on the path

170

also lies within a boat. The other is that a boat A is "the same boat as" a boat B if A and B share most of their parts (thinking of parts as we ordinarily do: as things that persist through time).

We certainly do use both criteria in ordinary life (though often only implicitly). Sometimes we're in a better position to apply one than the other, sometime we can use either, and sometimes neither helps. Occasionally the criteria lead to divergent conclusions, even in everyday life. [**Exercise: Give examples.**] But they usually coincide when it comes to things like boats. Our stories show that these criteria can diverge very dramatically, and even that our personal situation with respect to a boat can influence which criterion we are likely to prefer in a case of divergence. In the first version, the "continuity" criterion backs Billy's assessment and the "parts" criterion backs Sally's. In the second version, the continuity criterion backs both Billy and Sally, and perhaps this shows that we generally give it more weight than the parts criterion (according to which Sally would have wound up with the *Neptune*).

It is very natural to react to, say, the first *Neptune* story by wondering whether Billy or Sally is "right." But exactly what is the question about which they might be right or wrong? Let's call the three-dimensional physical object that Billy starts out with "A," the one he winds up with "B," and the one Sally winds up with "C." Now, by hypothesis (from the story itself), A is the *Neptune*, and one way of asking our question is "Who owns the *Neptune* at the end of the story?" It is extremely tempting (and natural) to understand this question as asking whether the object A is *identical* with B, or instead is *identical* with C. And in fact, legions of philosophers have seen this and similar questions in precisely these terms.

But we have just spent a good deal of effort developing a general conception of physical objects, seemingly on principled and independent grounds, according to which this way of understanding the question *simply cannot* be right. It can't be right because (in general) A wouldn't be identical with either B or C, regardless of whether the world is really like a river, really like a movie, or whether the river–movie decision is a matter of sheer convention: (1) If things work like a river, then A won't be identical with B since they have no parts in common. (A remote possibility is that they do have a very few tiny parts in common, but anyway they won't have exactly the same parts.) And A won't be identical with C since at least some of A's parts will be missing from C and vice versa, even if we're just talking about small numbers of molecules. (2) If things work like a movie, then A can't be identical with either B or C since A no longer exists when they do. (3) If things are purely a matter of convention, then just take your pick and refer to (1) or (2) accordingly.

It follows that either something is wrong with Q, or else the question really is not about identity. Now, if there were no plausible alternative way of understanding the question, then that might pose a real problem for Q. But there is another way. It is a way that enables (say) B to "be the *Neptune*" without being identical with A. That way is for B to stand in the "same-boat-as" relation to A, where this is a *relevant similarity* relation, not the identity relation. (Recall from chapter 4 the everyday examples in which the words "same" and "identical" – and even, occasionally, "is" – clearly express notions of relevant similarity rather than identity.)

When Billy acquired his boat, he thereby acquired a thing that instantiated the property of *being a boat*. But nothing can be a boat without also being a *specific* boat. There must have been a property of *being that particular boat* that Billy's boat instantiated, and that no "other boat" could possibly instantiate. And, of course, every other boat must instantiate a similar "particularized" property. We can think of these properties as "boat-properties." (There must also be person-properties, dog-properties, house-properties, and so on.) Now, whatever boat-properties are like in detail, we *already* know that a given one can be instantiated by different physical objects at different times, because our notion of being a specific boat clearly tolerates *some* leeway for what we ordinarily call "change of parts" over time. For a boat to "change parts over time" simply *is* for different physical object to count as "the same boat" at different times. We are now in a position to try to say a little more about why *Neptune*-style stories seem so puzzling, and a little more about the same-boat-as relation.

Of course, a crucial source of the puzzlement is that we are accustomed to thinking of objects like boats as persisting through time. This leads us to want there to be a simple answer as to whether B or C "is" A. But our recent metaphysical reflections have suggested that this is not really right. As noted above, the large objects that persist through time (on the river conception) only very rarely constitute ordinary objects like boats. For most of the time they are grossly scattered. (And on the movie conception, there is no genuine persistence in the first place.)

A second source of puzzlement is that we do not really have a completely sharp conception of ordinary objects like boats. Instead, our conception is somewhat vague and imprecise. But for almost all practical purposes, the vagueness doesn't matter. Undoubtedly, this is why we haven't bothered to sharpen it up. We generally avoid expending lots of effort for very little practical gain. The fundamental source of the vagueness is our language. The term "boat" is vague in the sense that competent speakers who know how to use the word will not always offer the same definition, nor will they always agree in classifying borderline cases. Nor will a single speaker always have a clear opinion in a borderline case. Our inner, mental representation of boathood – our "conception" – is also correspondingly vague, and correspondingly variable from person to person.

The best philosophical account of this variety of vagueness is that there are countless distinct and "precise" properties, each of which is pretty much as good a "candidate" as any other for playing the role of the meaning of the term "boat." That is, each of them conforms as well as any other to our actual use of the term. Our linguistic practice simply hasn't determined that one of them is the real meaning of "boat" and the others are not. Thus, when we use the term "boat," we do not express a single property. Instead, our use stands in a different, but expression-like, relation to a large cluster of properties that are very similar to each other. So the picture of language according to which every predicate expresses a specific property is really a considerable idealization, but one that is very much in the spirit of how things actually work in practice.

[Exercise: Think about the vagueness of simpler terms, like terms of color and shape. Convince yourself that it isn't that there is a *property* of redness or roundness that is vague, but rather that we simply aren't sharp enough in our use of these terms to fix a unique property in the first place. Instead, each of a whole range of properties, each fully precise and all quite similar to each other, is compatible with the great preponderance of our use of the terms.]

What *Neptune*-style stories do, in effect, is to present us with examples in which different properties from the cluster give contrasting answers, even though each is fully compatible with almost all everyday usage of the term in question. If "boat" did clearly express a property that, say, required spatiotemporal continuity, then there would be no puzzle. Sally would never have been tempted to think, in the first story, that she possessed the *Neptune*. Of course, the fact that "boat" is vague guarantees that "being the *Neptune*" is also vague. Any of a multitude of distinct properties could adequately serve as this particular boat-property.

Now, it is evident that any "same-boat-as" relation would have to be analyzed as follows: X is the *same boat as* Y iff there is a boat-property P such that X and Y both instantiate P. Because this formulation appeals to the vague notion of a boat-property, it guarantees that the same-boat-as conception has (at least) the same degree of vagueness as "boat-property" (and "boat"). So there really is no single *same-boat-as* relation any more than there is a single property of *being a boat* (or *being red* or *being round*). Instead there is a cluster of adequate candidate relations.

It is important to see that the kind of vagueness we have been discussing is not at all a *defect* of our language (or our conceptualization). To the contrary, it is a significant advantage. For, in addition to being able to express and function with specific properties (etc.) when the need arises, we are also able to function with clusters of properties when our purposes don't require greater precision.

Let's summarize our main conclusions. We have seen that traditional puzzles about "change of parts over time" tend to have three main sources. The first is an inadequate conception of what it is to be a physical object. We tried to remedy this with a general theory. We saw that this theory admitted of two divergent interpretations, one that allowed objects to persist through time (the river), and one that did not (the movie). We also saw that choosing between these interpretations was, at bottom, a matter of adopting an appropriate "convention." A second source of the puzzles was the everyday idea that "ordinary objects" persist through time. But we saw that our general theory of objects is incompatible with this idea, even on the interpretation that allows for persistence. A third source of the puzzles was the philosophical conviction – doubtless encouraged by the idea that "ordinary objects" persist – that these puzzles concern the relation of *identity*. We tried to show that they do not, but are instead about relevant similarity relations, noting that such relations are often commonly expressed using the same terms that, on other occasions, do express genuine identity. Finally, we noticed that, to a certain extent, the "grip" of the puzzles depended on the fact that ordinary terms like "boat" are vague, and we offered a philosophical account of this species of vagueness. This account, along with our other considerations, loosens the grip of the puzzles without removing the vagueness. But the vagueness of ordinary terms like "boat" was not seen as a defect in need of any remedy.

10

Is There Truth in Fiction?

All of us have heard, read, and discussed works of fiction. Fiction plays several remarkably important roles in our lives. It plays a vital role in our early language learning and in the development of our imaginations. It can provide a stimulating mental retreat from the concerns of our everyday lives. It can inspire and fascinate, disturb and repel, amuse and frighten, arouse and anger. It can even change people's lives. How is it that fiction, which seems by its very nature not to be literally true, can have these profound emotional effects on us? This is, of course, a psychological question. But it is a question that gets its bite from a philosophical source: the concept of truth. In this chapter we will take a look at the philosophical question of whether there is truth in fiction and, if there is, what it amounts to.

10.1   Introduction

There is a curious dilemma embedded in how we normally think about fiction and truth. Half of the dilemma is the fact that we often use the term "fiction" in contrast with "truth," as in the saying "Truth is stranger than fiction." We tend to think of fiction as a kind of falsehood, but a kind that is different from lying. Writers (and tellers) of fiction are generally not lying.

The second half of the dilemma is that we commonly make what look like unqualified assertions about fictional characters, assertions based on what the fictions appear to say. Thus we say "Lois Lane doesn't know that Superman is Clark Kent," and "The dagger was a figment of Macbeth's

175

imagination," and so forth. So we have a dilemma. Are such statements true, as we seem to be claiming, or are they false, as the fact that they occur in fiction appears to require?

One potential resolution is to hold that when we utter sentences like these, we merely mean to be reporting what the story says (or implies, or presupposes), and that in giving the report we simply haven't bothered to make this explicit. Although this idea is promising, it cannot be right as it stands. The reason is that the story doesn't *say* (that is, *assert*), for example, that Lois Lane doesn't know that Superman is Clark Kent, even if it contains the very sentence "Lois Lane doesn't know that Superman is Clark Kent." (In fact it is unclear exactly what proposition would be asserted by such a sentence even if it were intended as a simple assertion, but we'll let that rest for the moment.) The sentences in fiction are generally not written with the intention that the reader interpret them literally and accept them as true. Instead, somehow, they are intended to be understood "as fiction". Another example may help to make this more evident.

Many stories contain names of actual people, places, things, events, and times (in addition to names of "fictional entities"). Certainly authors generally intend these occurrences of the names to refer to the actual entities that the names refer to outside of fiction. Thus, in *A Tale of Two Cities*, Dickens is referring to the actual cities of London and Paris, during an actual historical era, but he isn't claiming that the events he describes *as if* they unfolded there, *actually did* unfold there. The sentences that appear to describe such events are imbued with a kind of "fictional intent" that immunizes them against the charge of falsity. Whatever Dickens was doing, he wasn't misrepresenting events in major European capitals.

We may be able to develop a clearer view of this matter if we think more generally about the connection between our language and the realm of propositions. (It may be helpful here to reread chapter 3, especially Section 3.3.) Usually, when we utter a declarative sentence, the utterance not only *expresses* a proposition, but also *asserts* it. Normally, if you say "Sue enjoyed the party," part of what you are doing is, in effect, claiming that the proposition *that Sue enjoyed the party* is true. (Whether you also happen to *believe* the proposition is an independent matter. If you don't, you're guilty of a misrepresentation.) But on other occasions we utter declarative sentences without asserting the propositions that they express. Let's look at two examples.

The first is sarcastic or ironic speech. In a political discussion, someone might say (with ironic intent) "Of course most politicians are paragons of honesty." Here the speaker clearly does not assert the proposition that most politicians are paragons of honesty. In fact, exactly the opposite is being asserted. So, sometimes an utterance may *express* a particular proposition while at the same time *asserting* its very denial. (In other instances of irony the asserted proposition may be something other than the denial of the expressed proposition. For example, it may just be an assertion of doubt about that proposition.)

A second example is provided by actors in plays. Say an actor delivers the line "Sue enjoyed the party." In his utterance, the name "Sue" certainly does not refer to the actress who is playing the role of Sue in the play. Furthermore, "the party" does not refer to any actual party that ever took place. [**Exercise: Suppose there is a party scene in the play. Is the complex event that includes the set, the props, and the actors' speech and behavior in this scene a *party*?**] These quirks of reference make it unclear exactly what proposition, if any, is expressed by the utterance. Despite this, it is very clear that even if the utterance plays the role of an assertion within the play, it does not actually assert whatever proposition it happens to express. That is, the actor isn't claiming that some (presumed) proposition — *that Sue enjoyed the party* — is true, even if his thespian effort is to infuse the utterance with all the typical qualities of a sincere assertion.

Examples like these make it evident that we do not always assert the propositions that our sentence-tokens express. So it should not come as a complete surprise, or seem like an isolated or suspicious phenomenon, if this also holds for the sentence-tokens of fiction. On the contrary, if this does occur, then it offers hope for a solution to the dilemma. It may be that when we are inclined to regard a sentence occurring in fiction as false, we are thinking of the proposition it expresses, and that when we are inclined to regard it as true, we are thinking of the proposition it asserts.

In what follows we are going to develop just such a view. Sentences occurring in works of fiction will be held to express — but not assert — the sort of propositions that similar, fiction-independent occurrences would express (and often assert). And these same occurrences in fiction will then be held to assert certain further propositions, ones that are closely related to (but of course not identical with) the propositions that they express. As suggested above, the expressed propositions will generally be false, and the

177

asserted ones will generally be true. Thus, fiction will be held to be structurally similar to irony, in which we saw that a proposition different from (but related to) the one expressed is asserted.

10.2 Two Thought Experiments

The specifics of the theory we are aiming for are motivated in part by adopting certain responses to two thought experiments, which we may call the *aboutness* experiment and the *duplication* experiment.

Aboutness. Suppose you decide to write a novel, a work of fiction. You set it in a place you have never visited, say some small town in the Australian outback whose name fascinated you when you were looking at a map in an atlas. You decide that your tale will unfold in the 1950s. Apart from the setting and the period, everything about your novel is fictional. That is, you invent the characters, you give them their names, and you dream up all of the situations and events that you describe in the story. Now, suppose that by a remarkable coincidence, there actually were people in that town in that period who had "the same names" you gave your characters. To magnify the coincidence to the level of the near-miraculous, suppose further that, in 1960, someone wrote a history of certain events in the town, and that this history happens to be word-for-word indistinguishable from your novel! (We may also imagine that the titles of the two works are indistinguishable, and even that your name and the historian's are "the same name.") Finally, suppose the historian was very meticulous and very lucky, and as a result got everything exactly right, so that every proposition asserted in the history was literally true. (Notice that a *history* actually does assert the propositions expressed by the sentences it contains.)

It is important to be very clear that we are *not* talking about a funny case of unconscious ESP, clairvoyance, time travel, or any other "paranormal" phenomena here, although any of these is surely conceivable. For example, you were not influenced by unperceived outside agents to write what you wrote, although this sort of occult "dictation" is certainly conceivable. In the present case it's really true that you invented your characters, etc., and that your creative activity was independent of people and events in the outback of the 1950s.

Now here is the crucial question. Is your novel about the real people that the historian's chronicle is unquestionably about? It would certainly be very peculiar to think that it is. For one thing, it would evidently imply that your work really wasn't *fiction*, despite your firm intention. For the names of the "fictional characters," as they occur in print in the copies of your novel, would actually refer to certain real people. But this conclusion evidently violates the empirical facts about how names of actual entities work. When we use a name to refer to someone or some thing, either it is a name that we have learned from someone else (whether by way of speech or writing), or else it is a name that we ourselves have given to the thing named (as when we name an infant or a pet). In both cases the name refers to the entity because some person or other originally, knowingly, and explicitly applied it to that thing, and if it is a name we have learned, then our learning traces back to this original naming.

Now, obviously, it wasn't you who was responsible for the original namings of the people in the outback, and neither did you learn the names from someone else (so that your use could trace back to the original outback namings). We therefore conclude that your use of the names doesn't meet either of the conditions that would permit them to refer to these nonfictional entities. It follows that your novel is not about any actual people who lived in the outback in the '50s. It also follows that if the sentences in your novel assert any propositions, then they do not assert the same propositions that are asserted by the sentences in the true history. Furthermore, your sentences do not even *express* the historical propositions, since those propositions really are about the people in the outback. (We will soon return to the question of just what propositions your sentences do express.)

We may even draw a stronger conclusion from the aboutness experiment. For it not only shows that your names in fact don't refer to any actual flesh-and-blood people, it also shows that they don't refer to any possible flesh-and-blood people. To see this, let's appeal to "possible worlds" in the metaphorical way considered in chapter 8 (especially Section 8.3). Do your names perhaps refer to flesh-and-blood people in some other possible world (even though they do not in the actual world)? Suppose that they do, and let W be such a world. Then these people are not the people of the actual '50s outback, or else the names really would refer to them, contrary to our recent conclusion. Now, it certainly seems that your names are at least as remote from the people in W as they are from the actual people in the outback. So the damaging considerations about giving names and learning names should still apply.

179

But also notice this. If W exists, then there must also be a world, W*, that includes all of the relevant W-people and events, and also includes you and your novel. We may also assume that in W* the relations between you, your novel, and the W-people are relevantly no different from the actual-world relations between you, your novel, and the actual outback people. But then, in W*, the novel names don't refer to the W-people – just as, in the actual world, the novel names don't refer to the actual outback people. But since it's the same novel as the one you wrote in the actual world, it follows that the names in the actual novel don't refer to the W-people either! So the (fictional) names in a novel don't refer to any "possible entities" at all. It is therefore a necessary truth that the fictional entities (and events) depicted in the novel *do not exist*. This is a pretty stunning outcome, for it means that fiction is not only false, but (in a certain crucial sense) *impossible*. We will have more to say about his later.

Duplication.   Imagine that, by an amazing coincidence, two novelists (A and B), who have never had any contact with each other, produce what is, word-for-word, exactly the same (abstract) document. As above, we may also imagine that the novels have "the same title," and even that the authors have "the same name," so that there need be nothing in a (physical) copy of the novel that would enable us to decide whether A or B was responsible for it. (Here imagine that the copies are unpublished typescripts.)

Now the big question is: How many *novels* are we dealing with here? The answer may not be quite as clear-cut as in the aboutness case. We learned from that case that the author's fictional intent prevented the book from being about the actual people dealt with in the history. In effect, all it took for the book to be fiction was for the author to intend it as such. **[Exercise: Can an author take something known to be a true account of actual people and events, and "reproduce it" *as fiction*?]**

Now, in the present case, we have two different people intending to produce fiction, and we have seen that that's all it takes for their works to be fiction. The fundamental question is then whether such a work of fiction gets its fictionality by "personalized" or (somehow) by "anonymous" intention. To put it another way, suppose we think of works of fiction as being prefixed by a kind of "fiction-proclamation." (In fact, many works do bear just such a prefix, serving primarily as a legal disclaimer of the intention to represent actual persons or circumstances.) In these terms, our question is whether the proclamation should be something like "What follows is intended as fiction by A [the author]," or, instead, something like "What follows is intended as fiction (by someone or other)." To the extent that such a proclamation would function merely to make explicit the author's fictional intent, it is hard to see how the latter could be the right answer. In fact, it seems that we can imagine peculiar circumstances in which the nonspecific proclamation was true while the specific one was false. In that kind of case, the author's work would not be fiction. It would be (asserted) fact masquerading as fiction. [**Exercise: Give a clear and plausible example of this phenomenon.**]

It therefore seems that the most natural answer to the duplication question is that A and B have produced two different, but "lexically indistinguishable" novels. Each bears the stamp of its author's personal fictional intent, and that suffices to make them distinct works of fiction.

10.3   A Sketch of a Theory

The aboutness experiment convinces us that typical declarative sentences that appear in a work of fiction generally do not even express the propositions that similar sentences would express in nonfictional contexts. But then what propositions do they express? And what propositions do they assert?

An initial possibility is that they don't express (or, for that matter, assert) any propositions at all. But this seems an overly drastic conclusion. After all, they are declarative sentences, containing words that are, mostly, familiar to us all. These words have the same meanings they usually have. (It's hard to see how we could even begin to understand fiction if they didn't!) Shouldn't these meanings add up to propositions in the usual way? To hold that they do not would be to assign an utterly mysterious role to the sentences, one that seems incompatible with our ordinary view of how meaningful components of our language fit together so as to produce more complex meanings (notably propositions, in the case of typical tokens of declarative sentences). So let's try to develop a view in which sentences in fiction do have (propositional) meanings, meanings that emerge, in the ordinary way, as a function of the meanings of the smaller units they contain (and the context in which they occur).

Declarative sentences in fiction are of two importantly different sorts — those that make reference to "fictional entities" and those that do not. Let's look at the latter case first, because it is simpler. As noted above, works of fiction often refer to such nonfictional entities as places, times, and historical figures. So let's suppose a novel contains the sentence, "In the summer of 1990 there were nine days when the official Chicago temperature reached 100 degrees." Now, if this sentence occurred in a nonfictional setting, it would express – and likely assert – a certain proposition. The truth-value of this proposition could easily be learned by consulting the Chicago weather records. Let's first consider the case in which the proposition happens to be false.

Then what about the occurrence of the sentence in the novel? Because it contains no explicitly fictional elements, like names of fictional characters, it is very natural to think it expresses the usual proposition, the one it would express outside of fiction. This view fits naturally with the idea that the meanings of sentences are a product of the meanings of their constituent parts, as suggested above. But it is also strongly reinforced if we think about what an author is typically trying to do with such a sentence. The aim is to get the reader to *imagine* Chicago having all those very hot days during that summer. Certainly this is going to be difficult to achieve if the sentence doesn't at least express that proposition. So two very different reasons lead us to the same conclusion: that such a sentence, occurring in fiction, really does express the usual, extra-fictional proposition.

But does it assert it? It is part of our conception of fiction that authors have vast amounts of latitude in telling stories the way they want to. They are even allowed to portray situations that violate the laws of nature. (Certain kinds of time-travel are examples here, and so is exceeding the speed of light. A more down-to-earth example is Superman's ability to fly.) So the fact that the *proposition* is false doesn't rule out A's including the *sentence* in the novel, even if A knows the proposition is false. Since the authors of ficton aren't telling lies, this is enough to show that the sentence does not assert that proposition, even though we have concluded that it does express it.

But now suppose the proposition happens to be true, and that A believed it at the time of the writing. These are the circumstances that would most favor the view that the sentence asserts the proposition. But the price for taking this view is much too high, precisely because it makes A's epistemic relation to the proposition relevant to the question of assertion. If it were relevant, then what is lexically the very same *document* would have been a different *novel* if A had held just one slightly different belief about Chicago's weather. But surely this can't be right. In general, it would mean that we would have to be aware of a wide array of A's beliefs in order to understand the novel even at the most basic level. Moreover, it would introduce a puzzling lack of uniformity on the question of what is asserted in novels. A sentence like the present example would assert the proposition it expresses if the author believes it, but presumably not if the author disbelieves it, since authors aren't lying. And what if the author has no belief at all? It is much better to think that any assertion made by a sentence of this sort is independent of the author's epistemic relation to the expressed proposition. We conclude that no matter what A happens to believe or know about the weather in Chicago, and no matter what the facts may be, the sentence simply doesn't assert what it expresses. (And we will soon take up the question of what it does assert.)

(It is worth noting that, at sophisticated interpretational levels, a knowledge of such extra-fictional facts as the personal beliefs of an author is sometimes needed for a complete understanding of a work, especially for grasping its "tone." For example, we may need extra-fictional knowledge in order to decide whether it is a satire. But we aren't worrying about sophisticated literary interpretation here.)

Now let's consider a sentence in which fictional elements are explicitly present. An example might be: "Everyone at the *Daily Planet* thought Clark Kent was from Chicago." This sentence contains three proper names. The first two are fictional, the third is not. We have already concluded that fictional occurrences of names like "Chicago" refer to the entities they normally refer to, so the present occurrence of "Chicago" refers to the actual city in northeastern Illinois. We have also concluded that names like "Clark Kent" do not refer to anything that actually exists and, moreover, could not refer to anything under any possible circumstances. To put it another way, nothing that could possibly exist is referred to by such fictional names. Yet the sentences containing these names are perfectly meaningful. So there is some proposition that the present sentence expresses. And that proposition is different from the one that would be expressed by "Everyone at the *Daily Planet* thought Lois Lane was from Chicago," if it were also to occur in the fiction.

How can these be different propositions if neither "Clark Kent" nor "Lois Lane" refers to any entity, either actual or "possible"? Here is a suggestion that we will not be able to develop in complete detail here. Names like "Clark Kent" and "Lois Lane" serve to express certain properties, the properties of *being Clark Kent* and *being Lois Lane*. These properties are distinct from each other, so the two names contribute different properties to the propositions the two sentences express. As a result of having

183

these different properties as constituents, the propositions are different (even though neither name refers to anything).

Properties like *being Clark Kent* and *being Lois Lane* are *in themselves* no different in any significant way from properties like *being Bill Clinton* or *being Margaret Thatcher*. But, unlike the latter properties, the former have no instances and, moreover, could not possibly have any instances. In this last sense, they are "impossible" properties. So they are like the property of *being a triangular square*. Nothing has it, nothing could possibly have it, and yet we understand perfectly well what this property is. We know what something would have to be like to instantiate it and, as a result, we know that nothing could possibly instantiate it. We also know that it is not the same property as *being a round square* or *being red and green all over*, which of course are also impossible.

Being a triangular square is impossible because it is in a certain way "self-contradictory:" Given elementary principles of Euclidean geometry, the assumption that something is both triangular and square entails an explicit contradiction. *Being Clark Kent* is impossible for a different reason, one we are now in a good position to see. It's impossible because it entails *being fictional*, so an entity could instantiate it only if it were a fictional entity. But we have concluded that no entity that could possibly exist would be fictional. (In different terms, no entity in any "possible world" is fictional.)

Properties like *being Clark Kent* entail *being fictional* precisely because authors intend them to have that entailment. Most authors would not express their intentions in these abstract terms, but instead would say, for example, that they "intended Clark Kent to be a fictional character." Since we have seen that no possible world contains any flesh-and-blood fictional characters, that's good enough. We are merely capturing the authors' fictional intentions in the most appropriate metaphysical way.

We will not try to give an analysis of properties like *being Clark Kent*, but will merely remark that it is possible to see them as meriting analyses that are uniform with the analyses of properties like *being Bill Clinton* (which we also refrain from giving). All such properties may be seen as playing a crucial role in the theory of proper names, because they are very naturally regarded as being expressed by ordinary occurrences of names, whether fictional or not. So let us agree that properties like *being Clark Kent* are perfectly coherent even though they are necessarily uninstantiated, and that they entail *being fictional*. Finally, we will also take it that all proper names, fictional or not, express properties like these.

Now consider the sentence "Clark Kent is over six feet tall," which might appear in a Superman story. Then the present proposal is that the occurrence of this sentence in the story expresses the proposition *that something exists that has the property of being Clark Kent and the property of being over six feet tall*. Since, in fact, nothing has the property of *being Clark Kent*, this proposition is false. And this is a good reason to deny that the occurrence of the sentence asserts this proposition. Here, once again, we are merely protecting authors of fiction from the charge of lying, since they certainly do know which of their characters are fictional (and hence do not actually exist). [**Exercise: What proposition does the more complicated sentence "Everyone at the *Daily Planet* thought Clark Kent was from Chicago" express?**]

We have now developed a view about what propositions are expressed by declarative sentences in fiction, whether they contain explicitly fictional elements or not. According to this view, sentences without fictional elements express the same propositions they express when they occur outside of fiction. But notice that this is also true for sentences *with* fictional elements, given that the occurrences outside fiction are really occurrences of the *fictional* sentences. Consider "Clark Kent is a reporter." Of course it could be that there is an actual person with the *lexical* name "Clark Kent," who works as a reporter. And people may sometimes utter this sentence with this person in mind. But when they do, they are not uttering the fictional sentence, because the name in the fictional sentence is a different (though lexically indistinguishable) name – it expresses a different property from the one expressed by the name of the actual person. (Since one of these properties is impossible while the other is not, they cannot be the same.) But people who are familiar with the Superman stories may sometimes utter the sentence with the stories in mind. Then they are uttering the fictional sentence, and thus are expressing the very same proposition that gets expressed in the stories.

It should be noted that a complete theory of what is expressed in fiction would have to deal with matters that go well beyond declarative sentences. For example, propositions get expressed in dialogue, in questions, and also implicitly in the unfolding of a story. Here is a simple case. Character X says "Why did you leave the meeting early?" and character Y answers "Because I didn't feel well." In this interchange, the fiction manages to express the proposition *that Y left the meeting early*, even though it does not contain anything like the declarative sentence "Y left the meeting early." And sometimes things can be expressed even more indirectly. Imagine a story about characters who meet at a university, fall in love, get married, and go on to share various adventures. It may never say explicitly nor even logically entail that these characters are human beings, but that certainly is part of the content of the fiction nevertheless. Thus, very crudely, we may say that a story expresses propositions directly, in the form of declarative sentences, and indirectly, by logical entailment and also by what we may call "reasonable presupposition." It would be a considerable task to produce a complete and plausible account of these matters, and we will not attempt to do so here.

We may think of the totality of what is expressed in a story as "the world of the story." The world of a story is thus a certain complex *proposition* having as constituents various properties and relations, some of which entail *being fictional*. Because it does entail the existence of fictional – and therefore impossible – entities, the world of a story is not a metaphysically possible world (nor part of such a world). It is a necessarily false proposition. It is helpful to think of the world of a story as the sum of what an attentive and cooperative reader (or hearer, etc.) will *imagine* during and as a result of reading the story.

Now let's pretend that we have available a complete theory of what fictions express, and focus on the problem of assertion. The above account of expression is mainly based on the aboutness experiment. But now the duplication experiment will play the major role. In responding to the duplication question (in Section 10.2), we found it useful to view fictional works as if they were preceded by a proclamation stating that "what follows" is intended as fiction by the author. (This led to the conclusion that works that were lexically identical by accident would be different fictions.) Using our new notion of the world of the story, we may now state this a little less vaguely. For "what follows" the proclamation, that is, what is intended as fiction by the author, can now be seen to be the world of the story.

The author has expressed this complicated proposition in the work, but is careful not to assert it. We, in turn, are not asked to believe that the proposition is true. Rather, we are merely asked to *imagine* that it is true. Now, suppose that A is the author of story F and that W is the world of this story. Then F expresses W (and also every proposition that W entails). But this cannot be all that F does. If it were, there would be nothing to guarantee that it was fiction. Even the fact that F expresses propositions that entail that some fictional properties are instantiated does not guaran-

186

tee that F is fiction, since it is possible to make the mistake of taking fictional characters to be actual.

The mere expression of a proposition is an incomplete linguistic performance. It is not even clear that it is something we are able to do in everyday language. The expression of a proposition apparently occurs only when we are asserting it, doubting it, denying it, considering it, asking about it, or the like. If there is no surrounding context to determine otherwise, a declarative sentence-token will generally be given a "default" interpretation as asserting what it expresses. So F does not merely express W. It must also assert of W that it is fiction, specifically, that it is A's fiction. Thus, whether it contains an explicit proclamation to this effect or not, the fact that F is A's fiction means that in addition to expressing W, it asserts the proposition *that W is A's fiction.*

A consequence is that every proposition that W entails is also asserted by F to be A's fiction. For example, if F contains the sentence "Everyone at the *Daily Planet* thought Clark Kent was from Chicago," then F asserts the proposition *that it is A's fiction that everyone at the Daily Planet thought Clark Kent was from Chicago.* And if we (outside the story) happen to utter this same sentence in discussing F, we are asserting the exact same proposition. Thus we see how it is that when a reviewer says, for example, "Then Superman flew to the scene and rescued the child," a true proposition is being asserted, one that involves F and A even though they aren't mentioned explicitly in the sentence.

We began with the question "Is there truth in fiction?" and we have arrived at an answer. Yes, there is truth in fiction, and falsity too. Works of fiction assert true propositions while expressing false propositions. And the propositions asserted happen to be *about* the propositions expressed. So we have a solution to the dilemma mentioned at the outset. It's a "false dilemma" because the sense in which fiction is true does not conflict with the sense in which it is false.

11
Cosmology

Webster's New Collegiate Dictionary offers two definitions of "cosmology:" "1: a branch of metaphysics that deals with the universe as an orderly system; 2: a branch of astronomy that deals with the origin, structure, and space–time relationships of the universe." Accordingly, depending on the sorts of questions we ask, cosmology is either a branch of philosophy or a branch of astronomy. Certain questions, like "What is the origin of the universe?", may appear to involve aspects of both. This chapter is concerned mainly with this sort of question, and mainly from a metaphysical point of view.

Let's start by agreeing how certain terms will be used. First, we'll use the term "the universe" to mean the physical (or material) universe, that is, all of spacetime and whatever exists and occurs within it, whether in the past, present, or future. This is probably what most astronomers have in mind when they use the term. Philosophers, however, often use the term more inclusively, so as to cover whatever may exist outside of spacetime as well (perhaps God, properties, numbers, etc.). We will reserve the term "the world" for this all-inclusive notion. The choice here is merely a matter of adopting one convention or another. We could do just as well with some other convention, but it is important to settle on one at the outset.

Now, the question was "What is the origin of the universe?" But what does "origin" mean here? Normally when we look for the origin of a spatiotemporal entity, we are seeking another spatiotemporal entity (or entities). If you're looking for the origin of the Nile, you go to Africa and try to find the spring or lake from which the waters of the river first flow. If you're trying to find the origin of a particular antique chair, you try to trace it to a certain artisan's workshop (or even to a specific tree or trees, if your interest is physical rather than artistic). The origins of material things involve, depending on our concerns from case to case: their physical causes, the material that constitutes them, the methods or agents that produced them, the spatiotemporal locations at which they first appeared, and the like. In every case we are likely to think of, the origins of material things involve other spatiotemporal entities. But it is clearly impossible for the universe to have an origin in this sense. Because it includes all spatiotemporal entities, there are no other spatiotemporal entities to serve as its origin. This suggests that the question itself has a confused origin, and that the answer must be: "It doesn't have one." This answer may seem shocking to some: for example, to those who say that the origin of the universe is the "Big Bang" – an unimaginably intense release of energy supposedly marking the beginning of spacetime.

But if there really was such an "original" Big Bang, then it was part of the universe. It took up a certain region of spacetime including a certain amount of time. Since "originalists" are assuming that the span of time taken up by the Big Bang was in fact the earliest of all spans of time (having that duration), it is incoherent for them to speak of conditions before the Big Bang. (Notice that this is not to say that there was nothing before the Big Bang. The point is that since time (supposedly) begins with the beginning of the Big Bang, the very concept *before the Big Bang* is incoherent.)

Much the same point may be made if we think in terms of causation rather than origination. (For a discussion of the notion of causation, see Section 7.1.) In the normal sense of the term, the *causes* of physical events are prior physical events. So, if the Big Bang was the first physical event (of its duration), then the Big Bang has no cause in this sense. (Whether it has a cause in some other sense is another matter.) When people say the Big Bang was the cause (or the origin) of the universe, the most natural (and charitable) reading of the claim is simply that the Big Bang is the cause (or origin) of the *rest* of the universe. But what is important is that this still leaves us with no standard causal source for the entire universe.

Of course it is possible to accept the claim that there was a Big-Bang-like event, and that the subsequent part of the universe developed causally from that event, but without holding that it was the cause of the rest of the universe. In fact many astronomers believe there is substantial physical evidence that there really was an amazing event from which matter and energy spewed forth leading to the distribution of stars and galaxies that we are presently able to observe. But such an event might merely have been the beginning of a cycle of expansion and contraction among a two-way infinite series of similar cycles. Then it would not be the first physical event (of its duration) since it would have been immediately preceded by (and presumably caused by) an era of contraction. (Cycles of expansion and contraction are just one scenario among many that are compatible with a non-original Big Bang.)

It is often argued that the universe must extend infinitely backwards in time, and that this conclusion permits us to retain the belief that every event has a cause. The argument in fact proceeds from the premise that every event has a cause. (Theories that postulate an original Big Bang of course violate that principle since their Big Bang has no cause.) So even if there was a Big-Bang-like event, it is claimed, it must not have been original. There must have been a prior event that caused it, say E1, which in turn was caused by an earlier event, E2, and so on. It is concluded that time must extend infinitely backwards, in order to accommodate the infinite sequence of increasingly earlier events, E1, E2, ... (Notice that the same argument can be made without a Big-Bang-like event. Take any event you like, say the eruption of some volcano. Then there must have been a prior event that caused it, and so on.)

But something is suspect about this argument. It appeals to the principle that every event has a cause, but it may be held that it does so on behalf of a theory that violates that very principle. For what about the event consisting of the universe as a whole, or even the universe up until now? Since there are no events prior to either of these events, they are both examples of events with no causes.

It might be replied that these are not really events because they extend infinitely backwards in time, that genuine events have beginnings in time. But there are two problems with this reply. First, it seems both arbitrary and *ad hoc*. Intuitively, events are just connected sequences of changes. There doesn't seem to be any independent reason to disallow sequences that happen to extend infinitely backwards (as long as there are such sequences in the first place). They're still sequences of changes. (Closely related to this point is that any pressure to find a "cause" of the universe should be equally strong regardless of whether the universe happens to extend infinitely backwards in time, in other words, regardless of whether it is an event in the restricted sense.)

Second, suppose we ignored this problem and accepted the restriction that a genuine event must have a beginning "in time." What would this mean? Apparently, it would mean that for any event at all, there is a time before it begins to occur. But consider again the original-Big-Bang theory. The claim was that it violated the principle that every event has a cause, and the Big Bang itself was the supposed example of an uncaused event. But in the present, restricted sense of "event," it isn't a genuine event after all since it doesn't begin in time! (We might say that the Big Bang "begins time," but since there is no time before it begins, it doesn't begin "in time.") It thus appears that when it comes to the question of causation, theories that claim that time extends infinitely backwards are not that different from theories that deny it. On either view, the universe as a whole is an event in the intuitive sense and fails to be an event in the restricted sense.

Let's try to put a slightly different light on the matter. Original-Big-Bang theories have to concede that the Big Bang has no (prior) cause, and hence that the entire universe itself has no cause and no beginning in time. But everything that happens after the Big Bang is caused by the Big Bang. In fact every event with a beginning in time may be held to have a prior cause, namely some or all of what happened before. But things are very much the same with the infinite-backwards theories: Every event with a beginning in time has a cause, but the universe itself has no cause and no beginning in time. Both sorts of theories therefore make lots of room for "local" causation, but neither answers the question "What caused the universe itself?" (or "What is the origin of the universe?") in a philosophically satisfying way. The reason is that the usual, everyday notions of cause and origin (especially their temporal features) make it virtually a technicality that the universe has no cause or origin. But the ordinary person who wonders why the universe exists at all is not going to be satisfied by this outcome, correct though it may be.

The ordinary reflective person and the professional philosopher alike want to know "why there is something (physical) rather than nothing," a question that we may raise without resorting to the temporally rooted notion of cause (or origin). So it may have been a mistake to frame the fundamental cosmological question in temporal terms in the first place. If so, it is a mistake that has often been made in the history of cosmological thought, even by some whose positions would be more plausible if they had avoided it.

Many believe that God – a nonmaterial being – is the cause (or "creator") of the universe. This is often accompanied by the claim that God is self-caused. Now, apart from how we might ultimately evaluate these claims, it seems clear at the outset that they do not involve the ordinary

191

notion of cause (even if some who have made them have thought that they do). On the ordinary notion, as characterized above, causes always precede and are distinct from their effects, and physical effects always have physical causes. (But, concerning the last, see the discussion of compatibilism and dualism in Section 7.2. [Exercise: How different would psychophysical causation be from divine causation? Different enough to make one plausible, the other not?]) The notion of cause appealed to in these claims does not have these three features. There are several possible reactions to this situation.

(1)   It might be insisted that it really is the ordinary notion after all, and that the ordinary notion doesn't really require the three features just mentioned. It's just an accident that most everyday cases of causation happen to have them. Causing, on this view, is *any* kind of "bringing about," where this notion is understood to be compatible with but not to guarantee these three features. [It is a good exercise to try to find a convincing argument against this position.]

(2)   It might be agreed that it isn't the ordinary notion (and that the ordinary notion does involve the three features). Instead, according to this position, what's involved is a different, special kind of causation, a kind that's also involved in miracles (and perhaps other apparent violations of physical laws.) It's a causal intervention from outside the spatiotemporal realm. The problem with this position is that it seems *ad hoc*. That is, it seems to be a notion that gets introduced simply in order to do a certain job (namely, getting the universe caused, getting otherwise unexplained events explained, etc.). The notion lacks the kind of independent support that would be needed for general acceptance.

(3)   It might be conceded that the fundamental relation connecting God and the material universe isn't causal after all. Perhaps it's a kind of atemporal "necessitation." We will now explore this idea in some detail. (It may be useful to reread chapter 8, especially Sections 8.1 and 8.2.)

First, some terminology: a *necessary existent* is an entity that exists as a matter of necessity, that is, one that could not have failed to exist. An entity that might not have existed is called *contingent*. So human beings, dogs, tables, mountains, planets, and so forth all appear to be contingent existents. In fact, every physical entity of our everyday acquaintance seems contingent. But many philosophers have held that *God* is a necessary being.

It is very natural to think that any entity that exists outside of spacetime must be necessary. For example, Platonists who believe that numbers, properties, and the like really exist outside of spacetime generally hold that they exist of necessity. [**Exercise: What then should we make of** *sets* **of** *contingent* **entities?**] This is a natural thought because our ideas of contingency seem to be rooted in spatiotemporal events. The reason we think that we are contingent beings is (roughly) that we think our parents might never have met. The reason we think a certain table is contingent is (e.g.) that we think the person who made it might have decided not to make a table, but to make something else instead (or to let the wood rot into the ground). In this way, the idea of contingency seems closely linked to the question of which causal chains of events are genuinely possible and which are not. Entities outside of spacetime (if there are any) are insulated from these sorts of effects, and so it is natural to think they exist necessarily. To put it a little differently, such (supposed) entities do not come into being as a result of causal processes, so their existence is not subject to whatever vagaries affect causal processes. In fact, since coming into being is itself at least a temporal and perhaps even a causal notion, it seems that such entities, if they exist, do not come into being at all: They simply exist, and their existence is timeless and unconditional. But this sounds like another way of saying it is necessary.

We should pause here to note that it is often held that the universe is "deterministic," and it is sometimes inferred from this that everything happens of necessity. But the inference is faulty. Suppose that the universe is in fact deterministic (say in the "causal" sense of Section 7.2) and let E be some specific event. Also let . . . E3, E2, E1 be a backwards infinite chain of determining events, so that E1 causes E, E2 causes E1, and so forth. Now notice that nothing so far guarantees that any of . . . E3, E2, E1 occurs in the first place. So nothing guarantees that E occurs. E may not be necessary even if E1 does determine that E occurs. What is necessary here is only the conditional assertion that if E1 occurs, then E also occurs (and, in general, that if En + 1 occurs, then En also occurs). In different terms, the determinism lies entirely within the system, but the system itself (and everything within it) might never have existed at all despite its deterministic character. Another way to make the same point is to claim that there are many different deterministic "possible worlds" – in some of them E occurs, in others it does not. So even if it has been determined for all eternity that our parents would meet and we would be born, it doesn't follow that our existence is necessary.

Let's return to the question of whether God could stand in an atemporal relation of necessitation to the universe. So far we have seen that as long as God is conceived as a nonmaterial being, an entity existing outside of spacetime, it is natural to assume "he" exists necessarily. The very use of the personal pronoun here should remind us that traditional conceptions of God are often to a certain extent "anthropomorphic." Human characteristics are often attributed to God, especially in artistic depictions, in teachings intended primarily for children, and in the music, prayer, and other aspects of ritual devotion. But the official theologies that underlie these diverse anthropomorphic attributions are generally inconsistent with them precisely because God is officially assumed to be a nonmaterial being. (Notice that his nonmateriality does not rule out his being a *person*. But it does rule out his having a beard or being a male.) So, although different religions may entertain somewhat different conceptions of God, as long as they (officially) conceive of him as nonmaterial, it is reasonable for them also to take him to be a necessary existent. (Of course some do so explicitly.)

Now let's introduce a concept of "necessitation" that might be relevant here. We will first conceive of necessitation as a relation between pairs of particular entities. We will say that an entity X *necessitates* an entity Y iff it is impossible for X to exist without Y also existing. In loose but suggestive terms, the existence of X "insures" or "guarantees" the existence of Y. In fancier terms, the existence of X is a "sufficient condition" for the existence of Y. Notice that if X necessitates Y, and X is itself a necessary existent, then so must be Y. This is the key ingredient of the "necessitation strategy."

An important thing to notice about necessitation is that it is neither a temporal nor a causal notion. If X is a specific triangle and Y is one of its sides, then X necessitates Y. The necessitation here is in no way temporal or causal. The reason X necessitates Y is that Y is an essential part of X. Triangles are constituted by their sides, so we couldn't have X without also having Y. Notice that although the concept of necessitation is neither temporal nor causal, a given case of necessitation may well depend on temporal or causal relations. A specific X might necessitate a specific Y because only Y could have caused X to exist. Thus a particular oak tree may necessitate a particular acorn precisely because that acorn is the only possible cause (or origin) of that specific tree. This example, if it is a good one, brings out another important feature of necessitation: There is nothing about the relation that prevents it from holding between (what are normally thought to be) contingent entities (even though we may hope to deploy it with respect to God or other necessary existents).

The present concept of necessitation does have one slightly strange feature: If Y is a necessary existent and X is any entity at all, then it is a consequence of the definition that X necessitates Y. It is impossible for X to exist without Y also existing simply because it is impossible for Y not to exist. There are ways to revise the definition so as to avoid this consequence, but for our purposes it is easier simply to live with it. It should become clear that it has no adverse effect on what we're doing here.

Now let's consider the idea that God necessitates the universe. A proponent of this position will maintain that it is in God's nature that he could not exist unless the universe also existed. The advantage of this view is its lack of commitment to suspect "causal" relations between the nonmaterial and the material, but how might a proponent go about motivating a theory of noncausal necessitation? It won't help to claim that the universe is an essential part of God (as in the case of the triangle and its sides), because we are assuming God is nonmaterial. (Of course a different theory might hold that God is only partly nonmaterial, but we won't discuss such a view.)

One idea is that God's *essential* properties include some *relational* properties involving entities outside himself, and hence that he necessitates these entities. (Relational properties are discussed in Section 3.1.) Everything that exists has relational properties. For example, among a given person A's properties is the relational property of *being a child of M*, where M is A's mother. Arguably, this property is essential to A, so that A could not have existed without instantiating it. If this is right, then A necessitates M. Of course, in the case of a mother and child, it would be a drastic error to infer that the child is in any way responsible for (or in any way provides an explanation for) the existence of the mother. But here we nevertheless see how even an ordinary thing might have a relational property essentially, and how having such a property can entail that an entity necessitates some entity outside itself.

So the strategy is to try to find a suitable relational property of God's. For this strategy to succeed, it will have to be very plausible to think that God has the property essentially, and his having the property will, of course, have to entail that the universe exists. In effect, God's having the relational property will amount to his standing in a certain relation to the universe as a matter of necessity.

One among several possible approaches along these lines – the only one we will consider – is based on the idea that one of God's essential properties is *appreciating value* (or *goodness*). Then, putting it roughly, the universe will wind up being necessitated because it contains value for God to appreciate. We will soon see that there are some serious objections to this account, one of which will lead to a modification. But first let's consider a point or two in its favor.

The world – the totality of what exists – consists (on the present view) of the universe, God, and any other nonmaterial entities (like numbers or properties) that may exist. We have already noticed that it is compelling to think that entities existing outside of spacetime are necessary existents. Now notice that it is hard to see how a necessary existent like a number or a proposition can be valuable in and of itself. In fact it is also hard to see how a contingent entity like a diamond or a Van Gogh can be valuable in and of itself. Although it has sometimes been held that existing is a "perfection" and that anything that has it is to that extent valuable, the present strategy rejects this position, and holds that value can only arise from "activity." Since entities like numbers and diamonds don't *do* anything, they don't have any intrinsic value. It may be valuable for us (or for God) to *contemplate* the numbers, or to *enjoy* diamonds and van Goghs. But the value seems intrinsic to the contemplation or enjoyment, not to the entities contemplated or enjoyed. Put somewhat crudely, it isn't that we like such things because they're intrinsically valuable; rather, they're "instrumentally" valuable because we like them.

Of course some nonmaterial entities (notably God) may be capable of activity, and it certainly doesn't follow from the fact that an entity exists necessarily that it acts as it does necessarily. God is generally conceived as "omnipotent," and a reasonable construal of this is that his activity is entirely up to him. Indeed, it would seem to limit his power unduly if his actions were constrained by any necessity other than what is imposed by logic. But it also seems to limit God's power by limiting the amount and variety of value available for him to appreciate, and this is the core of the idea that there must be a universe filled with value-laden activity if God is to realize fully his nature as an appreciator of value. There are two major (and somewhat related) problems with this view. One of them can perhaps be alleviated by a modification in the concept of necessitation. The other is a central theological problem that we will mention but not consider in detail.

The first problem stems from the fact that necessitation as we are so far conceiving it is a relation between God and our *specific* universe. If God is a necessary existent, and God necessitates our universe, then it follows that our universe – the way it is in every detail – is a necessary existent. From this it follows that everything that exists in our universe, every human, dog, table, and speck of dust, is a necessary existent. It also follows that every event that occurs in our universe occurs of necessity.

These outcomes are very unwelcome for two reasons. First, we don't normally think these things are necessary at all. Could we really be so radically and thoroughly wrong about how the concept of necessity applies in actual cases? Second, and perhaps more important, we seemed to conclude that value stems from activity. But can it stem from *necessary* activity? If you had no real choice about any of your actions, would it still be true that some of them are worthy and others perhaps unworthy? Would it be true for the "actions" of a robot? Surely there is a strong inclination to think that real value stems only from contingent activity, more specifically from "freely chosen" activity. To the extent that we agree with this assessment, we will find the necessitation strategy deficient precisely because it makes our universe (and each of its parts) a necessary existent. [Exercise: How plausible is the idea that all value must stem from free activity? Suppose someone is given no choice about whether to listen to beautiful music, and enjoys it nevertheless. Is the enjoyment not valuable? Or is the taking pleasure in the imposed music free?]

One possible solution to this problem is to introduce a more relaxed concept of necessitation. The fundamental idea is that God "necessitates" the existence of a certain *kind* of universe (namely one in which value arises from contingent activity). So, while necessitation, as considered above, holds between two specific entities like God and the universe, the new relation holds between a specific entity and a *kind* of entity. Let's call the new relation "k-necessitation" and define it as follows. An entity X *k-necessitates* a kind of entity K iff it is impossible for X to exist unless some entity (or other) of kind K also exists. K-necessitation is more relaxed than necessitation proper because the existence of possible universes different from the actual universe is not ruled out. God is claimed to k-necessitate the existence of a universe of a certain kind, the actual universe happens to be of that kind, but it isn't the only possible universe of that kind, so it doesn't exist of necessity. Thus there is room to hold that value arises from the contingent and purposive activity of contingent beings existing in the actual universe. The k-necessitation strategy thus avoids the worry about whether value could arise in a necessary universe by concluding that the actual universe is not necessitated by God and hence is not a necessary existent.

If the k-necessitation strategy has a drawback it is that the existence of this universe takes on a quasi-random quality. It exists, and there had to exist something of that kind, but it didn't have to exist. We thus have only a partial explanation of the existence of this universe (though we have a full answer to the "something rather than nothing" question). But, it may be replied, the price of a "full" explanation would be the conclusion that the universe is a necessary existent, and this is something we don't really believe in the first place.

A very serious problem that affects any divine necessitation strategy is the infamous "problem of evil." A traditional statement of this problem runs as follows. God is assumed to be all-powerful, all-good, and the creator of the universe. But it is claimed to be evident that the universe contains a great deal of "evil." (Some is the result of actions of conscious beings; some is the result of mindless natural events.) How can these four things be consistent? Some have held that they are not consistent, and have concluded that God, so described, must not exist. Others have argued that the appearance of great evil in the universe is illusory, or that the balance of goodness over evil is maximal (so that this is "the best of all possible worlds"), and even that genuine goodness in the absence of evil is impossible.

Our present thinking has taken a somewhat nontraditional course in that we are not assuming God to have "created" the universe, since that sounds causal, and since causal relations between the nonmaterial and the material seem at least suspicious. This is what gave rise to the necessitation strategy in the first place. Still, a variation on the problem of evil easily arises. What drives the current necessitation idea is that God is by nature an appreciator of value (or goodness). It certainly seems that a universe could contain much more goodness than the actual universe contains. (Perhaps it would help for it to contain less evil.) In different terms, it certainly seems that this is not the best of all possible worlds. Now, although this is not inconsistent with God's assumed nature as a value appreciator, it does seem at least awkward – and perhaps inconsistent – when combined with the assumption of omnipotence. For any limitation on the existence of goodness would seem to be a limitation on God's appreciation of goodness, and thus on his power. We will not consider any of the many possible ways of dealing with this variation on the problem of evil. Instead we will ask briefly whether there is a plausible "secular" variation on the necessitation strategy.

If the universe is necessitated by something other than God, then apparently it must be by the Platonic realm (or some part of it). Now, it is certainly *conceivable* that there should have been no (physical) universe at all. But it is at least somewhat odd to imagine there being no universe, but there nevertheless existing, uninstantiated, all of the innumerably many properties that only physical things can have (and all of the innumerably many propositions about physical entities, etc.). Yet we normally think of these Platonic entities as necessary existents. It is tempting to ask why there would be any properties like *having mass, being yellow, occupying spacetime*, and so forth, if there were nothing that could instantiate them. If the answer is that there wouldn't, and we refuse to abandon the necessary existence of these properties, it looks like the conclusion must be that the existence of a material realm is necessary because it is necessitated by an entity whose existence is necessary.

It is clear that, at least initially, we feel pretty strongly that there might have been no physical realm. Otherwise, the question why there is one would not seem so gripping. But there is a serious danger of letting the strength of the feeling get in the way of an answer to the question. For it should also be clear that the most satisfying possible answer would be that, although we didn't see this at first, it is really *necessary* that there is a physical realm. And one kind of route to this conclusion would be the one we are exploring: that it is necessitated by a necessary existent (whether God, the Platonic realm, or whatever). Of course, such a route can never seem plausible if we are totally committed in our initial belief that there might have been no universe.

In Section 8.2 we considered a property-theoretic account of how certain sorts of propositions are necessarily true or possibly true. The account rested on primitive "entailment" and "compatibility" relations between properties. Thus, for example, the necessity of the proposition that all dogs are mammals is explained by the fact that the property of *being a dog* entails the property of *being a mammal*. The crucial consequence of this entailment is that if something instantiates the former property, it thereby automatically instantiates the latter. But we did not explicitly discuss propositions that assert necessary existence. So consider the proposition that God exists necessarily and suppose this proposition is true. Then a property-theoretic account of it would go as follows.

First, the proposition certainly entails that God exists. For God to exist is for the property of *being God* to be instantiated. So here we have a property, *being God*, having a further property, *being instantiated*. Now consider a third property, the property of *being the property of being God*. (The only entity that has this property is the property of *being God*.) For God to exist necessarily is simply for this third property to entail the property of *being instantiated*. So nothing could be the property of *being God* without being instantiated. For a contrast, consider the property of *being Caesar*, and the property of *being the property of being Caesar*. For Caesar to *fail* to exist necessarily is simply for this property *not* to entail *being instantiated*. (So the property of *being Caesar* could have failed to be instantiated, even though things didn't actually work out that way.)

This same account applies to any assertion of necessary existence, including, of course, assertions regarding the Platonic entities. **[Exercise: Say precisely what it is for a property or proposition to exist necessarily on the present account. (Careful . . .)]** So a coherent property-theoretic account of necessary existence indeed exists. Now consider the property, P, of *being physical*. The claim that it is necessary that a universe exists is nicely represented by the proposition that it is necessary that P is instantiated. And, on the present account, this simply means that the property of *being the property P* entails the property of *being instantiated*.

We are therefore in a position to give a kind of "transcendental" explanation of why there is something rather than nothing. First, it is a matter of fact that physical things exist. But, second, these things could not exist and be as they are unless there were a Platonic realm including such properties as P. Third, because Platonic entities like P are not spatiotemporal, they are necessary existents. Fourth, and finally, the necessary existence of (for example) P entails that it is necessary that there exists a physical universe, because P could not exist without being instantiated. (In our earlier terminology, P k-necessitates the kind *being a physical universe*.)

The weakest link in this chain is surely the fourth. In order to accept the explanation, one must somehow find it absurd to think that a world might include all of the innumerable properties that physical things actually instantiate, but include nothing physical at all.

One way to find it absurd might be as follows. We think of the physical – that is, the property P – as a "fundamental ontological category." Perhaps the mental is as well, if it is something apart from the physical, as dualists hold. And, assuming that properties and the like exist, the Platonic is certainly a fundamental category. If there is a God, then perhaps there is a fundamental category of the divine as well (unless God is a very special form of the mental). However many there actually are, these categories exhaust all of the possible fundamental forms of existence, and do so exclusively, in the sense that anything that could exist would fall into exactly one of them.

Now we might consider a "principle of completeness," asserting that it is necessary that every fundamental category be instantiated. In slightly different terms, worlds with uninstantiated fundamental categories are impossible. Then, for example, the actual world contains at least some members of every category. And, of course, there is no possible world containing no physical entities.

What can be said in favor of such a principle? Certainly nothing very conclusive. But we will end our discussion with one final speculation. It is easy to believe that many ordinary properties are instantiated only contingently. But why do we believe this? It is tempting to think that our reasons are largely *temporal*: We can readily imagine, for example, that humans might never have evolved. (One way this might have occurred would be if the universe had somehow ceased to exist at the time of the dinosaurs.) Then the property of *being human* would have been uninstantiated. What seems to be crucial here is that the property *came to be* instantiated, that is, was uninstantiated for a while, then was instantiated. So we are able to imagine that if there was an initial period at which it was uninstantiated, its becoming instantiated at all must have been contingent.

But recall that we noticed earlier that the universe had no such beginning *in time* (regardless of whether it extends infinitely backwards). Similarly, it has no end in time (regardless of whether the future is infinite). So at least one very natural source of the feeling of contingency is removed. To put it another way, since there have always been and will always be physical entities – there is no time, past, present, or future, at which there are no physical entities – the existence of a physical universe is every bit as necessary as the existence of the Platonic realm. At the risk of being somewhat cryptic, if our reason for thinking the Platonic realm is necessary is that it is not located *in* spacetime, then this reason applies equally well to the universe as a whole. [**Exercise: Does this line of reasoning "prove too much" by establishing necessary existence for the *specific* universe we inhabit, right down to the last grain of sand?**]

So it may be possible to make something like a principle of completeness for the fundamental categories plausible. If one accepts the present thought on behalf of the physical, then it isn't hard to see how to extend it to the other categories, even to those of which we may be unaware (and even unable to conceive). For no such category can apply to physical things. Otherwise it would be a subcategory of the physical, and hence not a fundamental category. So no such category can come to be instantiated in time. To that extent it is difficult to see how its being instantiated could be a contingent matter. [Exercise: Can nonphysical entities exist "in time" though not in spacetime? Can they perhaps exist even in spacetime? Either of these possibilities might be seen to undercut the present line of thought.]

Index